The Proactive Caregiver
Stop Reacting to Life, Start Living Proactively

By Jessica Lizel Cannon

A Caregiver's Journey through Bipolar Manic-Depressive Disorder and Mixed Dementia

Request for information should be addressed to:
info@cannonlightmedia.com

Cover Design by Cannon Light Media, LLC.
www.cannonlightmedia.com

Written by Jessica Lizel Cannon
www.jessicalizelcannon.com
Request for speaking engagements should be addressed to:
info@jessicalizelcannon.com

Dedication

To my loving Parents, Husband, and Family

Life as a caregiver comes with many sacrifices. Often the lessons learned together are painful and well beyond our comprehension initially. Nonetheless, spiritual guidance has inspired me to share my lessons with others so they can see the light amongst the darkness Dementia can bring to a family. This journey is a life-changing blessing.

I thank my husband, Scott Cannon, and our family for standing by me with endless love and support through our caregiving journey. My parents brought me into this world and raised me, but you, my life partner, are supporting me in countless ways that ultimately help me help Mom age with as much dignity and grace as possible. Our sons, Andrew, and Corbin have learned by our example what sacrifice looks like and means for others, even when we may not want to.

I thank Diane Haney for helping me discover my true self by uncovering the diamond in the rough within me along this caregiving journey. We are stronger together, just as He planned all along.

Table of Contents

Preface

I began having lucid dreams with Angels in my early twenties. It took decades before I began to reflect on what those peculiar, yet often beautiful dreams were trying to tell me. My most recent years of dreams leading up to stepping away from the corporate world were alarming yet sparked my interest enough to pay closer attention to my waking life. The change was coming for our entire family, and not one of us prepared for this sort of change.

My dream begins with my parents and sisters in the living room of our childhood home, looking through 3 tall single-pane windows. The front yard flooded with water flowing into the neighbor's yard and down into the street. There had been at least half a foot of standing water that unearthed many lizards and garden snakes.

I ran outside to check the water hose to make sure the faucet was not broken or damaged in such a way as to cause flooding. To my surprise, I found the water hose loosely unwound lying on the ground, with water pouring quickly from it. I realized Mom forgot to turn the water off after she watered the plants. It looked like she mindlessly dropped the hose on the ground and returned inside.

Mom followed me outside to the porch when I instantly flared up to tell her this flooding was because she forgot to turn the water hose off again. She looked at me with annoyance and dismissal while she asked, *"It's only water; what's the big deal?"*

She only made me angrier as I fired back, *"The big deal is it is wasteful and destructive. Look at the yard and how much you have washed away."*

At that moment, I extended my arms outwards to pull her attention to the entire yard instead of the front porch area. As I looked around the yard, I noticed three little kittens drowning in the water. I quickly ran over to each one and plucked them out of the water to place them into the front of my blouse and dry them off. I took them into the house to find more towels to warm and dry them better. Once I stepped into the living room, Dad was there shaking his head with disappointment as he looked at Mom while saying:
"You're crazy! Do you know that? Crazy!"

My Big Sis was sitting on the couch when I handed her a towel with one white kitten. Then I gave Little Sis a towel with one black kitten while she stood at the front door getting ready to leave. I sat down with yet another towel and the remaining white kitten. We all rubbed the kittens dry and stared at each other with shock and disbelief, wondering what we were supposed to do with them next. Little Sis stood a bit longer at the door before saying she could not stay and left with the black kitten.

The four elements are earth (dry), wind (cold), fire (hot), water (moist), which are essential to all life. Water is accorded as a cleansing power. It is symbolic of healing, purification, regeneration, and trust. It symbolizes death as well as rebirth. It is life-giving but can also be destructive. Freshwater stands for life and good health, while polluted/stagnant waters are symbolic of bad health.

I am a firm believer that everything happens for a reason. As I mulled over this dream along with countless others over the previous years, I realized so many of them involved some form of water. Only the water was rushing into my life in an overwhelming flow, often in floods or scenarios where I was drowning. Until one dream, I stood tall, breathing underwater as naturally as breathing nature's fresh air.

INTRODUCTION

Romans 5:3-5 (NIV)
"And not only that, but we also rejoice in our afflictions, because we know that affliction produces endurance, endurance produces proven character, and proven character produces hope. This hope will not disappoint us, because God's love has been poured out in our hearts through the Holy Spirit who was given to us."

What once felt like a punishment for stepping into Mom's demented world, I now view it as an opportunity to choose healthier options proactively. I was reluctant to step into this caregiving journey. Still, I came to a better understanding of who she was, and I also learned valuable lessons towards preventing my journey from heading along this degenerative path. As an accountant by trade, stepping into this caregiving journey with that mindset, I applied similar techniques to organize, analyze, and compare Mom's medical and mental health data to help me understand how Dementia is a disease of personal accountability.

Mom showed signs and later certainly displayed several symptoms of a malfunctioning or deteriorating brain as she became progressively worse over her 40's and 50's. Stemming from my vanity, I feared her story would become my story as I am now in my 40's. I needed to know what she did or didn't do, what she ate or didn't eat, how much she slept or didn't sleep, what she believed, and especially what she denied.

Scientific and medical research points heavily to genetics. We attempted to piece family history together through spending time with Mom for five years up close and personal. I firmly believe her diagnosis is not genetically related.

If I told you that my great grandmother taught my grandmother how to crochet, then my grandmother taught my mother, and now my mother is teaching me how to crochet, you could see a long-time tradition. Likewise, if my great grandfather had Alzheimer's, then my grandfather and father had Alzheimer's, and now I think I might have it too, then you might only assume Alzheimer's was passed down genetically.

We would ignore all the other habits that were indirectly passed down as well. Being accountable is taking responsibility for how we live. And how we live may simply be a series of traditions and learned behavior from our ancestors.

More and more baby boomers, along with younger generations, are not only beginning to experience Alzheimer's, the most well-known form of Dementia, they are also starting to experience Early on-set Alzheimer's with mixed Dementia. In many cases, Dementia related health issues become the deciding factor for early retirement to either tend to health issues or become a caregiver for a loved one with these health issues.

What does this say about the American culture? What does this say about our health on a global scale? Some reports explain Alzheimer's is a result of mutations in genes typically defined as being autosomal dominant, meaning you only need to have one parent pass on the gene to their child. If this happens, there is no escape from an eventual Alzheimer's diagnosis. The future looks grim by genetics alone.

Other reports lean more to a buildup of beta-amyloid protein to burden the brain by causing the breakage of connections to neurons leading to memory loss. It is not genetics related because the buildup of beta-amyloid protein, which creates the plaque-causing Alzheimer's, is caused by the same foods causing heart health problems, cancer, diabetes, and other oral diseases. Mom was raised on much of these foods, binged on as a depressed adult, and craves more as she declines. We consume too many complex carbohydrates, processed foods, and sugars that lead to toxins in the body, leading to inflammation and plaques in the brain.

Dementia is a silent killer because we simply do not pay close enough attention to our health until we find ourselves in dire need of a visit to the doctors or emergency room. A reactive mindset and one we continue to teach our children indirectly.

Instead, we could be providing a proactive approach for a better state of physical and mental health. We learned habits from our parents, peers, and educators from kindergarten to graduating high school. Our practices get worse as we venture out into the world as young adults bombarded by marketing ads and overindulgence simply because we can or are programmed to do so.

When I started my part-time caregiving journey with Mom, it was a frustrating inconvenience to me. I struggled to reconcile why taking better care of herself was so hard. Her struggles to live a healthier life evolved over her adolescent and young adult life. So why did I have to step in to make the hard decisions for her?

As part of my spiritual career training, I was allowed to glimpse into the looking glass of past, present, and future consequences of not properly caring for ourselves.

I continued researching the mixed Dementia Mom now lives with and became a bit overzealous in using this knowledge to reverse some of her symptoms. Unfortunately, any reversal requires a willing patient, which Mom is not.

After living a depressed life and becoming increasingly willing to die, she continued with poor lifestyle habits, which proved a critical game-changer. I may not help her reverse any of her forms of Dementia. Still, I can use this research to prevent my demise while teaching our children to hopefully stop this generational disease of accountability.

By helping Mom live with mixed Dementia, I could backtrack her habits back to those held as a child and those she indirectly taught me. Nutrition, sleep, and lack of exercise played a significant role in her life and what she inevitably passed on to my siblings and me. The cycle almost continued. I know I have the potential to carry the gene, yet I also believe I have the potential to prevent it by not activating the gene in the first place. Genes can be turned on or kept off in this respect, but this takes purposeful living without excuses.

I began researching from an intellectual yet vain standpoint. Further into Mom's life regarding scientific, medical, and psychological data, I could not help connecting spirituality with this journey. Aside from my vanity, I became driven by hope. My genetics are not the determining factor.

In Chapters 1-3, I explore what living with mixed Dementia looks like for Mom and how the stages of Dementia evolved for more than a decade. Moreover, in chapters 4-6, I cover ways to prevent Dementia by breaking apart our cultural programming. We can learn how to break our current cycles by identifying the triggers that may lead us to substance abuse.

However, in chapters 7-9, I explore how Bipolar Manic Depression often masks Early-Onset Dementia symptoms and heart-breaking sibling rivalry. In chapters 10-14, I share what I learned from the medical professionals and what I deciphered through real-life trauma. I decided to take Proactive Measures regarding my gut health to change my lifestyle habits.

In chapters 15-16, I explore how to effectively switch roles from child to adult caregiver or spouse to spousal caregivers by explaining areas for pitfalls along with the five necessary legal documents you will need to provide on behalf of your loved one for medical and business purposes. Chapters 17-18 cover how to avoid falling prey to caregiver burnout and how to make your reflection time meaningful.

Chapters 19-20 covers areas of spousal distress from the In-law perspective to the spouses when caregiving makes you feel dead inside. What happens when you decide to find the new forever home for your loved one, and what you can expect when starting the process. Other state agencies are listed as possible resources.

Furthermore, in chapters 21-22, I explain how to survive the holidays with your loved one living with Dementia and what to expect when you begin to mourn the living.

Then finally, in chapters 23-25, I refocus on the importance of living in the present and redefining our expectations. Letting God work in your life for much-needed transformation is easier said than done but not impossible. Finding the courage to cultivate a relationship with God shined a loving light as I struggled to let go and survive the darkness a caregiver's life becomes.

This book is a compilation of Spirit-guided answers to persistent questions of "Why is this happening" and "How do we fix this?" A collection of what I believe every caregiver needs to know, regardless of age, to proactively navigate your journey of caring for a loved one living with Dementia and prevent your demise while caring for yourself guilt-free.

Chapter 1
Stepping into Mom's World

Exodus 20:12 (ESV)
Honor your father and your mother, that your days may be long in the
land that the Lord your God is giving you.

It is just after 7 AM when the sun begins to shine through my bathroom window as I step out of the shower. My morning alone time is ending. I need to hurry as I push the French doors open to allow the crisp air in to release the steam quickly. The mirror clears enough for me to see, so I can massage a touch of moisturizer on my face, a splash of color, and throw my hair into a ponytail. Quickly yank up my jeans and yank a blouse over my head. Now it's Mom's turn.

Right before I enter her room, I pause just long enough to take a deep breath, inhale with a mental affirmation - I can do this, exhale with a smile. As I gently open her door, I check to see which end of her is up at the top of the bed, since Mom now sleeps like a fish out of water. Mom senses me in the room and quickly pulls the covers over her head as she moans, *"Awe, five more minutes."*

I remember telling Dad the same when he came in to wake me before school.

I walk over to her closet doors, not trying to be as quiet now, to pull out her clothes for the day. She's still a big ball of blankets unwilling to budge. As I pull back the curtains, I begin in a sing-song tone.

"Good morning; we have a beautiful day ahead of us."

Mom throws the covers off her head then says, *"What's so good about it?"*

"Well, you are alive and breathing to live another day. Isn't that a good enough reason?"

I lay her clothes near the foot of the bed so I could slowly pull back her covers. Underneath, she is gripping tightly to her stuffed Snoopy dog. Her PJ pants were pushed up above her knees with one sock on and one missing.

"You may not agree, but you are indeed blessed to enjoy another day."

She finally opens her eyes with a bit of a smirk and says, *"Yeah, I guess so."* She pushes Snoopy back over by her pillows and tells him to stay there. She begins to push herself up from the bed, belches, scratches her head, and then sits up to catch her breath for a moment.

Sitting there with one sock on while the other one falls under the bed, she appears like a little girl, young in mind. I can see the little girl in her face before she slides off the edge of the bed. Once her foot hits the floor, she stumbles just a tad as she finds her balance and then heads to the bathroom. That little girl disappears right before my eyes as each heavy footstep of her 200lbs standing 5 feet tall staggers like a petite drunk woman.

My husband and son have now gone to work and school so that I can leave the door to the bathroom cracked just enough for me to listen in.

It sounds weird, but I'm listening for her to call out if she needs help and to listen for the sound of her flow.

I place the toothpaste on the counter with her toothbrush and remind her to get the back molars as good as possible. She grins with all her front teeth visible and says, *"yep, I take good care of my teeth."* Never mind that by the evening, she will not want to brush her teeth again. Mom had quite a bit of dental work done to rebuild her lower right jawbone before one of her many crowns could be replaced.

"All done?" I asked.

While she smiles to show me the proof of her job well done, I can see the mirror and wall on the left side of the dual vanity sprinkled with heavy droplets of water. I figured she had a hard time turning the water pick off again.

We go back to her bedroom, where she sits on the bed to remove her PJs and slowly get dressed. By the time she is done with the bathroom and changing clothes, Mom is winded, breathing heavily, and ready for a nap. If it weren't for the smell of breakfast of fresh cinnamon toast, she would try to go right back to sleep.

Her coffee is brewing while my tea is steeping. Her hot oatmeal is cooling on the kitchen counter with a bowl of fresh fruit. Mom is making me nervous as she sits down at the round slate tile table by tucking her ankle under her bottom like a teenager on the edge of the chair, only she does not have the balance that a teenager has. Before bringing her food over to the table, I take another deep, cleansing breath before pulling out her morning meds.

Mom asks, *"More medicine? Didn't I already take them? What are these for?"* She asks the same question every morning. I point to the calendar to show the day of the week before responding to this same question again.

"Yes, you did take them yesterday. Today is a new day, though," and then I smile again, believing that it is a new day with renewed hope even though we had already dropped into the repetitive dialogue.

"These medicines are for your heart and to help you to remember," is my usual response. I have yet to stop hoping Mom understands or perhaps jogs her short-term memory just a little.

"Oh, right. So, I can remember to remember," Mom finally says with a girlish smile. Then instead of taking a few at a time, she puts all eight pills in her mouth at once and then takes a big gulp of water. *"Down the hatch,"* she chuckles with a wince as if I gave her a shot of tequila.

Other mornings she pours the pills into her hand, asking what each one is for because she wants to know which one is the heart medicine. It is both understandable yet upsetting, but I know exactly why she wants to know which pill is the heart med. She does not want to take the heart medication anymore.

Sometimes when she stubbornly insists on knowing before swallowing them, I tell her the heart med is her B12 supplement. And just as expected, that's the one she tries not to take or takes last when I refuse to walk away until she does.

We have completed our first few challenges of the day, and I have still yet to place her meal on the table. She knows her oatmeal is waiting for her, so she barks, *"hurry up, I'm starving."*

The oatmeal cooled a little, so I fastened a cover over her chest. As I watch her squirrel the food into her mouth, I cringe and look down at my bowl, hoping she does not see my look of panic and disgust.

A memory flashes back to the days when I was at the kitchen table squirreling food into my cheeks at age 9. I rushed through the meal to get back outside before the streetlights came on, signaling my curfew. Mom used to lean towards me, saying, *"Chew with your mouth closed! Food should be chewed and not seen."*

As much as I would like to remind her of these table manners, I know it will only trigger unpleasant conversation, including a firm middle finger telling me to shut up and leave her alone. *"Mom, it's okay; you have plenty of time, and no one is going to take the food away from you."*

She is hovering over her bowl with sweaty hair on her face stuck to her brow when she snaps back to my voice, *"huh? Oh, I know that."* She straightens up a little and slows down enough to look out the window while she chews another bite with her mouth closed and cheeks protruding with food, like a squirrel.

She finishes with breakfast saying, *"Thanks Jess, that was good."* Pushing back from the table out of her awkward way of sitting, she winces from pain in her knee. Now she heads for the recliner for another day of watching countless reruns of The Golden Girls, Matlock, Raymond, or Two and a Half Men.

"Snug as a bug?" I draped a blanket over her lap then waited for her thumbs up. I place her water bottle with lemon next to her and remind her to drink every commercial. She rolls her eyes at me with a smirk and says, *"Yeah, sure."*

Within two hours of breakfast, Mom is fast asleep in the recliner. Her Kindle tablet has fallen into the recliner's side cushion, which she cannot reach. Without the tablet to keep her mind active, she falls asleep while watching tv. I used to think watching the shows and laughing at them would be enough to keep her awake and focused, but now her comprehension and attention span are less than they used to be—more evidence of the effects of Dementia with a harsh reality check.

"Hey Mom, it's time to take a potty break; come on." I beckon her over in my direction towards the bathroom and then wait for her gripes.

"Huh, what do you want me to do? Where are we going?" She begins to pull the blanket off her lap as she struggles to push forward to sit up in the recliner. Her core strength is all but gone, so I use my foot to force the recliner down to a seated position and then help her up. She is like a turtle on its back, unable to turn or rise without some assistance.

"Come on, lift that caboose," I chuckle as I give her both my hands to pull her up.

By the time she stands, she chuckles too and then asks again, *"so where are we going?"* I tell her it is not too far over here and then move towards the downstairs bathroom with a smile. *"Oh no! I don't need to go. Come on, Jess, let me sit down a bit longer."*

The frustration bubbles up again in my mind *"stop giving me a hard time and go pee; it's for your own good!"* Another deep breath to calm and release the thought.

"Well, humor me and try. I bet you have to go a little. Besides, if not, then at least you get a bit of circulation going there and back."

Mom sighs deeply then says *"fine,"* while she rubs her forehead with her middle finger as she walks past me with a clown-like grin.

Halfway over to the bathroom, she starts to shuffle her feet faster as she fumbles with her pants. *"I gotta go pee-pee."*

She makes it to the bathroom with dry britches this time. I pull the door closed and then hover outside to listen. I can hear a much healthier flow now. Another concern is how much fluid she gets throughout the day to flush her system versus the amount of fluid her body retains. Excess fluid around the heart is not healthy.

I can hear her grunts and realize that she has to pee and finally has a BM. While I know she will be there a bit longer, I can rush to the laundry room to switch loads, stop by her room to mark her calendar with 'BM,' and get back downstairs in time to check on her.

Thirty-five minutes pass by when I hear her spin the toilet paper. She is done and goes to wash her hands. As soon as I hear the water turn on, I holler through the door, *"make sure you use the soap to wash your hands!"* Such a simple reminder, and yet it must be said. We have already gone through a spout of Helicobacter Pylori bacteria before.

H Pylori is an infection caused by bacteria when exposed through saliva, vomit, fecal matter, and contaminated foods. Although it's cured with a round of antibiotics, it is also 12 more pills a day for three weeks! More medicines to push her way.

"I know, I know!" I hear the water turn back on again as she pumps

the soap into her hand this time.

"Wow, that must have been the power of suggestion." She says as she emerges from the bathroom, looking exhausted, and heads back to the recliner. Mom holds tight to her tablet while I drape the blanket back over her lap. Now she will be content until the next bathroom break, then lunch.

We make it through lunch and eventually an afternoon snack. The late afternoon rolls around, and I'm beginning to feel the day. My eyes start to feel heavy while Mom is beginning to perk up with laughter as the game shows come on tv. Jeopardy, Wheel of Fortune, and Family Feud are the afternoon favorites. She shouts answers at the tv like she has money to win. Before I start working on dinner, I stand behind her in the living room to enjoy the moment.

Suddenly, conversation flows as the answers to some of the game show questions jog a memory or two. It's nice. For a moment, Mom is back. Maybe not the mother I remembered from just 10 or 15 years ago but a lively young, spirited woman instead of a sassy 12-year-old or challenging 5-year-old.

Since the day is winding down, I must keep moving because my family will be home from work and school hungry. Another deep breath as I walk back into the kitchen, knowing she is content while preparing dinner. Although I have not been entirely alone, I feel lonelier than I have ever felt my entire life.

I plug in my earbuds to listen to movie soundtracks that can whisk me away to another place and time while I chop up vegetables. Life has become drastically different from my corporate world routine.

I should be grateful for the time with Mom, and yet there is an emptiness deep inside those ebbs and flows as the days pass.

I am physically capable of being her caregiver, but I am not always emotionally capable or willing. Trying to practice being in the present moment, I force myself to find one thing to be grateful for this day of caregiving over the stresses I faced in the corporate world. This one little gratitude practice can be quite a challenge some days. This day, I wipe my tears away as I think, *"at least it wasn't a shower day."* Those are much harder days to get through.

I continue to listen to stress-relieving music, as I used to do in my cube while I worked late, allowing my mind to wander away. I chased a work-life balance for many years, desperately wanting to write more often and have more time to myself. Now, as I have more time without month-end deadlines or annual audits, it still does not feel balanced.

Some days I can see God's plan for us together on this journey, while other days, that inner teenager cries - *"why me, why now?"*

Now I fight for privacy, quiet moments to meditate or cry. Finding time to research more on Dementia to learn what I can do differently has helped me feel vindicated from those who did not believe me about Mom's journey of living with mixed Dementia.

No matter what balance may look or feel like, I know life certainly has more meaning. I feel the presence of God more than ever before. I have grown more as a caregiver than I could ever imagine growing in the corporate world professionally. Contemplating the meaning of life regularly rather than being stuck in an autopilot state makes the days pass much slower.

Dinner is prepared and, on the table, as we all sit around discussing our day. I live for these moments now. Not just because I know our youngest son will be graduating from high school soon and moving on into the world like his brother but because I crave human connection now more than dark chocolate. Who knew? The conversation has become such a commodity that I often strike up conversations in the grocery store with total strangers.

Mom lights up about her days as a teacher with her students as she listens to our son reflect on his school day. I am both excited to see her engaged and annoyed. Where was this chatty Cathy earlier today? Does she not have anything to tell me? And then my mind takes a turn in a direction I'm not particularly eager to go in—the what-ifs.

What if she is upset with me, so she chooses not to talk to me? What if she avoids me, so she doesn't have to speak to me? What if she thinks I am mean because I will not give in to her sweet cravings all day, so she would rather stay silent.

The internal battle has begun. Another part of me responds. No, she is just bored and does not have much to say. Oh, heck no, she already has a minimal attention span and can barely understand the jokes on tv when she laughs and then quickly asks what they meant. Ugh! Am I going crazy now? Take another deep breath and clear the dishes while Mom goes back to the recliner for more tv.

Now that everyone is home and in the living room, it is time to find something else on tv for all of us to enjoy. Mom does not care to give up the tv, so she decides she is ready to go to bed. I agree because I would like to spend time with my husband now before it's lights out for the night.

Before spending time with him, I have to get through my second least favorite part of the day before she can go up. Checking her blood sugar and then bedtime meds should be simple, but it takes more patience than I feel I have left this time of day.

I set the small plastic cup and a small glass of water on the coffee table next to the blood sugar kit. *"Again, I already took my medicines?"* she says with a grimace of disappointment.

"Yes, you did. These are the bedtime meds." I guide the cup into her hand. By this time, it has been a long day for her, which is visible in the amount of strength in her hand as she loosely holds the plastic cup while leaning against the recliner's arm.

From this angle, she looks around me to the coffee table and sees the blood sugar kit. She yells, *"Oh no! Not again. I don't need that! I won't have any dessert."*

Sometimes I can use dessert as her incentive to check her blood sugar, but other times she flat out does not care for it if it means avoiding a finger prick. I hate having to do this because although I know why I need to do it for her, it sets her off into unpleasant theatrics. Most of the time, her words roll off me like water on a duck's back, but now and then, she says something that hurts and gets under my feathers.

"Fine! You're such a drug pusher," she says as she rolls her eyes and then tosses the medicines into her mouth. It's not like I would have to give her a shot of insulin after checking her blood sugar; it was to collect data to report back to her doctor. Mom has such a sweet tooth and is reluctant to exercise that we must closely monitor the pre-diabetic status. I am supposed to check before bedtime about 3 to 4 times a week and report back to her general doctor.

I pull the kit open to get the sterile lance in place in the glucose monitor and then open an alcohol swab. Mom begins to squirm in the recliner. Like a child sitting on the pediatrics table as the nurse comes near with needles in hand, the tears start to fall as they squirm to hide in their parent's arms. Only Mom is back to the position of being a turtle on its back, exposed, and she is not shedding any tears of fear. Nope, the sassy 12-year-old mouth opens as she suddenly has a burst of strength and energy to push herself into an upright position in the recliner.

Now I had considered using the line I heard when I was that kid on the pediatrics table or principal's office awaiting a paddle for bad behavior. *"This is going to hurt me more than it's going to hurt you because I hate seeing you suffer."* Nope. I will not tell a lie, not even a therapeutic lie, for this moment. She had many opportunities to seek a healthier lifestyle, but unfortunately, her choices created consequences for us both. My inner teenager, along with all my many inner voices, agrees.

Mom sits up and tries to stand, but she cannot. I stand in front of her to block any forward movement. This battle is one I cannot afford to back down. As I am reaching for her hand to clean her fingers, the only choice I can offer her at this point is, *"which finger will it be this time? Pointer or middle?"*

You can imagine her now sassy 12-year-old self-choosing the middle finger when she realizes there is no escaping the finger prick. She points her right middle finger up at me firmly and says, *"Jodona puñeta."* Which is Spanish slang for 'damn pain in the ass.' I chuckle with a smile and take a deep breath while I clean her middle finger because she is grinning like a Cheshire cat that ate the canary, loving the moment of flipping me off. It is all good for me because I know what's next. Flipping me the bird is going to hurt me much less than she thinks.

I must position myself with her arm tucked like a football under my left arm to keep her from squirming even more. Every time we do this, it rarely takes one attempt from all her theatrics. Just as I kneel beside the recliner, she starts to wail, *"oh no, I don't need this, OOOOOOhhhh, NOOOOO! Come on, Jess, I don't need dessert!"*

My son and husband sit watching across the living room, unsure if they should help or stay put. Mom is nowhere close to a turtle exposed on her back but rather a little bull trying to buck me off. Even with her squirming and somewhat giggling now, I still hold firmly and prick her finger. It took more than 8 seconds, but I got her.

"¡Pinche puñeta jodona!" spews from her mouth, and now her finger has just enough blood to get on the strip but not enough for it to detect. While I try to keep her from sticking her finger in her mouth by pinching it a bit, we laugh as I try to get more blood. Hoping we do not have to do this all again on another finger.

Her blood is so thick that it does not flow well, so I must do it again on a different finger. Just like clockwork, she says, *"Darn it!"* and offers me her left-hand middle finger with a smile. It has become a game.

We go through the same theatrics, but I get a better finger prick to take the reading of 157. All that exhaustion confirms she is still just above normal in the prediabetes range. It would have been better if we went for a walk to get some exercise, but the way she fought to avoid a finger prick gave her system quite a bit of circulation. Mom was more than ready to get to her bedroom and away from me.

I stand behind her on the stairs with a palm hovering behind her back just in case she leans too far back. She yawns. *"It's been a long day. I'm so tired."* She is about halfway up the stairs when she attempts to turn to look over her shoulder to have this conversation. It would be nice to chat any other time, but it makes me nervous on the stairs. As soon as she turns her upper body to face me, she loses focus and leans too far back, and starts losing her balance.

Out of fear of us both falling on the steps, I cut off her statement to remind her to look forward. I may break her fall, but I do not want to experience both of us going down the steps.

"Mom, keep going. We're almost up to the top. You can go brush while I get your PJs."

No sooner than the words leave my mouth, I know what her repetitive response will be.

"I already brushed my teeth. I don't need to do it again. I am so tired. I just want to get into bed to watch Two and A Half Men."

I know this all too well. I could choose to avoid this, but I would not let our son skip his bedtime routine. Her gums and cosmetic dentistry work cannot go unattended. Even though I anticipated this response, it does not change the fact that I am tired too. I still want to get as much time with my husband as possible before we go to bed as well. I also understand that I cannot rush her, so she willingly does what she needs to do.

We finally make it to the top of the stairs when she suddenly begins to pick up the pace to walk past the hall bathroom. There is a mental order to this routine that makes this work smoothly for us, but it does not stop her from fighting the steps. I quickened my pace as well to guide her shoulders into the bathroom.

She pouts and wails, *"Oh come on, Jess, I'm tired. I'll do this later."*

We both know that is a lie indicating this will be another battle. I try to appeal to her delicate ability to reason. Once she lays down for the evening, she will not get up for almost 10 to 12 hours. If she does in the middle of the night, that creates the risk of falling, and neither gets sound sleep.

"Well, if you did not fight me so much to check your blood sugar, you probably would not be so exhausted." Her protest to the finger prick would not have made much difference. She is physically exhausted all day long regardless of what she does or doesn't do.

At this point, I'm a bit irritated with how this evening is ending. Even though I know what Mom yelled out downstairs when I pricked her finger was not how she felt about me, it still hurts. In my mind, a scary singular 'what if' bubbles up. What if she passes in her sleep, and that is her last sentiment towards me? That I am her pain in the ass daughter. Big deep breath before I continue to attempt to appeal to reason.

"Just go ahead and pee so you don't have to get up once you lay down. Once you are nice and comfortable, you're not going to want to have to get back up." She gives me a sideways smirk which confirms the appeal to reason worked - this time.

"Yeah, that's true. I'm tired, and I don't want to have to get up for anything." I stepped away to close the door to mark her calendar under

BM, BS 157 quickly. No sooner than I grab her PJs and lay them on her pillow, I hear her flush. A tantrum begins if I don't get back in time to encourage the water pick before she brushes.

She steps over to her side of the vanity and immediately reaches for her toothbrush. I smile while pulling the brush from her hand to set it next to the toothpaste. *"Before you do that, use the water pick to get out as much of the dinner that was left behind, so brushing is easier."* She grimaces, and before she can refuse, I quickly add, *"because you take good care of your teeth"* and smile with a wink.

She smiles back and agrees as she reaches for the water pick with no fuss. *"I sure do!"*

Knowing she already had a weakness in her hand with the cup downstairs to take her meds, she now must use more strength to turn the water pick on and hold it. Even though I wiped down the mirror and vanity from this morning's use, it is quickly doused in water when she can turn the water pick on but doesn't have it in her mouth yet. *"Oh shit."*

Somehow as she was fussing about turning the water pick on, she accidentally increased the power of the water flow. It did not occur to her to use the pause button on the water pick wand, but to keep it from spraying the vanity and wall even more, she shoved it into her mouth. Her eyes widened as her mouth filled up. *"Are you trying to waterboard yourself? Spit it out, Mom."*

She pulls the wand out of her mouth, laughing hysterically. She is now spraying me, the floor, and the mirror as she insists on telling me, *"I don't swallow."*

I dive over her to reduce the flow and turn the water pick off. Of course, she's still laughing because I am now looking like a cat dunked in the tub. She finally catches her breath and says, *"okay, that's enough,"* as she turns to leave the bathroom. Not only do I now have a sticky mess to pick up because the water pick contained a dilution of Listerine, but she has also not brushed her teeth yet.

"Wait, not so fast, Miss, I take good care of my teeth. You still have to brush." Here comes the temper tantrum even though she was just laughing hysterically. *"Awe, Jess, Come on. I'm tired. No, that is enough."*

Big deep breath and hard eye roll before I ask, *"So you want to let all that expensive dental work go to waste? You want to allow more cavities, need for a root canal, or more bone rebuilding?"* I get a hard eye roll right back as she picks up the toothpaste and toothbrush. *"Fine!"*

Little does she know I have already turned on her tv and set the one-hour timer, so it goes off on her by 10 PM. This bedtime routine stretches out longer nights when she fights more, but just like the morning conversation, the evening is the same repetitive conversation or bickering.

When we get into her bedroom, she pushes the PJs aside and attempts to crawl into bed with her food-stained clothes while reaching for Snoopy. *"Whoa, not so fast, look at you go. Did that splash of water wake you up a bit?"* And in that short instance, I hear the change in her voice, indicating her mental age. The little girl that was sitting on the bed this morning is back.

She chuckles and says, *"Yeah, I got a sprinkle or two,"* and keeps trying to reach for Snoopy, and at this point, giving her choices is challenging my patience. I am tired and frustrated knowing that as soon as I tuck her in, I need to go clean up the bathroom again before I can finally sit down to watch some tv with my husband.

I tug on her arms to get her to sit back up and see the fatigue in her face but hear the little girl asking for a different channel. *"I want to watch something else."*

Okay, not a problem once I get these dirty clothes off her. I quickly got Mom and the channel changed to Everybody Loves Raymond, then tucked her in with Snoopy.

"Goodnight, Mom. I love you." I lean down to hug and kiss her on the cheek. Each night I tuck Mom in with a kiss goodnight; I flashback to when I was a child at 5, 6, and 7. I always wanted just a bit more time to stay up with tv or bedtime stories. I always wanted to be tucked in to feel safe and secure. Always look for the kiss and hug goodnight from Mom and Dad.

Mom stretches out her arms to welcome a hug. *"I love you more."* She flashes her girlish grin showing all her front teeth again. She rolls over to snuggle with Snoopy and blows me one last kiss as I close her door. I blew a kiss right back with a smile, thinking, *'Ugh, we made it through another day.'*

When I stepped away from the corporate world to take care of Mom, I honestly thought it would be the busy body type of work—maintaining her household and finances or being present at a doctor's appointment. I hoped to share more happy moments with her, so I was unprepared for mental and emotional challenges. No more than I was aware of how much this journey would change me.

It was amazing to me now how much not knowing about Dementia would affect our time together. Many families and spouses are stepping into this kind of role with limited knowledge about the journey ahead. My emotional challenges far out wayed the physical or medical dilemmas we experienced together. When it comes down to the facts, we all know too little to help and far less to prevent our demise.

I began to wonder whether Mom was born with heart disease or not, or perhaps that somehow her deterioration was on a time-release mechanism. Then I could not help wondering if Mom is living with Mixed Dementia now, then was I also born with mixed conditions?

What would my timeline look like towards the degeneration of my brain? Am I deteriorating now as I write? Would my brain deteriorate in the same pattern as her brain? Would I gradually decline as she has over the past two decades simply because of my genetic make-up?

Thankfully, I have more curiosity than fear, but the fear is still real. As I watch Mom's limitations decline and her behaviors radically change, my fear is a driving force to stop this from happening to our sons and me.

When I stepped into Mom's world on a part-time basis, I used to think that I could save her and my sisters. Now I realize the journey I am on includes self-discovery, which I must do alone. Alone, meaning I had to *choose* to face my past, accept my present circumstances, and prepare for a future living a soul mission that I never thought possible.

Chapter 2
What We Know About Dementia

2 Corinthians 12:9 (ESV)
But he said to me, "My grace is sufficient for you, for my power is made
perfect in weakness."

What is Dementia?

Dementia gets its name from the Latin words *de*, or "without," and *mens*, or "mind," which join to mean "madness" in the English dictionary. Other terms used related to dementia have been mental illness or mental disorder.

Dementia was discovered in 1906 by Alois Alzheimer, a German psychiatrist who looked at the post-mortem brains of affected younger people. He published the first case detailing a 50-year-old woman with dementia symptoms. Even though Oskar Fischer, another German psychiatrist, also discovered the plaques and tangles in older people in 1907, the credit was given to Alois Alzheimer in 1910.

It took doctors another 60 years to recognize Alzheimer's as the most common form of Dementia. They were unable to differentiate Alzheimer's from the average mild cognitive decline associated with aging in 1970. At this time, they began using CT scans to detect the shrinkage of brains related to Alzheimer's.

Another ten years passed before biochemistry doctors were able to see tau protein and amyloid-b as components of tangles and plaques in 1980. Tau proteins are a group of six highly soluble protein isoforms. The role of this protein is primarily in maintaining the stability of microtubules in axons and is abundant in the neurons of the central nervous system.

Then ten years later, in 1990, genetic mutations were declared as part of risk factors to consider. Stages of dementia began to be defined in the 1990s. Mental health has been given more attention and respect, but not far enough since then.

Although Alzheimer's is still the most prevalent type of Dementia globally, some doctors now believe this to be less of a disease and more related to lifestyle habits. My hope is restored in science, which helped my fear and anxiety connected to what Dementia is subsided.

Dementia itself is not a disease, rather a loss of mental function in more than two areas of the brain. Dementia is a term used as an umbrella term to describe a collection of symptoms from a range of conditions that cause parts of the brain to deteriorate progressively.

The Queensland Brain Institute in Australia has identified more than 50 conditions known to cause symptoms of Dementia. Tau proteins and genetic markers detected in patients are not the sole cause of Dementia. The reason is a progression or build-up from the abuse to our heart, gut, or head, ultimately affecting the brain. Head injury includes stroke, excessive alcohol consumption, and smoking.

Mom's dominant symptom was not memory loss, yet her first Neurologist gave a misdiagnosis of early-onset Alzheimer's after her diagnosis of Vascular Dementia. This Neurologist then prescribed Donepezil, the generic version of the brand name Aricept, to slow the decline of Alzheimer's, which seemed to cause her more brain fog. Mom was medicated rather than educated on how to slow the progression or what caused the advancement in the first place.

One week several years ago, when I was caring for Mom in her home and struggling with my house chores, poorly balancing life with kids in school, I forgot to give her morning medicines two days in a row. I beat myself up over it because it could have caused severe consequences from missing her heart medication and antidepressants. The odd thing was she was clearer in mind and more responsive than she had been previously. After weighing the facts of bipolar tendencies, sleep patterns, and lack of exercise, I realized that she was more alert by missing the dosages of Donepezil.

The difference in her overall demeanor made me want to stop giving the Donepezil to her. Mom's second Neurologist left the medications as listed to evaluate her as she functioned with Donepezil. I felt I had to agree with Mom's neurologist at the time. She heard my concerns with her reaction yet still thought it would help her. The side effects of nausea, vomiting, diarrhea, and excessive tiredness alone were not helping Mom during the day, so switching the time she took it from AM to PM was the only change to come about. The neurologist was hoping she would sleep through the side effects instead.

I did not care for the previous doctor because he seemed more like pulling out the RX pad than evaluating her. Mom was losing track of time and getting lost more while driving back then when he prescribed the Donepezil and determined she had mild early on-set Alzheimer's. He also decided she was fine continuing driving and living alone. Other side effects included depression, confusion, difficulty falling asleep or staying asleep, which did not help Mom function better, but he felt it would.

Donepezil is prescribed for people who have Alzheimer's to aid the ability to remember, think, communicate, and perform daily activities. It can cause changes in mood or personality, but those changes are from the side effects with potential irritability. Mom's attitude and behaviors did not change with Donepezil, but her brain fog was considerably worse. The drug is by no means a cure and only claims to slow the process of brain deterioration.

Later, when Mom lived in a memory care community, she had better professional care and was evaluated more closely. Mom's Gerontologist asked me why she was taking Donepezil because it did not treat her type of Dementia. I explained the same to her about being more alert without it, and this doctor agreed with me. Another moment I felt both vindicated and angry that the other doctors only assumed she had Alzheimer's and were quick to medicate, assuming Donepezil would work. It has the potential to make life more difficult for those living with Dementia.

After those two days, I placed visible reminders in her kitchen and timed reminders on my phone, so I would not forget to give her medicines again. She was not nearly as alert or responsive once she was back on the regular AM & PM medication cycle. The memory loss she was experiencing was part of Vascular Dementia which often naturally progresses into Frontotemporal Dementia.

The lack of education ends up robbing individuals of valuable time to reverse any possible symptoms that are not indeed Alzheimer's.

Medications like Donepezil may not help as expected when you do not know the actual type of Dementia your loved one is experiencing.

Scientists have not pinpointed why some people produce excess Beta Amyloid or tau protein while others do not. What are the contributing factors to why we naturally produce this protein?

We already have Beta-Amyloid protein in our systems. The protein intended as protection is found in our liver, pancreas, and brain. The problem is introduced when we consume excessive amounts of food that causes inflammation which breaks down the protective barriers to our central nervous system. That excess amyloid protein then enters the bloodstream for the central nervous system and collects on our brain like mold.

I believe we are unknowingly creating the conditions within our body to allow the protective protein to reach abnormal levels, creating abnormal behaviors or Dementia. What can we do to stop this gene from turning on or even passing on to the next generation?

Detecting Dementia

By studying families with early-onset Alzheimer's, scientists now realize that the buildup of beta-amyloid or tau protein can happen two decades before the first symptoms of the manifestation of brain degeneration. This discovery gives scientists tremendous hope in terms of a large therapeutic window to intervene and stop the beta-amyloid cascade.

According to the American Academy of Neurology article published in August 2019, a simple blood test can detect beta-amyloid protein buildup in a person's brain years before symptoms appear. The test checks the plasma in the blood sample for AB42/AB40. Individuals who may have received a negative PET scan result may still receive a positive plasma test, placing them at higher risk of the amyloid buildup.

I didn't have a positive plasma test. Even as I went in for routine annual physicals and preventative dental check-ups twice a year, I was not having any MRIs or PET scans done on my brain. It was not something I considered until I learned more at Mom's appointments. Aside from Mom's bi-annual well-checks, we were left with the guesswork on her exact diagnosis from her behavioral cues and changes in abilities.

My nagging 'what if' genetic thoughts were getting louder in my mind. Even if I wanted to silence those thoughts, insurance or Medicare did not cover these kinds of tests. To add to my frustrations, the companies that can administer this blood test charge based on income and begin around $1,250.

The blood tests are not designed as a preventative measure but are available for people 60 and older who think they have problems or want to be evaluated for Alzheimer's. At this time in my life, I still wanted to know if I would travel down Mom's path. This kind of 'wait and see' made me feel like it would keep me in a reactive state of living and losing precious time if I did need treatment.

I started to compare my behavior to Mom's, wondering if there was any pattern or similarities. A wide range of cues make this even more difficult because many of these cues are emotionally challenging, so I had to push myself to look deeper instead of avoiding or ignoring as Mom did.

It became a cycle of denial and depression for her. Once she was finally able to get past denial, then depression became another barrier. Conditions like chronic depression or cognitive dysfunction caused by chemical imbalances can mask Dementia-related symptoms.

What made Dementia hard to detect for us was the lack of knowledge back in the 1990s and the comparison between Delirium and Bipolar Manic-Depressive Disorder. Long before Mom was diagnosed with Dementia, she had been living with Bipolar Manic Depression. Mom fluctuated between episodes of depression that went beyond feeling sad to as low as showing hopelessness or suicidal thoughts. She did not attempt to take her life directly, but she did write a few farewell-type letters to Dad.

Over the years of her decline, Mom kept many journals. Writing and reading books filled countless hours during her insomniac nights. When it came time to downsize her home for the first time, I found a letter tucked away in her bedside end table addressed to Dad. I did not feel comfortable reading it, but these articles gave my sisters and me a glimpse inside her mind that she kept so heavily guarded.

In this letter, Mom told Dad how much she loved him and how broken her physical body was, which was why she felt we would be better off without her. She was permitting him to move on in life once she was gone. It made me sad to see the proof in her words of how hopeless she felt and very angry that Mom was unwilling to fight for us. She was no longer interested in life any more than in building beautiful flower beds, building luxurious miniature detailed dollhouses, or spending time with her grandchildren. She barely existed in the world, waiting for her time to end.

Bipolar Manic Depression is a mental health condition that causes extreme mood swings, including emotional highs (mania or hypomania) and extreme lows (depression or suicidal hopelessness). Doctors can only speculate on causality between a combination of genetics, environment, and altered brain structure or chemistry. If we get stuck on the idea of genetics, then we lose valuable insight into our environment and potential triggers from food, PTSD, or disrupted sleep cycles.

Mom had prescriptions for anti-depression, but she would quit cold turkey whenever she finally felt good and 'normal,' saying she felt fine and didn't need the meds anymore. She was unwilling or able to acknowledge she felt fine because the medication was working for all her reasons. The stigma she attached to this antidepressant medication made her feel like less of the survivor she claimed to be and broken instead.

Delirium Mimics Dementia

On the other hand, Delirium is a sudden onset of mental confusion resulting from medical or environmental conditions. Delirium-inducing conditions include excessive alcohol or drug intoxication or withdrawal from opioids. Delirium can also result from a stroke, heart attack, worsening lung or liver disease, or a concussion.

Metabolic imbalances caused by low sodium, calcium, or blood sugar can present as delirium. Sleep deprivation, sleeping pills, and pain relievers may also contribute to a state of delirium. Some more common yet unsuspecting conditions such as dehydration, poor nutrition, and urinary tract infections or pneumonia are dangerous when left uncorrected and contribute to delirium.

Some lifestyle choices known to cause cancer, like smoking, might make people think they do not have to worry about Dementia. If

Dementia is not in their genetic history, as far as they know, cancer treatments such as chemotherapy can expose your loved one to Delirium and Dementia. Whether it is surgery of the brain to remove cancer (should it be operable) or the chemo itself that causes the injury to the brain is unknown. Studies are still in the process of determining a patient's mental health before and after treatment.

Some medications post-chemotherapy can cause chemo brain delirium. These types of lapses in short-term memory may present with difficulty remembering names or dates and problems concentrating. This chemo brain reaction is also found with certain chemotherapy drugs prescribed to treat many types of breast cancer. Thankfully, for most patient's chemo brain improves within 9-12 months after completing chemotherapy.

Delirium is sudden and typically subsides when the condition causing it is corrected or regulated. When some of those conditions are left uncorrected or unregulated, patterns begin to create conditions for Dementia. It is difficult to determine which behaviors cause or are linked to Dementia.

Something as minor as vitamin deficiencies can create a state of Delirium and, left untreated, can become a progressive decline towards Dementia. As there is a loss of brain cells resulting in a drop in everyday cognition and function, it may be time to suspect more than temporary Delirium.

Because of the sudden onset of Delirium, your loved one has trouble paying attention or cannot stay focused. In the early stages of dementia, your loved one can remain focused throughout the day. However, Dementia and Delirium both present with your loved one becoming distracted easily, withdrawn, fluctuating in mental status, difficulties communicating, reading, or writing. Both cause memory loss. Paying close attention to what is triggering a change in behavior or loss of function is so important.

In addition to three cesarean deliveries of my sisters and me, Mom also had other significant surgeries, which created a state of delirium afterward. It was easy to see her physical frailty after surgery, but the days that followed made her state of agitation more noticeable.

When she opted for sleep rather than eating, it made her seem what we called "loopy" or just not all present in mind. After a decent meal, we could see her skin color brighten back up with more energy in her movements. Before the meal and after pain medication, she was not able to make sentences that made sense. Items she needed were referred to as 'that thing' or where 'that thing' was left the last time she used it. Perhaps a hairbrush or the tv remote - the clicker thing.

After dental appointments with more than a typical cleaning, I could see the difference in her mental state from a current mindset of maybe her mid-twenties to that of a five-year-old. If my sisters witnessed her before and after, they could only see her as being silly. It usually took two or three days before this kind of delirium wore off for Mom.

These mental moments after her outpatient procedures were temporary and gave false confidence when her behaviors were not connected to a procedure. Out of context or without sedation, this kind of behavior puzzled us with why she may have acted out of character or seemed dazed and confused.

Reversible vs. Irreversible

The more I understood my brain connected with the rest of my body, the more I understood there is no cure for Dementia and mainly prevention. The brain may seem like a superficial muscle in our head, magically coordinating our thoughts, emotions, and actions, yet it is still very complicated. Because of the way Alzheimer's has been introduced to the public over the years, so many people understand Dementia primarily as memory loss even though there are multiple types of Dementia with varying behaviors. For instance, there are reversible and irreversible forms of Dementia.

Depending on the severity or type, the following conditions are reversible forms of Dementia:

Brain tumor
Depression
Dehydration
Side effects from surgery
Metabolic disorders such as disease of thyroid, pancreas, liver, or kidneys
Side effects of medication
Infection such as Urinary Tract Infection, Pneumonia, Periodontitis
Circulatory disorders
Nutritional deficiencies, malnutrition
Substance abuse
Head trauma
Carbon monoxide poisoning (CO2)
Lyme Disease
Sleep disorders

Simple and normal pressure hydrocephalus (NPH) is an abnormal buildup of cerebrospinal fluid (CSF) in the brain's ventricles or cavities.

Irreversible Dementia:
Alzheimer's
Lewy Body
Vascular
Frontotemporal Dementia
Picks
Huntington
Creutzfeldt - Jakob (Mad Cow disease)

Dementia itself is not a disease but a loss of mental function in more than two brain areas. I will detail more in later chapters about Irreversible Dementia (Vascular and FTD) and what behaviors they present.

Genetics vs. Lifestyle

Food can be our medicine coupled with meditation, exercise, and restorative sleep to reduce the stress we encounter. In addition to your daily health regimen, seeking therapy to understand our emotions better will help us identify our cycle. We can then identify the triggers within our reactive minds we indirectly pass down to our children. I know I did.

Once I began to accept this caregiver journey and what I could be facing, I became obsessed with finding out how to keep my genes in check. A theme was building in my mind to explain better what Dementia is but less about why our brain deteriorates in the first place. I was not buying the genetics claim.

The more I read, the more this question kept surfacing - Is Dementia hereditary or a consequence of poor lifestyle habits? If others claim Dementia is a disease of the brain, then it seems that it is a disease of accountability. We would be held accountable for what we put our bodies through over our lifetime, plain and simple.

The idea that I potentially carried genes for Dementia related illness drove me nuts. I did not want to accept it, still don't, so I had to know. My husband knew how important this was to me, so for Christmas of 2018, I received a gift box from Ancestry.com. I spit in the tube and sent it off as quickly as possible, wondering if this would stop my obsessive worries about my genes.

My health status results revealed no links to cancer and reminded me that most cancer cases are not caused by inherited DNA differences but are more affected by lifestyle. The test searched for only 27 out of 2400 DNA differences based on the family history I provided.

Receiving my results gave me a huge relief knowing the test did not find any links to cancer even though my paternal grandmother passed away from throat cancer. From what I was told, her death was due to smoking and secondhand smoke. I am not a smoker and will never start.

The following section in my Ancestry.com report covered Heart & Blood health. One link was identified as being a carrier of Hereditary Hemochromatosis, which is a condition that causes iron overload disorder or too much iron to build up in the body. I have not had any issues with Hemochromatosis so far, which is nice knowing it is prevalent and treatable.

Another family heart history issue was cardiomyopathy. I did not have any cardiac issues, but the family history flagged me with a warning. Then I read over another reminder that lifestyle and nutrition can also affect those chances. I thanked my lucky stars and moved on to the next section of the report.

Carrier status is to identify conditions that don't generally show signs, but their children might if the child's other parent is also a carrier. For example, conditions such as Cystic Fibrosis, Sickle Cell Anemia, Tay-Sachs disease could be passed to our children if both my spouse and I carried genes for these conditions. I was not a carrier, according to my results.

So aside from the Hemochromatosis and family history of cardiomyopathy, I did not have anything come back indicating I needed to be concerned about Dementia. Throughout the report, I was given several reminders that lifestyle could create heart problems from high blood pressure or obesity. Since I'm not yet the age to consider spending $1,250 on a blood test for Alzheimer's, this test was more than convincing. My lifestyle will continue to be my proactive approach.

I had to stop and smile up at the sky and say, *"THANK YOU, GOD."* I chuckled to myself because I felt like he was laughing as he looked down back at me. In my mind, I could hear, *"well, duh?! I told you there was nothing to worry about."*

Unfortunately, trying to silence the noise in my head between the gap created by mainstream media and what I knew in my heart to be different needed more of a compelling argument with results.

It takes quite a bit of appreciation of our anatomy and scientific discoveries to connect that Dementia, more specifically Alzheimer's, is not mainly a genetic disease. As the author of "How Not to Die," Dr. Michael Greger points out, *"when you examine the distribution of*

Alzheimer's disease around the world, that argument begins to crumble."

You can only imagine how uplifting it felt to read this research and no longer feel like I was doomed to succumb to my genetics no matter what I did. This book helped reinforce what I was understanding from Mom's history and now my DNA results. We have the power and the resources to change our habits, mindset, and DNA structure to prevent this type of brain degeneration and heart disease. In the least, we can postpone the effects of aging to live more purpose-driven lives.

If we begin changing habits, our hearts need help healing emotionally and medically to maintain energetic reserves daily. Stop the out-of-control cravings because emotional brokenness is not all about what we are eating but more so what is eating away at us.

Ironically, Mom used to tell me as a teenager, *"it's not what you're eating; it's what is eating at you."* She was partially correct because it IS about what we are eating. When stressed and searching for comfort, eating and drinking are dangerous ways to cope with life, let alone replenish our reserves.

Dr. Michael Greger reports that in Japan, the prevalence of Alzheimer's significantly increased in correlation to the shift from a traditional rice-and-vegetable-based diet to one featuring triple the dairy and six times the meat. The closest correlation researchers found between diet and dementia was animal fat consumption; animal fat intake shot up nearly 600 percent between 1961 and 2008 in Japan. A similar trend linking diet and dementia was found in China.

With diets Westernizing globally, Alzheimer's rates are expected to continue to increase, writes one researcher in the Journal of Alzheimer's disease, "unless dietary patterns change to those with less reliance on animal products...."

Dr. Michael Greger continues to point out, *"In the United States, those who don't eat meat (including poultry and fish) appear to cut their risk of developing dementia in half. And the longer meat is avoided, the lower the dementia risk may fall. Compared to those eating meat more than four times a week, those who have eaten vegetarian diets for thirty years or more had three times lower risk of becoming demented."*

Are you convinced that food should be our medicine yet? Well, here is another uplifting and inspiring nugget of information from Dr. Michael Greger. He shares what he refers to as the 'Nigerian paradox.' Mind-blowing details on a genetic factor discovered back in the 1990s called Apolipoprotein E4, or ApoE4. If you inherit one ApoE4 gene from your mother or father, it has been shown that your risk of getting Alzheimer's may triple. If you get the ApoE4 gene from both parents, which about one-in-fifty people do, you might end up with nine times the risk.

The highest frequency of the ApoE4 variant occurs in Nigerians, who surprisingly also have some of the lowest rates of Alzheimer's. Nigerians also have extremely low blood cholesterol levels, thanks to a diet low in animal fat consisting mainly of grains and vegetables.

The question begs to be asked, lifestyle or genetics. What do you think?

I was amazed after receiving my DNA results and seeing where my genetic make-up originates. The chart on the next page shows I have 12% Nigerian genes.

Ethnicity Estimate

[Share

Spain	31%	>
Indigenous Puerto Rico	17%	>
Portugal	14%	>
Nigeria	12%	>
Mali	4%	>
Cameroon, Congo & Western Bantu Peoples	4%	>
Southern Italy	4%	>
France	3%	>
Northern Africa	3%	>
Ireland	2%	>
Wales	2%	>
European Jewish	1%	>
Basque	1%	>
Benin & Togo	1%	>
Senegal	1%	>

The potential for me to carry the ApoE4 gene is alarming. It is just as fundamental as protecting my heart, gut, and brain. My genes are what they are. It brings me peace of mind knowing I can hold myself accountable for every meal, beverage, dessert, or drug that is not value-added to my mind, body, and soul. Knowing this has made me feel like a better mother, wife, daughter, and person overall.

I could feel a spiritual shift from eating more like a vegetarian and felt better too. It was almost as if God was pleased that I was learning how to protect the temple he gave me to fulfill His plan in this dimension during my time on earth.

Even though researchers now know of 10 genes believed to be associated with Alzheimer's and now have blood tests available to help determine if you carry them, the tests do not provide a definitive diagnosis. Carrying the genes and having Alzheimer's are still two separate concepts.

I analyzed Mom and Dad's family tree from what I could map out and compared her family with our family. I picked apart the similarities and differences in connection to potential changes in my day-to-day life.

Suppose I could keep my genes turned off in the first place. In that case, I could potentially stop the caregiving boomerang of passing down mutated genes to my sons and future grandchildren, thereby breaking the connection to genetic markers. Instead, I would pass down positive, helpful habits with encouragement for seeking therapy as the occasional need for a mental tune-up arises.

Lifestyle factors such as smoking, excessive alcohol consumption, unhealthy diet, physical inactivity, poor dental hygiene, and the lack of adequate restorative sleep also contribute to Dementia-related conditions. If you have the genes, you are more at risk of developing Alzheimer's, but the genes do not mean you have Alzheimer's or any specific form of dementia. They may very well remain dormant with a choice of lifestyle changes.

Dementia in Connection with Dental Hygiene

"There's an old saying about the eyes being windows to the soul. But the latest medical and dental research shows that the mouth truly is a window into one's overall health. Looking out for a loved one's health means not only keeping an eye on their nutritional intake and physical capabilities but also their teeth and gums," as quoted by Dr. Joy Poskozim, owner of Joyful Dental Care in Chicago.

Dental hygiene is one area sadly overlooked when it carries a great potential for prevention. I had the opportunity to interview Dr. Joy, a very passionate Dentist who owns her dental practice, including a mobile dentist service for seniors. Dentists are also part of the research into the causes of Dementia. Discovery into poor dental hygiene suggests that even Alzheimer's disease can result from gingivitis when the bacteria and plaque in the mouth spread to the nerve channels or enter the bloodstream.

With all the possibilities and hypotheses surrounding the causes of Dementia, it can be as simple as correcting dry mouth. A dry mouth happens when your mouth doesn't make enough saliva. Medications for Alzheimer's disease, high blood pressure, depression, and allergies can also cause dry mouth. If left untreated, then dry mouth can lead to ulcers, sores, and cavities which can cause problems with digesting food.

Gum disease or periodontitis is associated with an increased risk of developing heart disease. Poor dental health increases the risk of a bacterial infection in the bloodstream, affecting the heart valves. If you already have a family history of heart conditions, then your dental health becomes extremely important.

Mom's 3rd dementia diagnosis came well after living with Vascular Dementia and Early Onset Alzheimer's. Her dental hygiene was not as excellent as it should have been. After several expensive trips to the dentist for fillings, root canals, crowns, and jawbone reconstruction, she learned only swishing with Listerine was not enough. Brushing at least twice a day with flossing 2-3 times a week finally became a routine for her to protect her investment in her teeth. Even after spending thousands, she eventually reverted to the same poor habits.

The buildup of bacteria in her mouth over time and chronic insomnia caused her body to be exposed to more Dementia, causing elements without the opportunity of restorative sleep. In retrospect, I wonder if her poor nutritional habits and poor oral hygiene did not create the gateway to her life with mixed Dementia.

Both habits could have affected her heart, gut, and brain without us knowing until the symptoms became painfully apparent. As she began to isolate herself at home over the years, she did not keep up with dental visits regularly anymore on her own. It is essential to help our loved ones keep up with regular dental visits for as long as possible. This type of self-care will help prevent tooth decay, gum problems, pain, and infection.

Often the specialists who our loved ones attend are not connected by joining networks of patient records or treatment procedures, including dentists. The right-hand does not know what the left is doing. It is vital to have a list of your loved one's medications on hand, ready to provide to the health care providers. Not only can certain combinations of drugs be harmful, but they can also cause dry mouth and other oral health issues.

Be prepared and proactive to help prevent poor oral health with mouthwashes such as Biotene or Act. Electric toothbrushes such as Oral B Smartclean 360 are inexpensive and well worth brushing in 2-minute intervals. Go one more step by keeping extra replaceable heads readily available to be switched out at least once a quarter or when an illness occurs. We live in the new health-conscious era of Coronavirus, so changing the toothbrush head to avoid cross-contamination, as suggested by Dr. Joy, will improve good dental hygiene. Floss regularly and smile often.

Chapter 3
How the Stages of Dementia
Get Dismissed

Philippians 2:4 (NIV)
not looking to your own interests but each of you to the interests of the others.

Studies of experimental treatments such as Eli and AstraZeneca PLC ended when they failed to show improvement in people with early signs of cognitive impairment. Pfizer shut down its neurodegenerative disease research in addition to Merck after disappointing results, according to Alice Park of TIME Health magazine issue fall of 2018.

An investigation continues to be conducted searching for the "magic pill" by Eisai, a Japanese company partnered with Biogen, based in Massachusetts. The Alzheimer's Association noted that trials on BAN2401 are the second experimental drug to show effectiveness in reducing amyloid burden in the brain. The first was aducanumab, which two companies developed and tested in a more advanced Phase 3 trial.

What doctors are beginning to learn is the cause of Dementia is not entirely limited to our DNA. If Dementia is pinpointed to mutated genes, then we are responsible for turning on the gene when we allow our physical and mental health to degrade.

On a global scale, Dementia is increasing as the western diet spreads across the globe. Michael Greger, M.D., FACLM, founder of nutritionfacts.org, states the balance of evidence in the United States, Japan, and even China lies in the American diet. As the Western diet spread globally over the past few decades, the prevalence of Alzheimer's has shot up.

This alarming fact made me wonder why people worldwide were being affected by the deterioration we call Dementia. How could they not see the preliminary signs to avoid the pitfalls?

Over the years with Mom, we did not see the signs because we were so busy with our own lives. We were still stuck in the old patterns of programming that promoted convenience over healthy choices. The early stages are not as recognizable because the subtle changes can easily be explained from various views.

Vitamin deficiency, sleep deprivation, malnutrition, and other metabolic issues can mask the early signs of Dementia. The numbers of those living with Dementia continue to rise worldwide because we need to pay closer attention to our bodies and our loved ones.

Once I was aware of the stages of Dementia and what they look like, I found peace of mind having a better grasp on where Mom was from stage to stage. The steps helped me know how, when, and where my level of care needed to be focused or changed. It also made me aware of how and where my habits needed to change. These stages are intended to be a general understanding rather than the hard-fast rule.

Many doctors in the medical profession stepped away from speaking about stages other than Intermediate, Mild, and Severe, or End-Stage because there is still quite a bit of variation with so many different forms of Dementia. Even with the top 4 most recognized and understood, there is still some variation and enough similarity to consider the stages.

Therefore, the environment and our loved one's historical data on habits, medical, mental, and emotional status become essential to observe. I compared who Mom had been over the years, but I could also compare normal and not by thinking through the stages. As you read on about my comparison with Mom's status with each the step, know that this information is not intended to be in place of a doctor visit or provide any diagnosis.

The environment is a crucial component. If you find any of this repetitive, it will be based around this concept for sure. I apologize for the redundancy; however, you must take away at least this one concept regarding the stages of Dementia.

What I was taught as I was raised through to a young adult was passed down from what Mom and Dad were taught as children and young adults. It was all they knew and believed they were doing their best.

My question of 'how did this happen' turned into 'how much time do we have left with her?' No one can answer the latter question, but the signs are there for observation. After dismissing her earlier symptoms for far too long, I know now what not to ignore as we continue this journey.

This level of understanding while experiencing the stages with Mom helped the silence to be bearable. I kept asking questions because I suspected her answers were more cover-ups. Then I finally accepted when she said she did not know something; she was honestly at a loss for words or lacked an understanding.

The Bible quotes the phrase to "be still" roughly seven or eight times. Psalm 46:10 *"Be still and know that I am God; I will be exalted among the nations, I will be exalted in the earth."* This psalm took me years before I could genuinely 'be still.' I kept thinking sitting physically still was contradictory to all that had to be done each day. For me, experiencing this kind of stillness is trusting God with where Mom's journey leads her.

"Silence is the language of God. All else is poor translation," as Rumi (Samadhi) quoted, is what being still now means to me. I had to learn how to build upon my spiritual toolbox. In our moments of silence, there was usually body language to follow. Many times, when we were not addressing Mom's behavior, we sat in silence or avoided each other because we had nothing else to make sense of what was happening and why much less how to fix it.

Denial can become a powerful force of persuasion. Belief and disbelief from one day to the next are of the mind. What we choose to see versus what we choose to believe can be annoying and distracting. This journey requires a sense of knowing and feeling through observation.

Our reality is all we know, so we must fight to believe, even if it is something that tests cannot prove. My need to understand Mom's needs became my reality, my obsession. Feeling that something is not quite right but coping with others telling me I was wrong or did not know what I was talking about made me fight even harder.

According to Tam Cummings, Ph.D. Gerontologist, awareness, and understanding of what Dementia is doing to which part of her brain are critical factors for all caregivers to grasp regardless of the type of Dementia your loved one might be enduring. Your loved one may not look ill, yet their behaviors or responses offer clues as to where they are in this process.

Dr. Cummings developed a tool for stages of Dementia, the Dementia Behavioral Assessment Tool (DBAT), which can be used to track the decline of your loved one. This tool can allow you to prepare emotionally and financially as the increase in the level of care presents. Dr. Cummings goes into detail, but I will only skim the tool-related directly to Mom. Many of these explanations can be read yet still not be understood because it is difficult to know what it looks like from person to person, stage to stage.

Judy Cornish, the author of The Dementia Handbook and Dementia with Dignity, founder of the Dementia & Alzheimer's Wellbeing Network (DAWN®), also correlates with practical stages. She gained knowledge of the steps as she worked with many seniors living with various forms of Dementia. Judy's description of stages is a bit more relatable when you think of the day-to-day changes we experience with our loved ones.

Stage 1 – Normal Aging (Age 40-55; Often missed due to lack of vitamins, hormonal imbalances, or infections such as UTIs); Also known as the Independence Stage.

A. No cognitive changes are evident. Normal aging, normal brain function.

1. Your loved one knows who they are and where they are. The concepts of time and place can still be understood. They can still understand relationships between people, objects, and environments. They can provide care for themselves. They may begin to lose knowledge of the recent past. Rational thinking

may start to slow, but others may see this as normal aging as our loved one slows down. They may also appear as stubborn independence.

2. Mom maintained a daily routine of living through the bare necessities while she was still teaching. She had a regimen that was her safety net of reminders to eat, bathe, change clothes, drive to/from work, and interact with people seamlessly.

3. Mom used to step out of the house to talk with the neighbor or plan holiday gatherings with co-workers, friends, and family to attend. Even though Mom was not primping with hair and make-up, she still attempted to dress nicely for work and church.

4. As time continues, their experience shifts cognitively in perception and awareness. These shifts lead to emotions and how their feelings are shown on their face. You can see other physical changes in their person's physical condition.

5. After a period, Mom's routine began to slip. The need to sleep longer than usual would take up time for eating or bathing but changing clothes and driving to/from work was still possible. What she needed to function gradually eroded down to sleeping more.

6. Mom was not one to take medicines on her own since it was not a necessity to her. This stage is when Mom's vascular issues started to appear more often. Dental Hygiene stopped being a priority. This stage was also when Mom pushed us away from helping more because she insisted on being a survivor. Her response was usually, *"I don't need that...."* She chose to sleep over attending our school events.

Stage 2 – Early Stage (Age 40-55/60) – Beginning of Cognitive changes (Can last between 5 to 20 years); Also known as Uncertainty Stage.

A. Mild Cognitive Impairment (MCI) with Minimal brain tissue loss.

1. Your loved one still knows who and where they are, yet subtle differences will begin to be noticeable. They may still be able to do well in casual social conversations, yet uncertainty or

---

increased loss of reason, logic, and judgment with a decreased attention occur more. They have enough awareness to recover from mistakes or correct themselves.

Sometimes this awareness may appear as denial, which may also be a sign of anosognosia. Anosognosia is a condition that causes someone to be unaware of their mental health condition and how it affects them. The reaction to bringing issues to their attention if they are experiencing anosognosia might spark family drama.

When we spend significant time with them, we can perceive the evident changes in their ability to function with their awareness of their functionality. They may begin to start and restart tasks or fail at completing the tasks yet still be able to complete activities of daily living.

Mom started to struggle with driving to/from work by getting lost along the way. Grading papers and posting grades or hunting down missed placed assignments began to take more and more of her time. Leaving work to be home around 5 PM slowly became 9 or 10 PM.

2. As time continues, typical daily tasks may be left undone or incomplete. Organizing plans, dates, and times becomes difficult, so they appear busy yet forgetful. Meanwhile, they begin to misplace objects, forget names they know, and notice the fleeting moments of cognitive loss. However, they can still decipher between seeking medical care or ignoring symptoms since they can still function effectively at work or home.

    Mom started to abandon many hobbies like building her flower beds and miniature dollhouses with intricate details. Leaving her purse in different places or misplacing her keys seemed subtle, yet it happened more often. She slowly stopped trying to talk with our neighbors and hid from them when they came to check up on her. Mom no longer cared to talk on the phone with family as long when they called.

3. Testing becomes a requirement to determine illness. Personality changes begin with social withdrawal and interest in their familiar environment, and daily routines become indifferent.

Thanks to muscle memories, they may score well on orientation tests even though they may be growing absent-minded or unable to concentrate.

Although we did not begin testing her at this stage, the personality changes were a bit tricky. Mom was usually "moody" or bipolar around us, and often her mood was blamed on simply being tired. Her workday was exhausting, which led into the evening with no energy left for any conversation or interest in interaction. She usually ate something and fell asleep on the couch.

Quick trips to the local hardware store on the weekends were eventually postponed. Familiar streets on the route to work gradually became unfamiliar. Mom began showing up late to her first-class period and then awarding the children for good behavior or not acting up while she was running late.

4. Carelessness with appearance, arrogant behavior, lessening facial emotions, and a sense of humor seems to be the occasional issue, so it is dismissed as tied to an event or specific moment (like we did). More frustration might be shown, or a sudden sense of humor returns when they cannot hide their symptoms.

Mom would appear depressed or angry and then later more aware of her forgetful or absent-mindedness only to shrug it off like it was not a big deal. While Mom was not the girlie-girl type with hair, nails, and makeup, she did try to put in some effort towards her appearance. She still dressed nicely for school during the week. Eventually, it became sweats and t-shirts with the attitude towards Dad of "take it or leave it!" She would make a snide remark and then return to bed or her office room if she could and avoid hanging around with us.

Dad became upset when she acted like that in front of us, but there was not much he could respond with that did not turn into bickering. She belittled him in front of us and then laughed it off. The emotional divide was taking a toll on them both.

Stage 3 – Beginning of Dementia (may last 1 to 4 or more years); Also known as Follow the Leader Stage.

A. Signs and symptoms become too pronounced to be normal aging with minimal brain tissue loss.

  1. Behaviorally, memory deficits are pretty evident, as are the attempts to conceal or deny their difficulties with cognition. Family members are confused because they appear to be fine as they use humor to hide their shortcomings. The family may begin to argue or disagree as we did when the mood works to cover up. They are no longer tracking time or days consistently. They may also be unable to recall simple daily items like what is in their refrigerator or what they want from the kitchen. They need daily caregivers and cannot be alone regularly.

      Mom would say, "How stupid of me?" and then laugh away whatever her action was. These moments became inside family jokes with inconsiderate teasing. I am not talking about the one time she put an egg in the microwave, shell and all, for it to explode and find out you cannot cook an egg that way. No. It was more moments forgetting she had to be somewhere important and why. Forgetting names and faces and even confusing pet names for ours created more laughable moments.

  2. Your loved one may begin to have difficulties finding correct words, misused words, or lose a train of thought mid-conversation. They may no longer try to be part of conversations or want to attend functions with specific participation. They may also begin to have problems performing at work.

      Mom started to make phrases using "that thing, you know, that thing…." If she could not think of the word in English, then she would say it in Spanish. I asked what it meant, but she would respond with "I don't know" because it either did not translate well or she still could not think of the English word.

  3. Driving begins to be a problem or safety hazard when traveling to new areas or in familiar surroundings, from minor fender benders to dents in the car. Household chores start taking longer or are not done at all. Paying routine bills becomes a challenge

to remember when to pay, how much, or even accessing online bill pay sites.

Mom's grandchildren began to mention she was driving on the wrong side of the road while out running errands together. An indicator for letting go of her car, which provided savings from a significant payment with insurance. It was a huge safety hazard and financial drain for a vehicle that was barely used.

Mom stopped trying to clean and began hoarding all sorts of things, like used toothbrushes, for example. Bills were forgotten or deliberately not paid so she could "save money" yet not understand the necessity of paying utilities or medical invoices. When she did remember to pay, she would consistently lock herself out of her online bill pay service. If she bothered to write a password down, then she could barely remember where she put it for safekeeping.

4. Poor judgment in making decisions like giving money away to charities or family and unable to choose appropriate clothing by the season or matching clothing. Misplaces items even more without being able to retrace steps to locate them. More depressed with a lack of spirit or spark for life with a vacant facial expression.

    Mom eventually insisted on having cash on hand to pay bills. She preferred to pay with cash rather than deal with credit cards, and money also made her feel more in control. She used to be so good at online banking until she could not get online anymore. Locking herself out of her online bank, laptop login, and eventually having to call one of us to take her into the bank became a regular occurrence. Then she decided the bills were not as essential to pay anymore but still wanted plenty of cash on hand to give away as gifts to others. She no longer cared about responsibility in maintaining her finances or protecting her credit score.

5. Increased anxiety with more self-awareness of their behavior makes them more withdrawn and self-isolated to avoid interaction with others—wide mood swings with increased agitation and hostility.

These were the moments we thought Mom was rude for no reason or being mean towards us, but this was also a tepid response that was not tied to her past Bipolar tendencies. At this point, Mom was always in dirty clothes when we visited or in bathrobes and pajamas. Clothing did not fit by being too small, missing buttons, or broken zippers, yet Mom insisted the clothing still worked even though zippers or buttons were left wide open.

It was a delicate subject because she either took offense when we pointed out her clothing malfunction or went off into an inappropriate conversation about being ready for a man to come to find her. Then on the flip side, Mom started to mention more often how aging sucked, and she was prepared for it all to be over.

6. There may be an increase or decrease in sexual desires. You might notice worsening coordination or balance. They may be sleeping more than usual with a change in normal appetite. If tested again, they would score well on orientation tests but not on cognition tests.

Mom's selection of food reduced to fewer types of food, or she ate her favorites as much as possible like ice cream, Little Debbie snacks like Nutty Buddies, and pizza. She ate because she was bored and seemed hungry all the time. She would not eat healthy unless she was given nutritious food or told that was the only option. When we provided her with healthy food, she ate smaller portions to save room for dessert.

If she was not watching something on tv, she usually was asleep throughout the day and night. The constant sound in the background helped her feel like she was not alone. She left lights off, saying it was to conserve energy costs, but the tv never went off. The tv became her companion to have constant sound in the house. Using the remote became a challenge as she mashed buttons and could not understand why the connection was lost.

Watching her walk from behind as we went on walks showed a noticeable difference in her gate. I would gradually step behind her to watch her steps. Like a car with poor alignment, she would stride across the sidewalk into the grass or gravel and catch herself when she finally noticed the change in terrain or stumbled.

She depended on someone walking with her to tell her when to turn because she became like a horse with blinders; she would not turn left or right unless you told her. She did the same thing when driving, which often made her get lost or end up on a highway for much longer than she needed.

Stage 4 – Middle Stage of Dementia (may last 1 to 4 or more years); Also known as Clinginess Stage.

A.   Moderate Dementia is believed to have roughly 4 ounces of brain tissue loss.

B.   Behaves like a 12 to 20-year-old; needs a caregiver for at least 8 hours a day.

   1.   Symptoms are more pronounced with no doubt of abnormal aging. Your loved one is struggling with current and recent events. They may look to you for help to answer questions as they struggle with immediate recall, simple math, dates, times, or personal history.

   Facial expressions become more of frowns or the grumpy cat face with little facial movement. They might have problems with sensory stimulation (loud noises) or interpret sensory data like their own image in the mirror. Making eye contact with your loved one becomes extremely important as their present moment changes every 3 to 20 seconds.

   Mom began accusing me of lying to the doctors or joking about her symptoms when asked what brought her in for a visit. She stopped trying to fill out forms when we arrived and handed all clipboards over to me to fill out for her. Mom claimed she did not have her glasses but worked a crossword puzzle or seek-n-find just fine without any glasses.

   We often said Mom felt like a sassy teenager. I frequently asked her what was wrong because she looked disgusted or confused, but she would smile or laugh and either say she farted then attempt to engage or be defensive and tell me to leave her alone.

2. Hygiene is dismissed or forgotten. Close friends, neighbors, and family may become difficult to recognize. Comprehension of reading and writing is lacking, contributing to difficulty in recognizing numbers for basic math. May have trouble expressing language yet cursing more often.

   Mom's limited conversation became about sex and meeting a man or many young men. Sometimes that kind of chat helped get her in the shower, and sometimes it became very colorful before needing to redirect. Sometimes she cussed, knowing which words upset us to hear, and other times she cursed when no other words came to mind.

   Mom grew more resistant and argumentative over showering no matter the time of day or season.

   I provided more books for her to read since she used to be an avid reader finishing a book a day if given the time, but now she did not have an interest in any topic aside from her crossword or seek-n-find word puzzles.

3. Difficulties extend to more complex tasks such as driving, finances, shopping, bathing, telling jokes or stories, or walking or falling more (higher risk with gate off). For many, the discussion of giving up their driver's license may be perceived as a prison sentence to their homes from total loss of independence.

   Mom gave up driving after a car accident, which resulted in shoulder surgery. It did not stop her from buying more cars because she preferred to be a passenger. Plus, these purchases became more impulse buys to prove she was still in control and independent.

   Mom no longer stepped out of the house to check her mail regularly, so utilities were cut off since notifications were often missed until we started checking her mail for her. When we brought it to her attention, she shrugged her shoulders since she no longer cared about bills.

4. Has a greater desire for sweet foods while difficulties increase with ADLs or IADLs. Anxiety/frustration over the loss of abilities is more apparent with a decrease in facial affects or emotion on the face. They may become lost while attempting to complete a task, so they stop.

    Mom stockpiled ice cream, junk food, and candy throughout the house. The wrappers left a trail of evidence of poor eating, which also led to a cockroach problem. Many times, Mom would reach into my plate or my son's plate to take food.

    She would go the day denying hunger if offered something other than sweets, then finally sit down to a meal and eat as if she had nothing in days. Mom then shoveled food in her mouth as fast as possible. While she shoveled, she hovered over her plate as if someone would attempt to take it away by chipmunking to stuff her cheeks. Moments later, she would ask if we had eaten lunch or dinner because she could not remember eating or the feeling of contentment.

5. Hallucinations or inappropriate social behaviors begin to happen. They still may score well on orientation tests, but dementia is evident on cognition testing by now.

    Each time Mom was subjected to these tests with positive results on the orientation testing, she would say, *"I aced it"* with an enthusiastic high-five but did not want to acknowledge or understand the poor scoring of cognition. Mom would listen and roll her eyes, then say, *"Yeah, so what. None of that stuff matters anyway."*

    Her response to many moments involved hurting someone's feelings or accepting any responsibility for her actions. My Big Sis experienced this far too often and was never given any kind of heartfelt apology. Mom showered her with cash on later birthdays and then laughed, saying she was too sensitive to hurtful comments. Unfortunately, hurt people - hurt people in return.

Stage 5 – Moderately Severe Dementia – Split between early and late-stage (may last 1 to 3 years); Also known as Overnight Care Stage.

A. A dementia diagnosis is typically made around this stage when they have lost roughly ½ to 1 pound of brain tissue.

B. Early-stage five behaves like an 8 to 12-year-old. Late-stage 5 acts like a 4 to 8-year-old. The beginning of the final stages makes it necessary to seek professional help, more so nursing care or 24-hour monitoring in memory care communities.

   1. Even though your loved one still knows self and family, they can no longer survive without help yet sporadically appear or act normal. Disorientation to time regarding date, day of the week, or season is apparent, so they need help choosing or layering clothing but can get frustrated with assistance. Family, friends, and even some doctors may say they look great or are physically healthy. Family feuding typically begins (if not before) between those around them regularly versus those who occasionally visit.

      My siblings and I began to fall apart over Mom's lack of abilities or difference of opinions to flat out denial. Mom could still recognize the holiday seasons by decorations or repetitive commercials on tv but lost track of what day of the week or month she was in otherwise and gradually lost track of the year.

   2. Craving sweets excessively over any other foods. They may begin to fall and struggle to stand or bend down to sit (toileting). Urinary incontinence begins sporadically monthly, weekly, to daily. Sleep disturbances overnight become excessive sleeping or napping during the day.

      Mom craved sweets like a drug addict, so they could not be accessible. Once I left a pecan pie on the kitchen counter after Thanksgiving by mistake. She grabbed a handful of the pie and ate like a starving child while laughing. Her response to me as I cleaned her hand was my fault for not letting her have as much as she wanted. I could never find the balance between moderation for a person with diabetes and 'enough' to please her.

Then Mom's falls were subtle at first, like catching her step on the floor or rising from her recliner or chair. She was no longer lifting her legs usually to walk rather shuffle her feet, and then she began falling over face first or in the bathroom. She did not have the strength to stand initially after sitting for long periods so that she would fall back down into the chair immediately. She would repeatedly fall back to the chair yet giggle and joke about being a weeble wobble without some assistance.

Every activity exhausted her, making it difficult to stay awake unless she could play interactive word games on her Kindle tablet to capture every bit of her attention.

3. Your loved one may begin to resist care even though they need it. They may appear to have Amnesia while becoming severely depressed with increased loss of facial affect. Hallucinations may worsen while they become accusatory. More assistance is needed for eating, toileting, bathing, grooming, and dressing. They may start to be lost in their current time and place yet still score well on a Mini-Mental Status exam, but not on a cognition test.

Mom avoided activities if it meant having to exert energy beyond standing up. Still, if I pointed this out, she suddenly had the burst of energy to fold towels, for example. Two or three towels seemed enough to show me she could, and then she was too tired again and needed to sit down.

Mom did not hallucinate during the day by seeing someone who was not there, but she had lucid dreams. One mid-morning, she dreamed about being in a house on fire which she had to jump out of the window. The vision caused her to fall out of bed partially onto the end table, where she could not push herself back in bed or fall the remainder way out of bed. I realized then I needed bed rails and unique locks on the windows. It was not the first time she was known to sleepwalk.

Offering help at this point was often turned down with the statement of "Leave me alone, I can do it, I'm not a child." Most of the time, if left alone, she would not do whatever the task was because the usual response was, "I'm tired, I'll do it later."

4. May begin having chronic Urinary Tract Infections (UTIs). Has increasingly more difficulty recognizing self in a mirror or recalling family members, losing knowledge from the past. May have trouble interpreting background noise and visual perception issues cause bumping into objects. Automatic "yes or no" answers without understanding the response. May start using vulgar curse words as temporal lobes become damaged.

   Mom stopped trying to carry on conversations and reverted to 'Yes' or 'No' answers, eventually to head nods or shakes. Each time I asked her to answer me with words, she would protest and say she was tired, leave her alone, or didn't know what to say.

   Mom began having UTIs every three months, making her more irritable than usual. She would ask for the little 'orange pills' or the over-the-counter AZO Standard urinary tract relief medication, which made me aware of the UTI. Then I would know to take her to the doctor. Eventually, she would not say anything but be more irritable until she began to vomit.

   Mom went for days saying she was nauseous and barely ate or wanted Ginger Ale to drink. This cycle happened for a year until I realized I had reached the point of not caring as well as a nurse could more intently. I had reached my limitations as an in-home caregiving daughter. I could not rush her to after-hours clinics every time she vomited and didn't know why.

   Mom also began watching tv with the sound louder than before and looked confused. She could not hear as well and refused to wear her glasses most of the time. Mom said no to hearing aids because she did not believe she needed them or was old enough.

5. If injuries occur, they may appear stubborn to therapists and family members out of embarrassment or confusion. Disorientation might cause your loved one to pull at their clothes, tap fingers or wring hand motions are common. Sundowning and wandering to find items throughout the house or even to leave 'to go home' begin to happen more regularly.

We called in-home health therapy to help Mom navigate the house and public more smoothly, but Mom resisted right away, stating she did not need help. Ironically, her reasonings for why she did not need help was because the falls were not so serious with an explanation for each fall or why it was not her fault. Explaining new bruising to the doctors was a challenge to get a straight answer over a fabricated excuse.

Mom also began repeatedly rubbing her thumb and middle finger together in a mindless, soothing manner known as pilling. She also would hang on tight to napkins or straw wrappers to fold and refold or wrap around her fingers.

After living with us for a couple of years, Mom mentioned going home as if our time together had been an extended visit. I was unsure which home she was referring to because she could only mention she wanted to go home. I tried to remind her that she was home already, with me gently, but she just rolled her eyes and said, *"that's not what I mean."* I was nervous to ask what she meant at that point, so I redirected once again.

6. Impaired language abilities make communication and comprehension difficult for both you and your loved one. Social skills may still be good, but they may not understand all the words spoken. They may become argumentative and accuse caregivers of theft for items misplaced. They may begin repeating statements as short-term memory is not as good even though speech and language skills are still functioning.

   Mom's conversations, when they were not about sex, were so short because it was frustrating to find the words. Or when it came to finding the tv remote or her Kindle tablet, it was the repetitive bicker of where it was left last, or maybe someone put it somewhere else to keep it from her. Most of the time, these items were under the bed covers or stuffed down the side of the recliner, but she would not stand up to look for them.

   Going out in public was more complicated because Mom would say whatever came to mind, no matter how derogatory, racial, or insensitive. A usual child asks out of curiosity, but Mom commented without regard and followed up with more insensitive responses when people showed shock or offense.

Stage 6 – Late-Stage Dementia (may last 1 to 3 years); Also known as Full-time Companion Care.

A. 1 ½ - 2 pounds of brain tissue loss.

B. Behaves like a 2 to 4-year-old with profound loss of abilities. Needs someone with them at all times.

    1. Short-term memory may be down to five minutes or less. Your loved one may be unaware of events or experiencing past moments as if they were present moments. Even if they may still recognize you, they may not remember the names of their spouse, adult children, or regular caregivers.

    As Mom entered this stage, it was subtle yet noticeable as her questions were more repetitive. For example, getting into the car for a trip to the store or doctor's appointment would begin with a question of where we were going. After a turn or two on the road, she would ask again where we were going. Minutes later, after she looked out of the window and did not recognize our surroundings, she asked again where we were going.

    When we used to host a holiday meal, she would try to greet the grandchildren but get names mixed up. At times she would call our youngest by her dog's name. And yet, when her staff caregiver kept getting Mom's name wrong, Mom said while shaking her balled-up fist through gritted teeth, *"Say my name wrong one more time!"*

    2. Speech and language deficits are more pronounced, making it difficult to engage in conversation or comprehend difficulties. They may be able to exchange greetings but not much else. They may be able to tell you basic needs like hunger or bathroom needs. If your loved one is multilingual, they will most likely revert to their first learned language growing up.They may attempt to engage in conversation but not make much sense.

    These are the moments I had to be comfortable in the silence and become increasingly aware of her body language with the time of day. Scheduling her meals, snacks, and bathroom breaks all had to be more routine. She was not very chatty but enjoyed listening to a conversation. Mom's first language is Spanish, which I do not speak fluently, but understand more than I can speak.

3. Your loved one might not be able to recognize or use everyday objects such as eyeglasses, dentures, hearing aids, or band-aids for their intended purpose. They will either remove them to put away in drawers or throw them away, thinking they do not need them.

    Mom lost so many pairs of readers or prescription glasses. She pushes them on top of her head and then asks where her glasses went. Every pair she owned that was not left on the driveway or thrown away by accident was missing one arm because of the way she pulled them off her face. Although she needs hearing aids, she would say she did not need them because they were for 'old fogies,' not her. Being able to hear and see is imperative for balance, judging distance, and avoiding more feelings of isolation.

4. Delusional, obsessive, or aggressive behaviors may begin or happen more frequently. Your loved ones may not recognize you anymore or start trying to pack their bags to go home. They may insist on completing a task their way. They may have a complete lack of sense of personal responsibility or their whereabouts.

    I started to buy Mom pants without any zippers or buttons. Elastic waistband pants were not only to help her dress more quickly on her own, but so she could not leave her pants unbuttoned or unzipped after meals or using the bathroom. She did not care who was around to see her glory. When I mentioned the clothing, she would laugh and say, *"Oh, I was going to tell you something, but I forgot."*

    Sexual behaviors became an unavoidable area. Mom reminded me the *"embers in the furnace may seem ashy, but they were still burning."* I went silent once this behavior started because if she was allowed to go on about needing a man, her conversation became very vulgar or descriptive of the male anatomy and why she needed it so badly.

It became a daily topic with the same responses. By the time Mom moved into her first memory care community, this behavior had worsened. She loved being silly before, so once the staff laughed, she was encouraged to speak that way even more until they became offended. Her vulgar suggestions with cussing became quite excessive and embarrassing.

Mom became increasingly more aggressive when she was told 'No' to sweets, sex talk, or dominating the tv in the community living room. Mom began spitting in faces, smacking residents, and bullying anyone that told her No. Everyone had to either stay clear or learn to be more creative with negative responses, making them positive.

This aggression led to Mom refusing to take medication and telling me she was done being in this world. She was ready to die. And yet, within the hour, Mom was ready to go shopping.

At this point, medication to manage behavior, as much as we tried to avoid it, became necessary to protect her and everyone else around her. Doctors prescribed Depakote to manage her manic outbursts.

5. Shadowing you for social contact or increased fear of being alone happens more frequently. Your loved one may find strangers and attempt to make conversation with them as if they were best friends.

Mom used to tell me to leave her alone, mainly once she was settled in her community. Then about six months after living there, she started to venture out of her room to find others for conversation. Her new best friends were the activities and executive director. Mom would often intrude into an office, regardless of if they were on the phone or an online meeting, to demand attention through belligerence with a smile. When I visited, she told me about the staff and their babies as family members.

When we had the same meal at the lunch table, she would follow me by selecting the same bite of food. If I went clockwise tasting each food group, then she mimicked the clockwise edges too. If I stopped eating and pushed the plate away, she would do the same but continue to pull bites of food from her plate.

6. If not attended to, they might look unkempt or disheveled with a face devoid of expression. Your loved one may refuse to change clothing or layer clothing incorrectly.

   Mom had the perpetual grumpy cat look or like she could not understand something unless you could make her smile or laugh.

   If you did not help her change her clothes or prompt her to brush her teeth and hair, she would not do so independently. By this point, I could only give her limited choices like two different color blouses to pick from, and then I picked out the rest of her outfit so she would not give up and stay in dirty clothes.

   Getting dressed seemed pointless to her when she knew we were not leaving the house but putting clothes on helped with physical activity and kept her smelling fresh whether it was shower day or not. Dressing eventually became too much to do alone without extreme exhaustion.
   When I had to dress her, Mom was aware and would say, *"I can't believe my daughter is dressing me now."*

7. Physical changes are quite a bit more apparent as your loved one becomes a fall risk because their coordination and muscle tone is impaired. Their posture is affected by the loss of core strength, which also throws their gate off.

   As Mom continued to age, she did not seem to look her age most of the time because, to me, she looked her mental age aside from greying hair or laugh lines. By the time she progressed to late-stage five and into stage six, it was as if she aged overnight. When I was able to take her on walks in our neighborhood, she tried to step over the sidewalk lines on her tiptoes. I resighted part of a childish verse to see how she responded. *"Step on the lines, break your father's spine. Step on the crack, break your mother's back."* Mom kept stretching over the lines and cracks and said in a little girl's voice, *"uh-huh, that's right."*

   Home health services eventually suggested a walker for stability, but she refused to use a walker because, you guessed it, she did not need one. I continued to walk alongside her with a secure grip on her entire arm tucked into mine. Even if I could have kept Mom home with us longer, the stairs became too dangerous as her legs and core muscles weakened. The stairs were an excellent way to get some exercise at first, and then they became too painful to navigate with her knees and back.

Her tiny steps changed with her gate from spread out heel-toe steps to short tiptoe or shuffled flat-footed steps. No matter the flooring, she would still seem top-heavy with bad posture having little to no core strength. The walk from the recliner to her bedroom up 15 stairs steps became quite the chore for her.

8. The occasional incontinence may be more frequent because they are unaware of the need to empty their bladder or bowels. Peripheral vision and depth perception are lost, causing your loved one to startle more easily. Trips to the bathroom in the middle of the night become dangerous accidents.

Mom had to be reminded and then helped to stand to go to the restroom throughout the day. If allowed to, she would not get up throughout the day. Each time I encouraged her to go, she insisted and argued that she did not have to go only to finally make it into the bathroom and find she needed to empty her bladder and bowels. She would snicker and say it was just the power of suggestion.

I had to be mindful when approaching her eventually in the living room or her bedroom to make sure she could hear me coming. Changing rooms from the kitchen to the living or returning from upstairs to the living room was not in her line of sight, so I tried to speak up to hear me over the tv. If she could not see me enter the room, she would jump with fright.

9. Sleep disturbances will cause your loved one to get out of sync by sleeping all day and staying awake at night. Staying awake for days or sleeping during activities is more common. Restlessly pacing or refusing to walk might happen as the brain tries to figure out how to maintain balance. A definite indication that your loved one's body is beginning the wind-down process of dying.

For years it was a struggle to keep Mom engaged and awake during the day so she would be tired enough to sleep during the night. It took me three weeks to get her sleep cycle back to normal when she first moved in with us. If she slept poorly the next day, she craved sweets even more than usual.

She resisted exercise the next day and hated changing clothes or even attempting to take a shower. Even when she had a decent night of sleep, she still was ready to nap within the hour of a morning routine. I used to think this was simply laziness until I understood what depression does to our physical body aside from psychological emotions.

I began to recognize a trend of less energy each month with more struggle to catch her breath after much movement. Giving up on exercise routines for her was rough because it was my acceptance that her journey was coming closer to the end.

10. Your loved one will require help with all activities of daily living by this stage. They may become combative as they cannot understand what is happening when you may be attempting to help them.

Mom used to argue or protest to help with her activities of daily living. I said back then she was too stubborn to accept help and wanted to prove she was a survivor, but later I understood the level of privacy, dignity, and mourning the loss of her abilities. Mom eventually allowed help from other caregivers and showed appreciation most days.

Other days Mom became feisty by flipping them off when it came time to go for a daily walk to the common areas. The talk of sexual desires dominated what little conversation she engaged in as she accepted help showering or dressing.
Overall, it was easier for her to accept help from the staff in her memory care community than me.

As painful as it was to decide to move her into the memory care community, I did receive some relief in being able to visit and reclaim somewhat of a role as daughter once again. One video call, when her caregiver approached while we were chatting, she said, *"You know who that is? That's my daughter, the love of my life."* It brought tears to my eyes that she said it; after all our fights and struggles to connect over the years, she finally said it.

I could see her routine was not different from when she lived with me. As the staff gave me updates on Mom's moods or level of engagement, I felt vindicated. I experienced many moments when I felt Mom was difficult on purpose. As her depression fluctuates and she decides not to take her medicine, they look to me to be the daughter with encouragement.

Understanding Mom's past helped for some time, but as Mom progresses, the days are more about understanding her present status. When her new friends in the community pass, Mom decides she no longer wants to take her medicine in her way of grieving.

Mom has started to ask about my sisters more as she winds down. Finding a truth that will satisfy her for their absence is heartbreaking. Somehow, I think she knows the end is nearing, and she wants to connect again. Now the weight of grieving is something we share through reminiscing more together.

Stage 7 – Very Severe Dementia (may last 1 to 3 years); End Stage

A. 2 pounds or more loss of brain tissue

B. Behaves from a 2-year-old to an infant newborn by the end of this stage.

  1. Effects of amnesia, aphasia, agnosia, and apraxia have almost run their entire course. Your loved one will no longer resemble the person you knew before. Hospice services must be scheduled, if not already.

  2. Cognitive activity is deficient with speech and language deficits making it impossible to initiate or maintain any conversation. Your loved one may still be able to show awareness of simple gestures, pantomimes, facial expressions, react to familiar musical tunes, or the sound of your voice.

3. Expressing pain may be with sounds, non-meaningful words, or no response at all. Dental pain may cause a loss of appetite.

4. Your loved one may no longer recognize you, a spouse, or another family member. They may not recognize or use everyday objects or be aware of any danger

5. They may seem fidgety or look vacant without any focus.

6. They may seem comatose and look incredibly ill.

7. They may experience significant weight loss and drool more as the swallow reflex diminishes. Difficulty in swallowing makes eating and drinking an ongoing challenge, and can lead to weight loss, malnutrition, and dehydration.

8. They may not be able to get out of bed or balance their head.

9. They may lose the ability to see the environment around them, so it all appears two-dimensional or flat.

10. They may become bed-bound with the risk of skin infections from bed sores or tears. They will most likely sleep for 20 hours a day.

11. The last ability to go is to smile, which typically happens a few months to a few weeks before the active dying begins. The brain is no longer capable of telling the body how to sustain life.

12. Breathing may slow until it stops.

As I continue to share this journey, Mom has stepped down to stage six. Due to her existing congestive heart failure status, I can only hope and pray her heart stops while she sleeps for her to return to Dad peacefully long before.

The defibrillator settings will have to be adjusted down to the lowest setting to allow that to happen. That is one decision I do not want to have to make. I find peace in that our journey is not over yet. By the time that decision must be made, I pray to God I will be ready.

Knowing the most common form of death for someone living with Alzheimer's is aspiration or pneumonia did not make me feel any less concerned for her heart. The deterioration of the brain eventually causes difficulty in swallowing because an individual inadvertently inhales food particles, liquid, or even gastric fluids.

Our mouth and throat contain numerous bacteria, which many experiences because of difficulty maintaining dental hygiene. This bacterium is then carried deep into the lungs. There they multiply and grow, which leads to pneumonia. Due to the impaired immune systems of Alzheimer's patients, pneumonia often is fatal.

Even though most diagnoses are not definitive until a postmortem autopsy, there are improvements in affirming diagnosis sooner than later without invasive testing.

According to the Journal of Clinical Investigation (JCI Insight) article published on August 17, 2017, noninvasive detection of Alzheimer's Disease with high specificity and sensitivity can significantly facilitate identifying at-risk populations for earlier, more effective intervention. An ophthalmologist using a high-resolution imaging technique would be able to detect beta-amyloid plaques in the retinas of patients with Alzheimer's disease.

A great leap in technology for earlier detection with the application making it practical for large-scale diagnosis and monitoring. There is one caveat to obtaining a diagnosis earlier. Due to the unforeseen expenses of the disease, insurance companies will not insure you once you have been given a firm diagnosis.

Be sure to have life insurance and long-term care policies in place before seeking the tests. You may lose relief in finally obtaining a diagnosis if you are not covered before testing. Plan accordingly with more information in chapter 16, Caregiver Compliance, and Chapter 20, Finding a New Home.

Rather than give into more anxiety, I decided to put my energies into proactive measures. Not focusing on what-if scenarios takes deliberate practice in releasing fear of the unknown to God.

Remaining in control was my first approach as I stepped into this journey because I needed something to grasp by trying to analyze every little detail, but that approach gave me a false sense of control. That mindset brought about more emotional stress.

When you understand how the environment your loved one lives in affects them in each stage, then learning how to relinquish the ideology of control comes more naturally. You will instinctively know what your loved one needs as you become a proactive caregiver too.

The Caregiver's journey is about transformation for both you and your loved one. Taking the time to address her and my own needs helped me identify the areas to prioritize first. I was then able to feel my way through to allow space for normal reactions

Chapter 4
Creating A Cultural Shift

Psalm 91:7 (ESV)
A thousand may fall at your side, ten thousand at your right hand, but it will not come near you.

The Need for New Programming

Several years before I stepped into Mom's world, I was still trying to be a visitor. My career was blossoming. I reached a point when I wanted to give back to her for pushing me and challenging me to be more, do more, and want more out of life even when her ways seemed harsh. I took the day off from work on her 56th birthday to take her out to lunch, go shopping, and get her hair styled. What I did not know at the time was that this would be the first and last moment I could share a regular mother-daughter outing. For the first time, she opened up to me emotionally, woman to woman.

We had a great time in the mall going from the salon to the clothes department so she could pick out an outfit before heading over for lunch. I wondered if, after my adolescent years, we would ever be able to become friends. As we walked through the petite clothes section in JCPenney, she talked about what it was like growing up in a family with ten kids. By the time we arrived at the restaurant for lunch, we were talking like old girlfriends. I loved it but did not know how to react to all she began to share with me.

She was no longer my mom who had difficulty raising me but a woman who lived through traumatic adolescence. I looked across our small table for two into the eyes of a woman who was still heartbroken and full of shame. She hid her shame through the aggressive and often unsympathetic responses to my sisters and me. At this moment, I was given a glimpse into her wounded child behind the dark sarcasm.

Mom shared one moment about what her father told her years ago when she started to date Dad. Grandpa Raphael was not fond of Dad at first. He told Mom that Dad was useless and wouldn't amount to anything.

Thankfully, Mom did not listen to him and married Dad anyway. The damage was done, and the mental programming was set regardless. Every time they argued over finances, she recalled her father's words on Dad being useless. She was programmed for independence and to never depend on him. Years later, as Mom & Dad's marriage fell apart for various reasons, she threw those words back at him. *"My father was right about you!"*

Grandpa was not correct. Dad was not useless, but the programming made it easier not to accept any responsibility for her actions or allow for her emotional healing. She saw him through Grandpa's eyes instead of from her heart.

She was convinced that because her father had a poorly functioning heart and died at 69, she had to have a poor heart and die at 69. Never mind that grandpa smoked cigars and drank heavily. Her programming manifested her poor heart health by thinking she had limited time to live so she could eat whatever she wanted.

Dad had a similar type of programming. Dad told me, *"If I knew I was going to live to be 70 years old, I would have taken better care of myself."* He was too quick to think he would die around the same age as his father at 55 by design alone.

Type 2 Diabetes had taken over my grandfather's life, but even this could have been prevented with lifestyle and nutritional changes. Something Dad learned far too late as he developed type 2 diabetes later in life as well.

Ironically, Mom continually mentions how aging sucks as she must take more medicine or acknowledges limited mobility because of her weight. Not only has she lived past her 69th birthday into her 70s, but now she lives with congestive heart failure (CHF) as well. Knowing a vital piece of her past that revealed her broken heart in more than physical heart health shed quite a bit of light on my heart health.

Mom used to tell me therapy does not work, and it is a waste of time and money, which she still believes to this day. She will not trust anyone enough to express the cause of her post-traumatic stress.

Therapy is a vital self-care commitment in my generation and was the first approach to breaking my programming. As a caregiver, I needed to understand my stress triggers indirectly caused by Mom's actions or words. I had to learn how to trust the process to confess, purge, and heal from many areas of my life.

Committing to therapy did not mean I would be in it for life or automatically be prescribed medication. Mom's old programming led her to believe therapy would inevitably become medications to fix your brokenness. Therapy helped me understand my transformation.

I returned to therapy again during later years of caregiving when family values that I was raised with were causing me more grief. My therapist said, *"I hear a script."*

I immediately stepped into denial because I was convinced that I knew better.

I had become stuck in this programming: family comes first, or blood is thicker than water even if blood was manipulative, controlling, or a bully. There were no actual guidelines wrapped around this value, but it was used more as a pressure point or manipulation than a lesson of compassion, consideration, or love.

I could not believe it. How could I not see this until now? So many times, over the past couple of years of caring, I felt torn. I was conflicted between what I knew was right and best for Mom's well-being but kept trying to please everyone. I knew I could not please everybody, but I felt powerless when family drama flared from a difference of opinions.

My old programming had me put family over my needs, concerns, or desires. My stressful reaction was to plug the emotional bullet holes left behind from their words and abandonment with food, pain killers, and alcohol. Just like Mom and Dad used to do and their parents before them.

It made sense the more my therapist explained how businesses do the same thing when they create a family-like structure departmentally. We are programmed to work extra-long hours, not take breaks to meet deadlines, or take on projects beyond our limitations for the good of the 'family.' Until, of course, the family must make budget cutbacks and let you go.

I knew what this type of manipulation looked like in the corporate world, but it looked different somehow with my actual blood family. This realization was freeing, but now I had to learn how to replace the old programming with new healthier programming. There is more to simply letting go of the past or trying to forgive and forget. There is a process of identifying triggers to understand why I react to situations, people, or self-soothing choices.

I came to understand the 'how' and 'why' behind Mom's programming related to her behaviors in the present, which alleviated quite a bit of stress for me. We kept referring to her as being a crazy woman in earlier years. Before we had any knowledge, Mom was living with Dementia. Wouldn't it be easier to dismiss the erratic behaviors of silly female hormones? Maybe. Boy, we had it all wrong. Men have these pesky hormones too!

We can prevent our demise by paying closer attention to our bodies, plain and simple. If we could ask ourselves what does our body need right now? Or what does our soul need right now? We could learn to hear the gentle whispers of the Spirit.

I tried to apply most of my childhood programming regarding food, water, rest, and emotions as a young adult. The problem came from the marketing of fast food and meeting demands to earn a living to provide for my family. Convenience and cheaper options reprogrammed my attempts at doing what I thought was good for my health and my family's health. Part of this kind of reprogramming is redefining Maslow's hierarchy of needs and the old paradigm around physiological needs.

Let's take another look at the food pyramid taught in elementary school in Figures A & B.

Figure A.

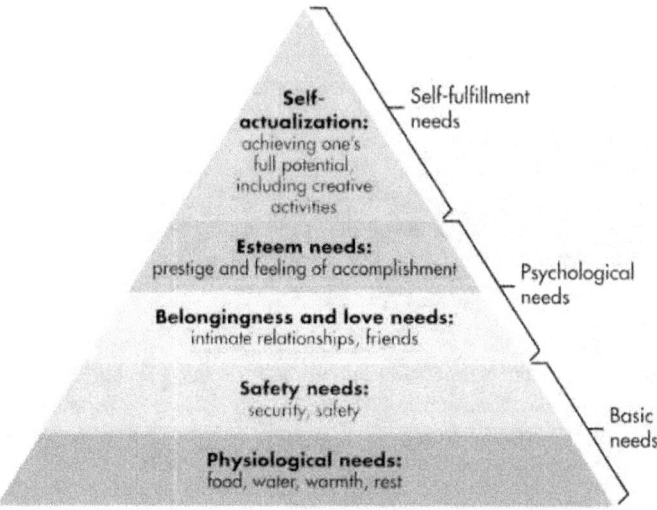

Figure B.

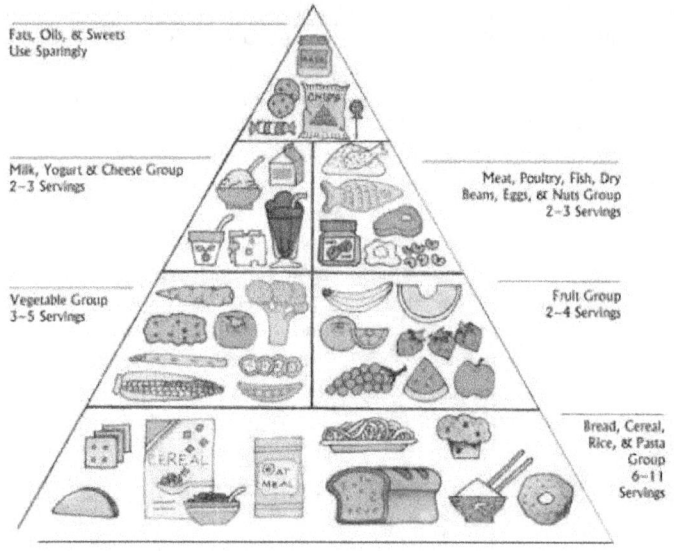

Figure C.

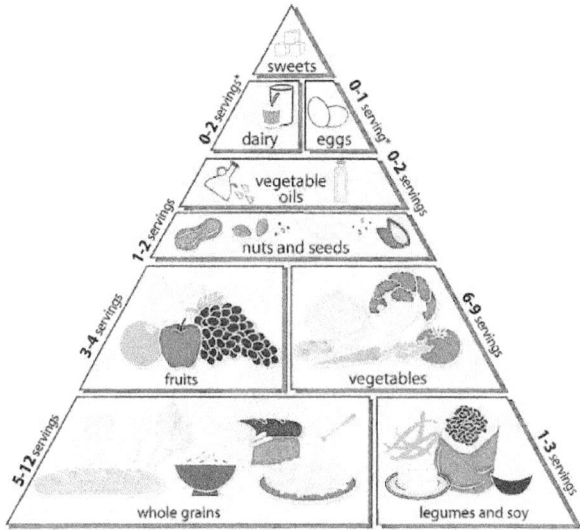

sweets

0-2 servings* dairy   eggs 0-1 serving*

vegetable oils 0-2 servings

1-2 servings nuts and seeds

3-4 servings fruits   vegetables 6-9 servings

5-12 servings whole grains   legumes and soy 1-3 servings

* A reliable source of vitamin B12 should be included if no dairy or eggs are consumed.

Figure C. represents part of my reprogramming. Now it started to sink in for me when I finally started to pay closer attention to my youngest son's pediatric well-checks. Every year I filled out a form for him checking off the boxes of how many servings of fruits, vegetables, and dairy he was eating weekly. I always thought we were doing good because he was growing well, but when he had an emergency appendectomy at ten years old, I realized we needed to do better.

We were teaching him it was okay to eat many junk foods we could buy in bulk or get quickly from a drive-thru window. As a parent and guardian of his health, I felt like I had been asleep at the wheel. Now we explain the benefits of what we have learned to buy, cook, and keep on hand, so we are not telling him what to do but why we choose to live differently than before.

Then later, as I took Mom to her well-checks, her GP asked me the same questions in addition to how much exercise she was getting. It hit me again that we could be doing better. Even as a grown adult living with mixed Dementia, these physiological needs were still as important for her to thrive. She still needs sufficient fuel for energy even if her days are less active than I would hope.

The more I attended various doctor appointments with Mom, the more it became clear to me that living with Dementia resulted from the effects of conditions we all too often dismiss and flat-out ignore.

We must consider everything going into our mouth for digestion from the value-added perspective to our body instead of taste or self-gratification alone.

The Figure D shows a more realistic breakdown of what I describe later as Mediterranean lifestyle nutrition—same great taste and self-gratification without the harmful effects.

Figure D.

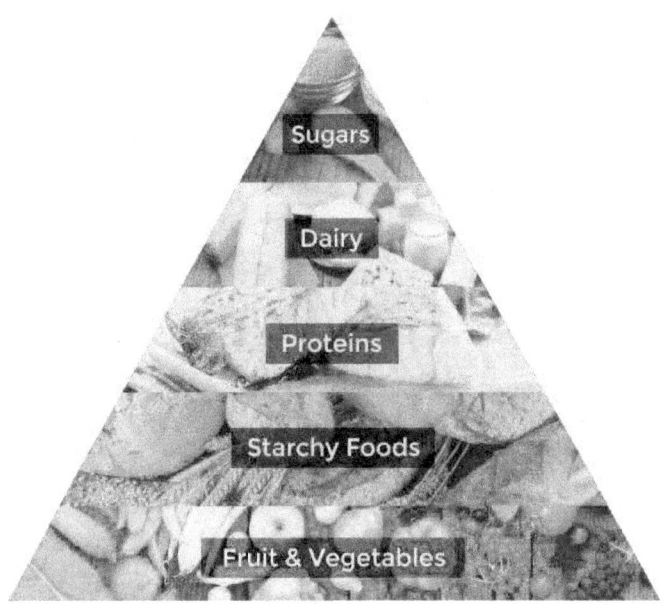

An abundance of processed foods is designed for addictive taste, which only loads our guts with a temporary sense of contentment. Those types of food are loaded with free radicals yet provide no beneficial nutritional value at all and cause more emotional problems. Even though everyone will vary based on height and weight, our brains still need balanced nutrition to not only fuel it but protect it as well.

I geeked out as I learned more about this because it kept reinforcing my idea that if, by chance, I carry any identifiable genes for Dementia, then I can use willpower and self-control to keep them off or unmutated.

According to the Global Health Center, *"Free radicals are atoms, ions, or molecules that contain an unpaired electron. The unpaired electron makes them unstable and highly reactive. In a process called oxidation, free radicals steal electrons from other molecules—fats, proteins, cell membranes, and even DNA—altering the fundamental structure of the affected molecule. One unstable molecule may not sound like a significant concern, but oxidation sets off a chain reaction by damaging a cell's DNA, structure, and ability to function, creating a mutation. Over time, oxidative damage accumulates and contributes to aging and a variety of degenerative diseases."*

Every cell in your body requires it for cellular metabolism. Cells use oxygen to convert food into energy the body can use during cellular metabolism, called ATP (adenosine triphosphate). Free radicals are a natural byproduct of cellular metabolism. The waste after it takes what it thinks the body can use to fuel its engine.

Cellular metabolism is not the only source of free radicals. Free radicals are generated by inflammation, stress, illness, and normal aging. Hazardous environmental sources such as pollution, toxic metals, excessive alcohol, cigarette smoke, radiation, industrial chemicals, and medications expose us to free radicals.

Avoiding free radicals altogether is neither possible nor desirable. At low concentrations, free radicals are beneficial to the human body. Your immune system uses them to help defend it against germs.

As in all things, however, proper balance is critical, and problems begin when free radicals are wildly out of balance. When free radicals overwhelm your body, it leads to oxidative stress. This kind of stress is damage that results from an imbalance between free radicals and your body's store of antioxidants—breaking our immune system down and exposing us to abnormal aging.

According to the free radical theory of aging (FRTA), organisms age because of accumulated free radical damage to cells and DNA. However, the free radical theory of aging remains controversial. Oxidative stress contributes to degenerative conditions such as arthritis, heart disease, hypertension, Alzheimer's, Parkinson's, muscular dystrophy, and more.

All our bodies go through this oxidative process as we react to the challenges of life. Family habits began to make sense to me. Mom experienced trauma in adolescence, which broke her proverbial heart, so she turned to sugar as her coping mechanism.

When I experienced similar trauma later in life, I turned to many things that would keep me numb from emotional pain, which eventually caused me physical pain. By not understanding the science behind how Mom's body or my own was trying to function correctly, we caused more damage than genetics.

By examining Mom's past, I realized I needed to examine myself seriously. I needed to give up guilty pleasures in comfort food and stop numbing myself to life with alcohol and pain meds, also part of my old programming. If this concept of changing our diet sounds like a broken record, then maybe, it is time to listen with a different perspective.

Not only is the cycle continuing, but it is also growing by alarming numbers of caregivers in the U.S. alone. The research conducted by AARP and published June 2015 states, "*We can estimate there are 34.2 million adults in the United States who have been a caregiver to an adult 50 or older in the prior 12 months.*" Overall, caregivers in 2015 were up to 43.5 million.

AARP updated this report in May 2020 by declaring the increase of caregivers to 1 in 5 or 21.3%, increasing caregivers overall to 53 million adults in the United States alone before the worldwide Coronavirus pandemic.

The caregiver gender remains heavily among women at 61% and men at 39% as of 2020. Most caregivers are caring for a relative or Parent In-law. The choice to become a caregiver was split between those who felt they did not have a choice at 53% and those who felt they did have a choice at 46%.

While there are varying conditions of care recipients, the top three are old age, mobility issues, and Alzheimer's or dementia which increased to 11%. In addition to a primary condition, caregivers reported their care recipients to have Dementia which is up from 22% in 2015 to 26% of caregivers in 2020.

Below are comparison figures between 2015 to 2020 of caregiver statistics according to the May 2020 AARP Caregiving in the U.S.

Figure 1. Prevalence of Caregiving by Age of Care Recipient, 2020 Compared to 2015

	2020 Prevalence	Estimated Number of U.S. Adults Who Are Caregivers	2015 Prevalence	Estimated Number of U.S. Adults Who Are Caregivers
Overall	21.3%*	53.0 million	18.2%	43.5 million
Caregivers of recipients ages 0-17	5.7%*	14.1 million	4.3%	10.2 million
Caregivers of recipients ages 18+	19.2%*	47.9 million	16.6%	39.8 million
Caregivers of recipients ages 18-49	2.5%	6.1 million	2.3%	5.6 million
Caregivers of recipients ages 50+	16.8%*	41.8 million	14.3%	34.2 million

Significantly higher than in 2015.

The more time passes with the same course of action or old programming, the need for younger caregivers becomes alarmingly noticeable. As the need for family caregivers increases, many in the millennial generation and gen Z will need to care for aging family members.

With a small number of millennials involved in direct care for aging family members, questions remain on how this demographic is prepared to work or create a living, career, or families of their own with an aging America.

Figure 5. Percentage of Caregivers of Adults Who Are in Each Generation, 2020 vs. 2015

	2020 (n = 1,392)	2015 (n = 1,248)
Generation Z (born 1997 or after)	6%*	–
Millennial (born 1981 to 1996)	23%	23%
Generation X (born 1965 to 1980)	29%*	25%
Baby Boomers (born 1946 to 1964)	34%	39%*
Silent/Greatest (born 1945 or prior)	7%	13%*

Significantly higher than comparison year.

Note: Results are rounded and don't know/refused responses are not shown; results may not add to 100 percent.

Graphs below represent Millennial family caregivers by age group and race/ethnicity according to the May 2018 AARP Public Policy Institute article published by Brendan Flinn.

EXHIBIT 1
Millennial Family Caregivers by Age Group

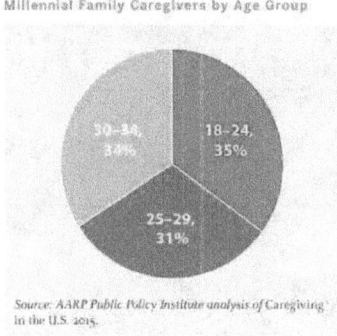

Source: AARP Public Policy Institute analysis of Caregiving in the U.S. 2015.

EXHIBIT 2
Millennial Family Caregivers by Race/Ethnicity

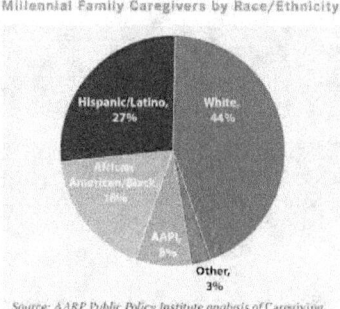

Source: AARP Public Policy Institute analysis of Caregiving in the U.S. 2015.

Figure 87. Demographic Summary of Caregivers of Adults, 2020 and 2015

	2020 (n = 1,392)	2015 (n = 1,248)
Caregiver Gender		
Man	39%	40%
Woman	61%	60%
Age of Caregiver		
18–34	24%	24%
35–49	23%	23%
50–64	36%	34%
65–74	12%	12%
75+	7%	7%
Mean age	49.4	49.2
Race/Ethnicity of Caregiver		
White	61%	62%
African American	14%	13%
Hispanic	17%	17%
Asian American	5%	6%
Other	3%	2%
Caregiver Education		
Less than high school	6%	8%
High school graduate	26%	28%
Some college	22%	22%
Technical school	11%*	8%
College graduate	21%	20%
Graduate school	14%	15%
Caregiver Marital Status		
Married	54%	57%
Living with a partner	7%	8%
Widowed	4%	5%
Separated	3%*	1%
Divorced	8%	8%
Single, never married	21%	19%

* Result is significantly higher or lower than in 2015.

Note: Results are rounded and don't know/refused responses are not shown; results may not add to 100 percent.

According to the National Alliance for Caregiving, in collaboration with AARP in November 2009, 23% of family caregivers cared for loved ones for five years or more and reported their health as fair or poor. The stress of caregiving for persons living with Dementia has been shown to affect a person's immune system for up to 3 years after the caregiving ends. Without changing habits then the caregiver increases their chances of developing a chronic illness themselves.

Before the November 2009 reports, in a report of findings in September 2006 Evercare Study of Caregivers in Decline, 72% of Family Caregivers report not going to the doctor as often as they should, and 55% say they skip doctor's appointments for themselves. 63% of caregivers report having poor eating habits than non-caregivers, and 58% indicate worse exercise habits than before caregiving responsibilities.

As researchers uncover more information about the brain, society still sees this as a disease manifested by genes. What society is not hearing is Dementia may take decades to develop. The 20 something-year-old who thinks, *"No big deal, I have time to be reckless and change habits later"* is just that – reckless. Yes, we are only young once (YOLO), but those young choices can set us up for expensive long-term consequences.

Our 20s pass us by, and before we know it, we're in our 30s and 40s when the damage is done. The *"No big deal"* thought process is similar to waiting to save for retirement *"when I make more money"* later down the road. 10 to 20 years regarding Dementia is the difference in having an opportunity for reversal or treatment to maintain slower decline over no decline towards abnormal aging. It's also the difference in more savings to cover the growing inflation of long-term expenses, but we get into that later.

Breaking the cycle

What Mom's journey has made very clear to me is that a healthy heart will give way to a healthy mind. Likewise, an unstable or unhealthy mind will damage the heart. I did not consider my mind as unhealthy when I worked in the corporate world. I was juggling life and meeting demands. It was not until I began my therapy did, I gain insight into how I had been categorizing life in general. I learned how to coexist just like Mom did but justified my way of living as better. I had my area of denial that only appeared as my inner parts were triggered.

It may sound simple enough because most people know maintaining a healthy diet with regular exercise is the best way to keep our hearts in top shape but knowing is not enough. I knew it and came up with so many excuses why I did not have the time to commit to exercise. Those excuses were life experiences at work, marital issues, parenting issues that created a cycle around situational depression. The exercise would have helped me burn through so much frustration and anxiety, but the depression made me surrender to the couch to sift through social media on my phone. Ironically, I suddenly had time to surf Instagram and Facebook but no time to exercise. Honesty - more so, the lack of honesty was my crutch.

Women with heart problems are about three times more likely to develop Dementia than women without heart concerns. The link is not as significant in men. When I think about how much women typically juggle, it makes sense knowing women are more likely to sacrifice their bodies without any doubt or concerns.

Since I was more concerned with not becoming what I perceived as the flawed parts of my parents, I could not see that I had already become what I had feared most. Complacent, disconnected, and feeling trapped in a mundane dead-end routine in life while self-medicating. My lack of honesty or denial kept me in a mental and emotional fog.

I started having flashbacks of Dad hiding a glass of wine or a shot of whiskey in the spice cabinet to sip while cooking with weary, emotionally tapped eyes. If not in the kitchen, then on leftover nights, he did yard work for as long as he had daylight to burn off his frustrations. It felt like what I witnessed so often was the normal thing to do.

After growing up watching Mom work and sleep life away during my adolescent years, existing on autopilot, I did not want to do the same. I may not have been sleeping life away, but I was using compartmentalization as my excuse to balance emotions, not life. Those emotions temporarily improved when I overindulged with food, alcohol, and pain medications. I was self-medicating and feeding a cycle of being energetically or spiritually blocked. What seemed like help or self-soothing at the moment was hurting my system.

Working long hours in a finance department contributed to the sedentary life that made me crave salty or sugary comfort foods with lots of caffeine to fuel my engine. I lost all sight of life outside of the corporate cube until my lower back and hips began to ache from sciatica nerve pain. As time passed, the middle of my back began to spasm with pain. I had no choice but to listen to my body. Even though I could take pain medication before bedtime in hopes of achieving pain-free sleep, I could not take those pain relievers during work and still focus. My programmed cycle took a toll as my Solar Plexus was blocked, indicating my loss of personal power.

I was beginning to have more restless nights filled with worries over her present and our future. I quickly recognized that my daily patterns were adapting to her way of life in the wrong way. I did not like who I was becoming and how it made me feel.

Mom's words continue to replay in my mind *"It's not what you're eating; it's what is eating you."* I continued to have excuses or reasons to ignore the dreams and messages to correct my course sooner than later. Consuming mainstream information, I was not making the connections. As a caregiver, my eyes, mind, and heart opened to make these connections finally.

Later, food cravings became my indicator or check engine light to tune into my body. I am not referring to the typical PMS cravings or pregnancy cravings. These food cravings linked up to my feelings of emptiness or loneliness and depletion from stress. I was able to see through my habits why so many others try to fill their guts with everything else but what it deserves, like honesty, acceptance, and love.

It may be hard to see how honesty is connected to a greasy pizza or juicy burger and fries. This kind of honesty means taking a better look at the layers below a basic craving. I craved acceptance and love with willpower to avoid depression simply because I fought to prevent becoming my mother. The more I tried to avoid the foods she ate, I craved them even more.

Trying to avoid depression made me feel like I could control not stepping into Mom's shoes, but this also meant I lost sight of who *IS* in control overall. The interesting thing is that focusing on what I did not want to become manifested it into my life. A new program had to be written into my heart.

Chapter 5
Protect Your Future with The Caregiver's Trinity

2 Peter 1:5-7 (NIV)
[5]For this very reason, make effort to add to your faith goodness; and to goodness, knowledge; [6]and to knowledge, self-control; and to self-control, perseverance; and to perseverance, godliness; [7]and to godliness, mutual affection; and to mutual affection, love.

The awareness of my old mental programming and my multiple inner parts helped create a powerful breakthrough. My mind was usually stuck in either the past or daydreaming and worrying about the future, rarely in the present. My present was spent in one stressful situation after the other and often several stressful moments combined. Not having a solid grip on current moments was my justification for chemically induced sleep which became part of my old programming to stay numb in the present.

A friend of mine asked me if I read before bedtime to relax. I did for some time which usually included romance novels or sci-fi mysteries. I even spent time reading bedtime stories to the boys of fantasy worlds like Harry Potter or Wings of Fire to help them relax. Reading these novels became my escape from reality, but it did not help me sleep any better. No sooner than I placed the book on my nightstand and turned off the lamp, my mind flipped back to some other time and place from the past. I had countless unresolved situations with many regrets.

She suggested I read a book by Eckhart Tolle called "*The Power of Now.*" After listening to my rants of the day, she pointed out one quote of his that says, "*Unease, anxiety, tension, stress, worry — all forms of fear — are caused by too much future, and not enough presence. Guilt, regret, resentment, grievances, sadness, bitterness, and all forms of non-forgiveness are caused by too much past and not enough presence.*"

By sharing this quote with me, it put names to my sources of sleepless, restless nights. Of course, naming them was not enough, so more therapy sessions were scheduled. Selfcare had to become more of a priority beyond hygiene or salon visits and include more self-discovery. The only way I could let go of the fears and distractions of becoming my parents was to figure out who I am, what I need, and find new programs or values to live by as an individual, mother, wife, sister, friend, and caregiver.

My paradoxical transformation came in both simple and complex ideals. Laying a new foundation was as simple as applying the Pareto Principle or the 80/20 rule. This rule applies the concept that 80% of the results you will achieve are determined by 20% of the lifestyle habits you develop. In other words, a small number of important actions will lead to the most significant changes in your life and health.

I have found by experience that the best way to break the cycle surrounding genetic challenges or nature versus nurture is to change your programming by emphasizing your 20% of the 80/20 rule. The following areas I now teach as the Caregiver's Trinity. This Trinity is made up of Lifestyle, Spirituality, and Financial Stability.

1. **Restorative Sleep (Lifestyle)**

I have heard many caregivers speak about poor sleep or achieving very few hours of sleep. I have even heard others say, *"I'll sleep when I'm dead."* Yikes! They do not know what happens within our bodies when we sleep. Guarding your sleep cycles is the most important form of self-care for every individual.

Sleep deprivation causes problems with memory recall, clear thinking, mood, depression/anxiety, and chronic fatigue or pain. Restorative sleep is essential for revitalizing and restoring the physiological processes that keep our body and mind healthy and properly functioning. Our waste removal system takes place while we sleep like a computer update when you initiate an effective shutdown.

Even though we stop growing by the time we become young adults, our internal systems are so magnificent they continue to need 7-9 hours straight of restorative sleep to do what cannot be done in our waking hours. Throughout the night, we are powered down so the body can routinely heal the brain by growing cells, tissue, and nerves to regenerate and boost our hormones and immune system. Hormones that assist our flight or fight mode called cortisol or stress hormone are restored. The body also rebalances other hormones such as Serotonin, Dopamine, and Melatonin during the deep sleep or delta stage of our REM cycle. In addition to replenishing our hormones, our blood is cleaned, and our organs are detoxed.

Dopamine and Serotonin are involved in our sleep-wake cycles. Dopamine helps us be more alert, while Serotonin prevents REM sleep during the day and induces sleep at night in tandem with Melatonin. We need our Serotonin levels to remain balanced because it is also required to produce Melatonin. Melatonin is a hormone our brain produces in response to darkness to help our circadian rhythms or internal clock function naturally. All part of our autopilot mode dictates sleep, waking, and eating time—basic survival modes.

An imbalance in either Serotonin or Dopamine can begin to affect our mental health, digestion, and sleep cycles. A decrease in Dopamine production, which occurs with Parkinson's, often causes drowsiness. The drowsiness is caused because of the imbalance between excess Melatonin and not enough Dopamine. Our loved ones struggle to find balance in the day, which adds to the stress of caregiving when we do not know how to meet their needs.

I used to think Mom was just lazy, and it was too easy for her to nap on the couch while she let me clean her house, cook her meals, and do her laundry. It fueled my anger, thinking she would not even try to help me and then make me feel sad and unappreciated. I did not know then that our pineal gland regulates Dopamine and Melatonin. Our pineal gland is in the brain's center and senses light and darkness signals from the eyes. She was not entirely lazy and more imbalanced hormonally.

Growing up, Dad kept curtains closed to keep the house cool during the brutal Texas summer. He used to point out that Mom's moody cycles happened for her more over the summer. She did not have a routine to keep her on autopilot or balance her circadian rhythm.

When Mom lived alone, she kept the curtains closed, day and night. Since she was not exercising or doing much to exert any energy to feel the release of dopamine, staying in dark rooms with only the brightness from the tv contributed to her brain fog. Again, no routine.

Each time I arrived at her home, the first thing I did was open her blinds and sometimes the windows, if weather permitted, to bring in light and fresh air. She could not stay awake 24/7 and barely woke long enough to grab junk food, use the restroom, and then go back to sleep on the couch. She switched from insomnia in prior years to not staying awake as Dementia progressed over 10 to 20 years. We were merely reacting to her and trying to fill in the blanks with what little knowledge we had about aging with Dementia.

Her body was consistently struggling to repair and detox, which was also affecting her heart. Not only did her sleep problems create cognitive function issues, but it also worsened her depression, fatigue, body aches and pain, and emotional health overall. I often worried that I would become what Mom had over the years through her lifestyle choices. When my sleep cycles were off, I started to experience migraine headaches, body aches, moody blues, and problems with concentration.

Protecting my routine to achieve restorative sleep made a difference in my ability to focus and maintain energy before changing other lifestyle habits. I wanted to do more than survive the days with Mom and still have energy left for the family each day.

Create an evening ritual that may include efforts in sleep training to achieve a better routine. Empty your mental To-Do list in a journal and include a daily gratitude declaration in this journal. Try reading a book, taking a hot Epsom salt bath, stretching before bed all help with winding the body down.

Your bedroom environment is most important to ensure your bed is optimized for comfort, the temperature is preferential (not too hot/cold), and outside light is not intrusive like streetlamps or bright televisions. If you must watch tv in bed, then set a timer on the TV to turn off at your designated lights out time. I found watching the news before bed too stimulating. Comedy can make us both tired from laughing or wake us.

2. Nutrition - Healthy fueling habits (Lifestyle)

My parents purchased items in bulk like rice, beans, pork chops, packaged lunch meat, and other processed foods with shelf life, including cakes and cookies. When I moved out and started my family, I did the same. It was all I knew. Growing up, we had a membership at Sam's Club and bought several more items in bulk to manage paycheck to paycheck.

In the first two years of my marriage, before having our second son, we became Sam's Club members as well. I purchased bulk items just like my parents and gained so much weight. I reacted to stress by eating my worries through salty or sugary treats, which provided little energy.

As a child, I had so much energy playing outside and swimming quite often, so I never had fatigue issues, even with a diet made up largely of rice, beans, and fried pork chops with fried plantains.

As an adult, the limit to outdoor activity and healthy produce, which provides natural sources of Vitamin D, did not register as a necessity. I had a day job and family that became my driving force. I was not exposed to these valuable lessons back then and never considered it until I became a full-time caregiver.

Until October 2015, a year before stepping away from the corporate world to become a full-time caregiver, I had a heart attack scare. I was 40 years old and kept dismissing the symptoms my body was signaling because I kept allowing self-talk to avoid the reality of my check engine light. Something was wrong.

In the middle of the night, I jolted awake and sat up in bed when I felt like someone had just punched me in the chest. It scared me because it was so sudden, and my right arm was hurting badly. In my state of delirium, I got out of bed to get two Aleve and then crawled back into bed. I had work in the morning and decided to call the doctor once I got settled in at the office. I pushed snooze on my check engine light even though I was scared, but fatigue clouded my judgment. My guardian angel must have smacked his forehead and shook his head.

Once I arrived at work, I dropped right into my normal routine by reading through emails and eating breakfast. My right arm and chest pain crept back in within an hour of eating, reminding me I needed to call the doctor sooner than later. I was still trying to multitask and putting my needs off. I stepped outside to make a quick call assuming I would just schedule an appointment for a checkup and maybe get a prescription for something.

When I explained my symptoms to the nurse, she urged me to go straight to the ER. I was shocked, but when she explained that women present with different heart attack signs than men, I knew I could not dismiss my symptoms anymore. These are the kind of signs that are not normal aging to accept and move on grudgingly. I called my husband and told him to meet me at the ER and explained on the way.

My scare of having a heart attack, thankfully, turned out to be my gall bladder instead. I had four large dice-sized stones wreaking havoc on my system. The procedure to remove the stones became a significant eye-opener to my nutritional habits.

Gallstones are hardened bile or digestive fluids which contain too much cholesterol (yellow) or bilirubin (dark brown or black). Gallstones may be considered another genetic-related medical history, but your current diet affects them more.

That's how it works, though, right? We generally do not place enough attention until there is a medical problem. We allow ourselves to be in reactive mode instead of being in a proactive mindset.

Caregiving is a very demanding job emotionally, but it takes your physical health and strength to sustain yourself during these long days. Good health rings truer for those caregivers living with their loved ones living with Dementia or special needs. They are on duty 24/7.

Once my gallbladder was removed later that October, my digestive system had to reacclimate. Eating healthier started as the reactive response, which gradually turned into a deliberate proactive lifestyle. My lifestyle finally changed, and then I became more energetic in my early 40's than I ever was throughout my 30's.

The moment of feeling a punch in the chest was another one of my divine interventions. I was not paying close enough attention when I was in autopilot mode. Self-medicating my physical pain or trying to find a state of numbness for emotional sadness was only masking my problems. Now I have the physical, emotional, and mental strength to care for Mom. It forced me to eat healthier and look within when I avoided it for far too long. It was preparation for a journey ahead that challenged my will to live in chaos.

By Divine design, Big Sis and I eventually became my mother's caregivers. She grew up on the same diet I did. She, too, had her gallbladder removed only two months after my procedure. It seemed like such an odd coincidence at the time, but hindsight has revealed the preparation to becoming a stronger, healthier caregiver a year in advance. We were in training for the greater task ahead of us and didn't even know it.

I began to eat better, exercise more, sleep better, and feel clearer in my mind. An opportunity was presented for me to help my heart more than I ever considered doing before. Tuning into my body more taught me a great deal about nutritional habits in connection to emotional stability. I started to refer to my body as a high-performance sports car, like a Ferrari.

Before, I did not realize I was doing this, but this shift made me see others in public and think of which type of vehicle they were or who had more emotional junk in their trunks. Walking through the grocery store, passing by people with their children for a short trip, made me see food as a weapon or medicine.

Our gut is our second brain. The gut is more than part of the digestion process since it affects our mood, health, and thinking. The food we choose to eat is more often a subliminal choice directed by the bacteria in our gut, microbiome. Therefore, some diets are often referred to as detoxifying. Understanding how food is our medicine is made more clearly under the Proactive Measures chapter. When I understood what my body needed, I knew to make better nutritional choices when grocery shopping and eating out in restaurants.

3. Exercise - what it does energetically (Lifestyle)

When I was an athlete in school, I had a defined practice regimen for each season of volleyball, basketball, softball, and track. All I knew in terms of exercise was strength training rather than cardio and flexibility. Sports helped keep me out of trouble in middle school and high school by burning off excess energy, but it was not the type of exercise I needed as an adult.

Now my focus was on core strength or middle body, glutes, and cardio for heart health. Weight was an issue for me after each pregnancy because I wanted to lose the baby weight fast. After my gallbladder was removed, I quickly realized I could control weight better through nutrition and tone through light exercise. My outputs in energy had to be as much as if not more than my inputs of calories.

Lifting weights for strength training as an athlete is more rigorous than the average adult trying to remain firm. Muscle mass is very important to maintain as we age, but it does not necessarily mean bench pressing your bodyweight. However, if you are trying to lose weight, moderate strength training would be beneficial because muscle mass burns fat more for active adults than cardio alone.

Exercising in the morning as opposed to the evening makes a difference in effectiveness for many. I had better results with weight loss by doing light Yoga in the mornings on an empty stomach rather than waiting to go to the gym after work. In addition to weight loss, yoga helped me begin the days with enough calmness and energy to avoid feeling stressed as my caregiving duties began.

Finding a balanced routine for Mom that allowed me time to exercise helped me meet both goals for her circulation and my strength building. It was a bonus when I included Mom in the exercise, but I knew when to pick my battles. I knew a light workout would benefit her mood and blood circulation, but she did not need to work out by her rationale.

She said several times, *"I never said I would die skinny."* I tried to reason with her by explaining losing 15lbs could relieve 4 pounds of pressure on her knees alone. That pain was not an issue for her when she was comfortably stretched out on the recliner watching tv. As soon as she had to stand to go to the restroom or go upstairs for the bed, I heard her painful moans and groans with each step she took or bending down to sit on the toilet.

I had been enduring sciatica nerve damage from degenerative disks in my lower spine after giving birth to our second son and sitting for too many hours at work. I needed low-impact exercises, so even running was out of the picture for me. Everything I chose had to be simple, inexpensive to maintain, and easily accessible.

Taking Mom to a gym with me was nice for a limited time but soon became too much of a challenge and frustration. My next attempt at low-impact exercise was swimming and walking.

Although I could get Mom to go for a walk, it was rarely for long and often wore her out faster than I could get a brisk walk in for less than 30 minutes. Convincing her to wear a bathing suit to do some water aerobics with me happened twice over three years.

I started to do Vinyasa Yoga poses to help me with the sciatic nerve and lower back muscles. It gave me such relief that I started to learn even more poses. As a former athlete, I dismissed engaging in Yoga practices because I felt it was not vigorous enough, but I was not considering the mental workout either.

This type of exercise is a low impact but a great strength training form of exercise. When I started with a beginners Yoga class, I could barely touch my knees, let alone my toes. I was tense and needed to learn to breathe through each pose, just as I learned breathing techniques in Lamaze class. I started with 15 minutes each morning with basic stretches. I gradually added a pose each week and built up to a 45-minute morning workout. The warm muscles and lengthy breathing exercises every morning started to make me feel wonderful, so I started setting my alarm clock earlier to get in more time. My workout increased, and so did my flexibility.

Light cardio exercise for at least 300 minutes per week or roughly 42 minutes per day would be more than enough for me. The fresh outdoor air walking, rowing, or swimming laps is also beneficial for toning and blood circulation. Blocking out time to work out without making Mom tag along or worry about her stability made Yoga the best commitment to exercise mentally and physically.

Yoga is a low-impact cardio regimen that builds muscle tone and encourages Dopamine levels in our body naturally. The benefit is not one size fits all. There are at least 13 different types to choose from, including beginners, advanced, and even prenatal yoga styles.

Even this kind of low-impact workout helps the blood circulation and heart muscles contract in such a way that helps get blood to the brain more efficiently. Smaller blood vessels will widen to deliver more oxygen to your muscles to help avoid muscle atrophy. At the same time, blood circulation helps carry waste products like carbon dioxide and lactic acid away from the muscles, which creates soreness post-workout.

My routine of value-added nutrition with daily Yoga made an unexpected change to my daily energy levels, overall moods, and acceptance of what my caregiving journey had become. This little bit of 'me' time provided far more than flexibility. As time passed, I felt less stressed and more capable of meeting Mom's and our family's needs.

I was able to find a place of calm that carried through my life beyond caregiving. The calmness contributed to a new level of creativity and well-being overall that happened in my space at home. My brief morning workouts gave me a sense of control over our space at home which had become isolating.

I still get out to go walking and swimming when the opportunity arises, but I mainly focus on setting time aside to allow for deliberate movements with cleansing breaths. I can help my body to release endorphins with natural painkillers.

I have experienced the benefit from various styles of Yoga which incorporate left-right movements to unblock negative energy from stress, grief, or trauma. Reducing my stress took more than physical movements because I had to engage my mind as well. The flexibility, however, reduced my physical strain from stiffness and weak muscles. If we do not maintain flexibility as we age, we lose muscle cells that contribute to muscle atrophy. Over time, we become weaker, which challenges basic movements of extending our arms and legs, walking across a room, or even maintaining our balance.

4. Meditation - Reduces stress, cortisol levels and connects inner self to source energy (Spirituality)

I used to have problems quieting my mind enough to fall asleep. Oddly enough, I could function during the day while entertaining a variety of thoughts or daydreams. When I began to engage in Yoga with breathing techniques, I also learned to redirect my thoughts through meditation.

When I first began with beginner stretches, my mind would jump to negative thoughts about my body's pressure points or how I could reach faster results. I got so frustrated at the thought of emptying my mind. The days between work as an accountant and caregiving were filled with all sorts of negative thoughts that brought me more pain and suffering.

I could wash dishes and still be stuck in a mental image of my cube at work or my finance spreadsheets. I could function in the present while rinsing each dish and still be in another place and time. I looked up when I sensed movement at the window in time to see a squirrel run along the fence. This little rodent could flick its tail and pull me to the present for a breath or two. Once it hurried further down the fence line, my mind was back into the past yet again.

Redirecting my thoughts was just as much of an exercise. At first, I sat in a comfortable position on my mat, trying to silence the monkey in my mind. I could not help thinking about my daily To-Do list or appointments scheduled during the week for Mom or me. Distractions would not turn off in my mind.

So, I started to meditate with Bible prayers like the Lord's Prayer and Psalm 23. Eventually, I could close my eyes and focus on my breath, the feel of my heartbeat, the touch of my skin, and then I could *feel* the present moment. With each cleansing breath, my pulse slowed, and the calmness returnèd. I was not concerned about my surroundings because I was finding a peaceful escape. I needed this moment to be imprinted on my mind, so I knew exactly where to return while I waited in the doctors' offices with Mom or struggled to get her into a shower.

I can meditate now just about anywhere I choose, but, in the beginning, I had to create a space that helped reinforce my desire and mood towards calmness. I trained myself to be more disciplined, which provided healthier sleep patterns, better concentration, and increased pain tolerance from sciatica. I either lit a candle or burned some lemon, lavender, and eucalyptus essential oils in my quiet space.

With your eyes closed, you can dampen one sense and increase the others. I found my Zen place. That was all I needed at the time, relaxation and calmness. The monkey in my mind was finally calm with my angry inner child. The calmness then allowed for curiosity to surface about why my inner child was so angry.

Every morning before Mom woke up, I went to my space to meditate for at least 15 minutes and about 20 minutes of yoga poses. I did not expect a new sense of self-awareness and spiritual connection. In this space of calm, I began to feel and hear the Spirit speak in my thoughts.

I realized later the Spirit had always been with me, but I was too distracted by the chaos in my life before caregiving to acknowledge Him.

I eventually went outside in the mornings under my meditation tree with a cup of green tea. I started with my cleansing breaths, spoke the Lord's Prayer or Psalm 23 aloud, and then just listened to birds, wind, and tree branches flexing in the wind. I could feel the warmth of the sunrise on my face even though my eyes were closed. I began to feel so much peace and appreciation for nature that I began to see shapes and imprints of movement in the universe in my mind's eye.

These images were so basic, yet I felt an overwhelming sense of awe because I felt that I was experiencing time and space in the present moment in a different dimension. I was connected to source energy. Without the chaos and anger, I felt the love and connection from the universe.

I wanted more! Such a beautiful, new, and different perspective than anything I had ever experienced. I wanted to stay anchored in the present moment, no matter what my day with Mom became. Unfortunately, I could only get moments of peace like this in the mornings before starting my day with Mom. My meditation routine was just a brief moment rather than being a part of me yet.

Finding time for meditation became another form of self-care for me because it gave me the kind of peace and connection I could not maintain during the day in the beginning. Frustrations or other distractions would take over. I now end my meditation by telling the universal space around me, *"Peace be with you, and I take you with me."* In time, I could whisper this thought during the day and feel a response of *"I am always with you."*

I now can meditate just about anywhere I choose. Once I close my eyes and breathe deeply, I can recreate my Zen space. I can redirect my thoughts to those geometric shapes and even a silhouette of Jesus' face that expresses his warmth and reminds me he is always with me. I am not alone on this journey.

It did not matter how long the days were with Mom once I had a solid morning routine. Practicing redirecting my thoughts helped me to find my Zen space in my mind when I became frustrated with Mom. I could walk away as needed at home, but out in public was a different kind of mental strength to find a sense of calm.

When the environment made it feel impossible, I would begin to feel the burning in my neck and shoulders. I knew if I was feeling the stress of our outing, then Mom's stress was amplified even more. If I could provide a smile with a sense of calm, then she responded better. Finding a genuine smile came after being able to breathe and search for Jesus in my mind. Somehow, I knew He was waiting for me to reach out, ready to wash peace over me.

5. Financial Stability - Build a Budget that includes Long Term Planning

When Mom was initially misdiagnosed with moderate stage Alzheimer's, my first concern was how much longer we had with her before she no longer recognized us. Even though others had told me, caring does get better by that point. I could not imagine a time when it got better because she no longer knew me.

The physical challenges of downsizing were coming closer into view on the horizon of our journey, which is when I began to understand the financial burden to come as well. Growing up, Mom always taught us to save for rainy days, but this would be a hurricane in comparison. As I started to research the cost of additional caregivers, aside from family to reduce burnout and tension, the shock of cost hit home. Mom was always a diligent saver, but she saw Long-Term Care (LTC) policies as insignificant because she already invested in retirement savings and life insurance policies along the way.

The sad reality is her retirement savings were not adjusted for inflation, nor did she consider long-term needs. When she signed her official retirement papers, the amount of her actual savings had been spent within the first five years of retirement. As a teacher in Texas, part of the retirement benefits currently includes a $10,000 life insurance policy intended to be enough for burial expenses. Thanks to inflation, today's burial expenses are now closer to $15,000 to $25,000. Of course, the choice of funeral homes and regional factors may vary, but these funds are earmarked for afterlife expenses. The $10,000 was never intended to help cover LTC expenses.

As Dementia progresses, your loved ones will require a more advanced level of care. This type of care can range from in-home assistance with Activities of Daily Living (such as bathing, dressing, toileting, or eating) to skilled care provided by nurses, therapists, or other professionals in a residential facility. A frustrating reality is Medicare does not cover the cost of LTC, but it now covers planning with a medical professional. Medicaid pays for nursing home care; it will also cover a limited amount of at-home care in most states.

Unfortunately, Medicaid requires you first to exhaust all your resources and meet their eligibility requirements. The United States, United Kingdom, and Canada sell policies associated with LTC insurance, which generally covers care not covered by health insurance, Medicare, or Medicaid.

Based on the estate documents gathered as discussed later in the Caregiver Compliance chapter, you will have a better idea of your loved one's financial status to determine how much they can afford. This information should explain their current expenses along with what assets they have and any limitations, if any, for liquidating them.

By this time, I was starting to think downsizing was the easy part. Even though I am a CPA, I still had to reach out to other financial and legal advisers. Managing Mom's trust taught me how much I did not know about finance when it came to understanding Long-term Care policies, Convertible Life Insurance Policies, market fluctuations, and how to become an intelligent investor.

Part of the sibling rivalry that began with my sisters placed a painfully bright spotlight on the efforts to help Mom financially. I could finally see that Little Sis, with all her limited life experience at that moment, was focused on the present moment, which was changing every six months for Mom. I was focused on her future cost of living and the inevitable needs her level of care was heading. The cost of care was only going to keep rising as her physical and mental health declined. Protecting her assets was necessary and difficult to do without creating more family drama.

Factors to consider regarding LTC insurance

Age and health – policies cost less if purchased when you are younger and in good health. If you are older or have serious health conditions, you can expect to pay more or not get coverage at all.

Income vs. Premiums – Assuming you were able to get affordable insurance now, would you be able to continue paying the premiums in the future with a lower fixed income? Considering potential premium increases as adjusted for inflation, would family help cover the cost if you needed it?

Savings and Investments – A certified financial advisor or an attorney who specializes in elder law and estate planning would be able to advise you on ways to save for future LTC expenses. They would also provide you with the pros and cons of purchasing LTC insurance that fits your family situation overall.

Tax Benefits – Benefits paid out through an LTC policy are generally not taxed as income. If you itemize deductions, then medical costs in excess of 7.5% (U.S. IRS rate as of 2020 thru 2025) of your adjusted gross income (AGI) can be deducted, including the premiums for LTC policies from your federal income taxes.

Individual vs. Employer-Sponsored – Most people buy LTC policies through an insurance agent or broker. Still, you must make sure they are licensed to sell in your state and know the type of care you are covering. You do not need to purchase more than your needs. Researching the type of Dementia and advice from their doctor will help grasp actual needs and worse case scenarios. Most policies will cap at $300K since companies know the true expenses involved in aging with Dementia.

Convertible Life Insurance Policies – If you are not familiar with the different insurance policies, begin research in your area to find providers. When I met with Mom's agent, I was overwhelmed with the number of options. I immediately got frustrated and wanted him to tell me what policy to purchase with the lowest cost so we could just set up payments and be done with it.

Policies are not one size fits all. These types of policies provide the benefit of obtaining less expensive term life insurance now while maintaining the option to convert to a permanent policy at a later date (between a specific age such as 65 to 70) as insurance needs and financial resources change.

The added benefit of Convertible policies is some policy providers offer the ability to convert Term Life Insurance into a Whole or Universal policy. The conversion creates a new policy, which might require an updated health screening. The timing of the conversion must be considered carefully regarding changes with health conditions.

Term Life Insurance – Provides the insured person coverage for a certain period. They are usually less expensive because they base their liability risk on life expectancy and the likelihood they would have to payout. Once the coverage period is met, the coverage is over unless you renew, which means increasing rates. As you age, liability risk goes up for the provider because likelihood becomes a probability. This type of policy does not carry a cash value and will not pay your beneficiary until death.

Whole Life Insurance – Also called Universal Policy, is considered more permanent since coverage is provided for the insured's entire life, so expectancy of payout is absolute. This policy is more expensive and most likely requires health screening to determine lifestyle, health status, and life expectancy. These types of policies are flexible and provide cash value buildup.

Insurance rates rise with age. The insurance carrier determines premiums each year based on actuarial tables. Each year the mortality rate changes and can place a bigger drain on cash values. You can choose to put more savings in the early years and less in later years as income becomes fixed, but this depends on when you purchase your policy and how many years you must allow the cash value to build.

Hybrid Policies – Offer both long-term care and life insurance. Our aging needs are causing an evolution in traditional products to become more linked benefit products. As more people develop long-term illnesses, this throws off the actuarial calculations of life expectancy. A person living with Dementia may have a functioning body long after the mind is no longer there. Life insurance covers them in death but does not cover the increasing cost of LTC unless you have a hybrid policy, which allows for a specific amount allotted to LTC with remainder funds for death benefits, for example.

Since LTC costs are rising, most companies allow you to draw down on life insurance to cover them but cap the amount you can draw and still receive a death benefit. These premiums will vary with whole life and typically include an annual inflation adjustment around 3% to 4%.

When to Consider a Policy

Insurance is intended to be the financial peace of mind for as many *"what if"* scenarios. We know every day when we get into our car, we have a daily risk of being in an accident and possibly even death. Yet, we take it for granted because we think our premiums paid give us the hassle-free, risk-free, and carefree ability not to become a statistic.

Insurance rates are determined by the statistical probability of future events, like car accidents or natural disasters. There is solid data for actuarial professionals to determine the type of incident, time of day, conditions involved, and other demographics such as sex and age to calculate the number of occurrences and likelihood or probability.

When you include unpaid caregivers and private care, the data is unavailable, and the cost is undeterminable. Estimates are low at best. LTC policies are very expensive for millions on a fixed income. Potential LTC expenditures represent a significant source of financial uncertainty for older adults. The growing trend is fear in covering costs, so instead of buying policies, adults aged 65 or older are spending down their assets to become eligible for Medicaid.

We are in the Silver Tsunami wave of LTC needs regarding Dementia. This wave is building as more baby boomers retire and younger adults in their 40's to early '50s are experiencing Dementia or early-onset Alzheimer's. Unfortunately, knowing when to purchase a policy depends on unique circumstances because some may choose to stay the course. In contrast, others attempt to fight it.

Long-term care (LTC) insurance policies cover the cost of services and may cover custodial care, home health care, hospice care (not covered by Medicare), assisted living care, adult day care, and skilled nursing care. These are services not eligible to individuals through Medicare or Medicaid, so paying down assets to become eligible will be a huge disappointment.

Although Medicaid, a federal and state program, does pay for nursing homes, it is available only to the poor or if you can *"spend down"* your assets to show you are needy and therefore eligible. Even then, this does not cover the luxury brochure as seen for most senior communities, which are still private pay. Trying to find what any of us consider nice for our loved ones to have a better quality of life may not be found in communities accepting Medicaid. There is still a huge gap in caring for our seniors and the mentally challenged versus profiting from the business of our aging society.

I had to face the financial facts that Mom, aging abnormally with Dementia, cannot survive in an assisted living facility because living with Dementia requires more of a memory care community. Right now, memory care communities are more often private pay than those that will accept Medicaid. The cost of the memory care community does not include the additional cost of home health care and skilled nursing.

Having the policy to cover these costs will be beneficial if it is considered supplemental towards existing assets. While the optimal age to purchase life insurance is under 35, millennials are the least likely to purchase a policy. Among the 57% of U.S. citizens who own life insurance, more than half of those policyholders are 45 or older.

YOLO, 'you only live once' - is not a good mindset to apply to when considering the cost of aging. Overindulgence, while we are young, is to be expected as we experiment and experience life. The problem is we pay for it later, which is why learning to live a healthy lifestyle is as much a financial decision as it is spiritual and nutritional.

Dual-income households have more than doubled from 1960 through 2012. More than 60% of U.S. households contained two wage earners in 2012, a 35% increase from 1960. Inflation is not only affecting our present purchasing power but the future as well. Anticipating monthly life insurance premiums or additional long-term insurance takes a back seat to retirement savings among U.S. residents 25 or older.

Furthermore, 40% of Americans do not own life insurance. More than half of that population say that payments for conveniences such as cell phones, cable, internet service, and social life take precedence over future life insurance premiums or LTC.

By the time I got my head wrapped around Mom's Mixed Dementia, she was already declined for LTC and life insurance policies due to her heart condition. Looking for burial plans made as much sense financially to have some preparations in place because it does not take an underwriter to know this outcome is imminent, especially sooner than later for a person living with Frontotemporal Dementia.

It is a painful reality because learning to live more frugally at an early age was not an issue for Mom. She learned by observing her parent's struggles to save for more than the rainy day, but unfortunately, no one expected this to become such a financial storm.

Chapter 6
The Domino Effect

Proverbs 4:23 (NIV)
Above all else, guard your heart, for everything you do flows from it.

Heal the Heart to Heal the Mind (Physical)

As children, we had no clue our hearts were such magical organs. We would not have appreciated the explanation from Euro Stem Cell that *"our heart is the first organ to form during development of the body. The blood and circulatory system, powered by the heart, together form the first organ system to develop. The circulatory system is essential to carry nutrients and waste around the embryo to keep its cells alive."*

We most likely would not have been able to grasp that some of the waste our body has to filter is directly from what we provide for nourishment and energy in the first place. Garbage in, garbage out is a motto I have come to understand as an adult.

Our heart is responsible for pumping oxygen-rich blood with antioxidants to all organs and tissue through the circulatory system. This system is like a luxury sports car needing high octane fuel rather than cheap gas to gum up the transmission and fuel injectors. We all have Ferrari's, and yet most treat them like a beat-up Pinto.

VS.

Stepping into Mom's world gave me a glimpse into her heart health physically and emotionally by what her diet had become. Trying to get her to exercise for added blood circulation has continued to be a struggle but the larger picture, or her 20% of the 80/20 rule, is the garbage she was putting into her body. Seeing her routine gave me the first clue to her constant nausea and dizziness. I first tried to break this down as much as possible to help her find relief from the upset stomach and acid reflux when I discovered she was eating rotten food from her refrigerator.

So many years later, into the long-term effects of her poor lifestyle choices, she experienced the slippage of time. If she could not discern what day of the week or how many days had passed since she had the leftovers in her refrigerator, she assumed it was still fine and ate the food. Later after vomiting or having bouts of diarrhea, she would assume she was allergic to something in the food, perhaps green bell peppers, before having the rationale thought that the food went bad and should have been tossed.

Seeing this was heart-wrenching - pun intended!

Mom went from one who hates to waste anything, especially food, to one who evolved into a mindless hoarder over the years of decline. You might be thinking now, *"I would know better not to eat rancid food."* So, hold this thought for a moment.

If we take this back several years, maybe a couple of decades, then we go back to her habits before Dementia started to affect her rationale. Mom's food habits or energy sources seemed to come from more of a mood-based response than hunger. Having favorites for treats was something we grew up with, but Mom indulged in sweets whenever she was hungry.

Sodas, sweet teas, and juices were the choice of fluid before she considered a glass of water. Aside from drinking her coffee black, every beverage she consumed was a sweet drink down to her favorite Choco Vine wine. We want our kids to avoid the dreaded sugar rush and inevitable sugar crash because we know the consequences of an amped-up child, but it is a bit more difficult with an adult.

High levels of sugar cause spikes in our blood sugar that go beyond a burst of energy to create sudden headaches, fatigue, irritability, increased heart rate, and anxiety. It sounds like the manic highs and lows we experienced Mom having back in the 90s when she ran on fumes or sweets alone.

We used to have pizza on Dad's paydays with a movie rental from Blockbuster as our weekly treat during the '80s and '90s. This treat, of course, was more of a treat for Dad, so he did not have to cook on a Friday night. Saturdays were typically backyard barbeque meals with potato salads smothered in a heavy mayonnaise dressing. Weekend food after a week of fried pork chops, fried bananas, with a side of salty rice and red beans. Sometimes we had sides of canned corn or green beans. Just about everything we ate was what you saw on TV commercials, aside from Dad's childhood Puerto Rican cuisine that Grandma taught him how to make.

Dad craved the salty fried foods, did not limit portions, and eventually had high blood pressure and diabetes, which caused other ailments. Mom craved the sweets and would eat desserts all day if she could get away with it.

I remember one morning, we had a dozen donuts for breakfast and snacking. At this point, Mom was trying to cut back on her sweet foods. She took the donut to the kitchen sink, turned on the water slowly, gently sprinkled it with water, lightly patted the frosting, and then dried it with a paper towel before giggling while taking her first bite. She thought doing so was cutting calories instead of maybe having a piece of avocado toast or something else altogether.

Again - garbage in, garbage out. Mom and Dad's diet fluctuated by what they could afford in bulk and what they craved the most. Life was stressful enough going paycheck to paycheck, but the lack of healthy foods left them tired. Not being properly fueled made pushing through the day feel like walking through a muddy swamp with weights on your back. This way of life made our hearts work much harder than they needed to.

Now grab that thought again—the one about not eating rotten food.

What do you find yourself craving often? What do you treat yourself with when payday rolls around? What do you tend to eat when you are stressed or feel sad?

It may not have been rotten food, but it is probably worth a second thought to consider the healthy alternative while you still have the rationale mind. Think alternatives that are sustainable, flexible, and value-adding for your heart over the compulsion to self-soothe with food.

I reached for my self-medication through food and alcohol. My childhood reward system usually included food which became another habit I had to unlearn. Chocolate chip cookies are my reward for making it through another day of stress, regardless of the source. The problem was in knowing how many cookies it would take to relieve my stress. No internal gauge tells you how much is enough when feeding pain or trying to soothe emotional stress with food.

I was overindulging in what I considered comfort foods (salty-sweet or starchy and greasy) and then topping it off with a hefty chocolate chip cookie. In my mind, I earned it, but I did not expect the cravings to take over. As I stressed more over Mom's care, I ate more, craved more, and bought more cookies. They tasted great, but eventually, I was left feeling depressed because I did not feel like I earned the stress, and my clothing sizes kept going up. It did not stop me from paying myself off with more cookies because I did not connect to self-soothing with food until much later.

There is also a flip side to this since we also must make sure we are eating enough. Daily nutrition becomes a challenge because when women think of fast weight loss, they usually deprive themselves of caloric intake instead of changing their diets altogether. Adding specific portions of fruits, vegetables, and plant-based proteins is a unique selection, but the choice must be made to meet your energy and health needs.

Dad told me about this flip side because Mom weighed 96 pounds soaking wet back when they met. She used to drink Coke Cola all the time and ate very little. She was not a young lady concerned about her curves. Mom was a tomboy that was used to getting by with very little sustenance and quite a bit of sweetness. Manic behavior back then could have easily been dismissed as a sugar high with the subsequent crash. Limiting the amount of soda and eating better was a temporary fix after they married.

During her first pregnancy, she became overwhelmed with morning sickness, which led to strict orders from the doctors to avoid salty and spicy foods. Dad became the house chef, having to learn how to cook for her. He cooked what he knew how initially, which he grew up on as the staples of a Puerto Rican diet, more fried food.

Dad eventually began to barbecue chicken and other cuts of beef before dabbling with a wok to make Chinese food. Of course, we could not have Chinese food without the fried egg rolls he bought in bulk.

It seemed so little at the time to help Mom through her pregnancies nutritionally, but it made a big difference food-wise. Hormonally was truly a different perspective. Not knowing what she was experiencing meant mood swings were blamed on the hormones of the pregnancy. Then after each of our deliveries, the hormones continued to be an issue and viewed as only postpartum depression. A condition perceived as normal because the expectation was this would lessen as time passed, and her body would return to a normal hormonal state postpartum.

That expectation was a bad assumption, but when we did not know any better, we continued to find small things to explain the uncomfortable moments all away. That is how it all began, one dismissal after the other. We were unaware that postpartum depression was a potential sign of Frontotemporal Dementia, formerly known as Pick disease. FTD, primary degenerative dementia for which no cause is established.

According to The American College of Obstetricians and Gynecologists, family history or genetic abnormalities are found in about 50% of cases published by Elsevier Inc. This connection was not made and published online until January 17, 2004, as a Case Report titled Dementia Presenting as postpartum depression by Diana L. Dell MD and Jonathan J. Halford MD. A diagnosis is frequently missed or delayed because it occurs in a younger age group, presents with unusual signs and symptoms, and is far less prevalent than Alzheimer's disease.

The problem was by the time Mom reached her 3rd pregnancy, over eight years later, this cycle of highs and lows, then extreme lows, left her depressed often and craving more junk foods. She kept wanting to give Dad a son after having three girls, but three more attempts ended in 3 miscarriages. Having a son was just not meant to be.

Her depression seemed to consume her entirely, with the only thing bringing her a smile was a bowl of ice cream. Her favorite is Blue Bell's Pecan Pralines, but it did not matter the flavor as much, so Dad bought what he could in bulk. He did anything to see her smile. He struggled to keep up with her cycles of mental health because it would take more than ice cream to keep her going.

Later, when Mom was living alone, her daily snacking seemed manageable because she was eating but not drinking water. Avoiding water is dangerous to your kidneys, urinary tract, and heart. A Urinary Tract Infection (UTI) is a silent killer for adults living with Dementia. This infection can seep into the kidneys and eventually our blood which inevitably affects the heart. Getting her to drink water is still a daily struggle, so it took some creative encouragement. Hearing her mention headaches throughout a day without the typical allergy issues queued me into her water intake.

She may not have been concerned with the thickness of her blood, but I was very attentive to her fluids. I tried to encourage water even more during the day before a doctor's appointment when I knew they would be taking a blood sample. Her blood thickened without the water, making the nurse hunt for a viable vein to pull enough blood to fill a vial. Mom often sat and squirmed in the chair while the nurse checked the right arm, then the left, and then finally settled on a right or left hand. We already knew she had low blood pressure with poor circulation but seeing it flow so slowly to fill a vial reminded me of when I heard others refer to her blood as molasses.

I learned a little life hack by using ice trays filled with thinly sliced strawberries and Ocean Spray juice (low sugar content) to make ice cubes is very helpful. Mom not only drank a full glass of water with 2 or 3 strawberry ice cubes in it, but she also used her straw for fishing out the strawberries to eat as well. Strawberries provide antioxidants, vitamin C, and fiber. Changing up the flavor of juice helped once she appeared to be burned out on a particular flavor.

As lifestyle is established through healthier nutritional selections, then sleep should fall in place. Rather, it would be best if you were falling to sleep easier and achieving more restorative sleep. Poor sleep will not only keep your body from the natural repair and restoration overnight, but it will also hinder our bodies' hormone production levels of Leptin and Ghrelin. These hormones signal our brains for us to eat less and more, respectively. When these levels are out of balance, it is too easy to go from poor to horrible diets.

Forget making any healthy New Year's Resolution when you cannot make more effort to maintain deep restorative sleep for at least 7 hours a night. Since it takes roughly 21 days for a new routine to become a habit, then good sleep will help to reinforce the early rise for a workout regimen and stop the craving for junk food to make it through the day.

Getting good sleep is not only important for your energy levels because it is crucial for your heart health as well. When we are rested, we are better equipped to handle the basic stress of the day. Our energy is not depleted so quickly when we care for our loved ones while handling the stressful moments as they arise during the day.

Our body's reaction to stressful moments releases adrenaline, which increases our heart rate, elevates our blood pressure, and boosts energy supplies. Adrenaline can be a good thing to help us maintain the demands caregiving presents, but we are not meant to remain at high levels of adrenaline rushes.

If we are in this heightened stressful state for lengthy periods, we begin to produce the cortisol hormone overly. This hormone is responsible for increasing sugars (glucose) in the bloodstream, enhancing our brain's use of glucose, and increasing substances' availability for repairing tissues. It is mainly used for short bursts of energy to help us in times of danger. Most bodily cells have Cortisol receptors which affect different functions in the body.

On the good side, Cortisol can help control blood sugar levels, regulate metabolism, help reduce inflammation, and assist with memory formulation. It has a controlling effect on salt and water balance to help control blood pressure.

We can get too much of a good thing. Staying in a high-stress mode known as the fight or flight will eventually cause you to experience suppressed immunity, hypertension, high blood sugar, Insulin resistance, *carbohydrate craving*, metabolic syndrome, type 2 diabetes, fat deposits of the face, neck, and belly, and reduced libido to name a few.

The vicious cycle begins because excessive Cortisol levels will build up in your body, causing you to eat more and experience poor sleep, which affects the Leptin and Ghrelin levels. You will crave all the wrong foods, gain weight, strain your heart, and lose the will to exercise because it will make you feel sore and exhausted day after day.

Mom fell into this cycle while teaching because she did not understand the importance of sleep in tandem with healthy nutrition and exercise. She was stuck in a state of fight or flight to manage the classroom and then too exhausted to enjoy family or life in general. This cycle added to her depression that slowly exposed her to Vascular Dementia.

When all you can think of is sleeping on your day off, should you get one, then it is time to pay closer attention to your hormones, sleep patterns, and nutrition choices. Unbalanced hormones could cause undue stress on your heart, creating the perfect storm for heart disease, among other diseases such as Diabetes and Dementia.

Common signs of being aware of excess Cortisol are severe fatigue, muscle weakness, depression, anxiety, irritability, loss of emotional control, cognitive difficulties, new or worsened high blood pressure, headache, and even bone loss leading to fractures over time. This stress hormone is intended to help your body function well in times of stress. Suppose you live in high-stress environments as a caregiver without a healthy diet and exercise to relieve stress. You are creating a lifestyle to expose yourself to Dementia regardless of genetics.

The life of a caregiver can be planned to be proactive to avoid this, but it does take discipline to keep a healthy heart and knowledge of how to tailor a new lifestyle with flexibility. You are worth it! Without a healthy heart, the brain eventually suffers along with your loved one, dependent on your care.

According to Aging Care expert Minding our Elders, in 2007, grim statistics showed 30% of caregivers die before those their loved ones in care. Our health becomes a side effect to unprepared caregivers. With caregivers skipping their own doctors' appointments or well checks, they have no idea of the damage their bodies are living with until serious trauma occurs, such as a heart attack.

Observing Mom's daily habits revealed what was happening to her current demented state of mind and how she arrived at this point of her life's journey. It is also what showed me if I did not choose to change poor habits of my own, then I would face the same demise.

Every time I would remind Mom how young she was, which meant she still had time to change habits, I would get the same depressed response. *"We're all going to die someday, so why does it matter?"*

And the one she tried to laugh her way through was, *"I never said I was going to die skinny."* As much as I tried to smile with acknowledgment in her typical 'leave me alone' response, I struggled more and more. It matters! Everything matters!

Her quality of life matters regardless of what stage of Dementia she is living within. Just because she gave up on her life did not mean I would give up on her as well. It is difficult to find the happy medium between allowing her to make choices and encouraging better choices without triggering an unwanted behavior or response.

Knowing this, while giving in to her bad habits, I was now helping her meet her end sooner than later. Our emotional battle continues because although I was not giving up on her, I had to let her go each day and convince myself it was all about her quality of life. I created better habits to live with that brought about more tension during our days because Mom did not care. We had to find a happy medium and keep trying each day.

I finally reached another plateau of understanding that although I could not break her cycle, I did have an opportunity to break my cycle. I tried each day to get her to eat better and exercise more but accepted both of our limitations week after week.

One unexpected change came when it was my turn to go to the doctor. Since I had no one else to stay with Mom, I took her along with me. It became a nice little outing, even if it was the doctor's office. Mom was able to watch me be the patient for a change. They asked me many of the same health questions they had asked her and did pretty much the same examination.

It was a nice reminder that she was not the only one getting poked and prodded. The appointment was all part of preventative maintenance. The only difference was I heeded every bit of suggestions or advice the doctor provided where Mom would roll her eyes and dismiss it.

I would get so frustrated with each moment Mom rolled her eyes and said, "I don't need it." Regardless of what she felt was not needed, there was an almost immediate follow-up with a complaint of pain.

Instead of doing something about the pain to locate and fix the source, she would rather take Advil and forget about it. I was doing the same when I was highly focused on building a career and unaware of the number of hours I was sitting at my desk. The problem that we both overlooked is the increased risk of a heart attack, stroke, and high blood pressure due to taking pain and inflammation OTC medications or Nonsteroidal anti-inflammatory drugs (NSAIDs).

All these realizations made my inner child sit back and relax. This caregiving journey was indeed happening for me instead of to me.

As a side note, Accounting is the action or process of keeping financial accounts. This profession holds companies for-profit and not-for-profit accountable for their transactions. It's more than being good at math, as most people reduce it down. An accountable mindset is what I stepped into this journey with, not a nurse or a physical trainer. Our free will choices create negative wear and tear ripe for Dementia to hold us individually accountable. No matter your age, we can all learn to be a healthier, better version of ourselves. A better example for our children. A better teacher. A better spouse. A better friend. Ultimately, a better caregiver.

The more we understand how much Mom's heart affects her overall health, the more I believe Vascular Dementia came first then progressed into Frontotemporal Dementia (FTD). It seems like a road map depicting the poor circulation towards which area of her brain eventually suffered. This damage was done over a lifetime of poor diet with little to no exercise and depression left unchecked.

Mom was convinced her father's ailments would become her own in due time, so there was no point in prevention which added to her depression and personal neglect. Dad lived by the same poor logic, unfortunately. I have met other caregivers with this same kind of logic.

"What is the point if we're all going to die anyway?" Mom would often say. This attitude made her completely miss the point of quality of life over quantity. Instead of sitting around waiting to die, she could have been living life as God intended in a community with others beyond being a classroom teacher just trying to survive another day.

I recognized the symptoms of excess Cortisol for myself, yet Mom's behavior became a daily puzzle once I understood what to look for because living with Dementia is stressful. Living with mixed Dementia makes it difficult to recognize symptoms of Dementia to decipher a specific type. Unfortunately, symptoms of Fibromyalgia are similar to common Dementia indicators. Without observation of daily changes, then you must become a medical detective.

We ignored the healthy heart life choices, which made us ignore the progression of Dementia that could have been prevented or postponed in the least. Since Mom had lived with manic bipolar depression for so long, we could not decipher one from the other.

Healing the Mind Through the Proverbial Heart (psychological)

If you are wondering what the Proverbial heart has to do with Alzheimer's and other forms of Dementia, then step away from the medical perspective for a moment. The psychological perspective gives insight into why we have poor diets or seek ways to be numb in our reality. This approach may also be helpful to understand why personalities are magnified as Dementia progresses aside from the loss of basic senses. We need to get down to the root cause of the cravings and broken hearts through the proverbial heart.

I spent five years cleansing my emotional heart from a childhood that created my initial broken heart. I also spent a considerable amount of time replacing the deeply embedded poor programming in my mind that convinced me I am not enough with an insistent imposter syndrome. I had to venture into the place where guilt and shame clashed in my mind to find the root cause, which took me back to my heart. The pursuit of love and acceptance is powerful.

I lived life in a structured passive risk-free life that kept me away from people as much as possible as an accountant. Caregiving requires an up close and personal space to care in, so my past life would not help Mom or me any longer. Stepping into her space more intently, I started to see similarities between Mom's eating habits and my habit of finding a state of numbness.

If you have not been able to cleanse the emotional heart before stepping into a caregiving role, then take advantage of an opportunity to make more sense of this journey by establishing a relationship with a therapist sooner than later. Clearing out the debris in my heart helped me to see Mom as an individual with emotional needs of her own instead of through eyes of anger or resentment.

Mom's care needed to be more hands-on many years before surrendering to this journey. I was not prepared to go where it was taking me. Not only was I denying she was having issues with abnormal aging, but I also denied how much Mom and I had in common.

Trying to accept her reasoning to avoid any form of psychotherapy and respect her choice only added to my frustrations with her. I started to lose empathy and respect for her when I knew how much therapy was helping me. I did not want to be sucked into her dark world of existence, and yet I knew I needed to meet her in her world. There was no benefit in forcing her to meet me in my world. I tried.

Every time I tried to come close to the point of acceptance with a thought of *"that's just how she is."* The acceptance went out the window when another part of me would think, *"I know, but WHY is she like this?"* Then another part would say, *"I know why she's like this, and it will not change until she allows the therapy process to work."* Nothing but more frustration because this internal dialogue made me feel helpless as we tried to make it through daily routines. Especially shower day routines.

I judged her harshly for living the way she had for so many years. The anger within me could only see she brought this all upon herself. My inner child stepped up quickly to point out how unfair this mess was for me. The timing of all this alone seemed unfair. The feeling of unfairness came from somewhere that needed to be unpacked and the anger, insecurity, resentment, perfectionism, and need to control everyone around me.

My inner child seemed to surface more on Mom's shower days for some odd reason. And then the flashbacks started to happen even more than the occasional dream at night of a time I did not want to address. No, this feeling went beyond the ick factor of seeing Mom naked in the shower. No one wants to see their parents this vulnerable, but there was something brewing and trying to surface from the depths of my psyche.

The Spirit within continued to remind me that this journey was not about me, yet I could not understand how it was not. There was an onion in my heart waiting to be peeled. Each time the Spirit tried to open my heart to shine the light, my inner parts reacted without being aware of them to keep my true self hidden and protected.

Even sharing this with you now, a little part of me feels like I am betraying her by telling you our secret.

Yet another part of me feels how silly it sounds to refer to myself in so many ways, shameful and embarrassed. I have learned this is the way the proverbial heart works. It works with the mind to protect us by creating another version of us to coexist with us. I know this sounds a bit like split personalities. Still, these parts within me are different versions of me emotionally stunted at the age various traumas happened—both the source of my caregiver stress and solution to breaking old programming.

My heart was broken when I was only four years old by someone in my extended family, I had no reason not to trust. Those flashbacks were from early memories in the bathroom of my paternal grandparent's home in Puerto Rico. Somehow Mom's reaction to me on shower days from saying *"I don't need another shower"* triggered my memories of saying *"I don't want to get into the tub"* as a child.

The single bathroom in this small three-bedroom house was where I had been trapped and violated as a small child. A wheelchair narrow enough to pass through the threshold of the doorway was wide enough to block my escape. I was trapped with my little body full of Cortisol and panic. The first moment I could recall when his touch became what it should have never been towards an innocent child, which gave birth to my inner runaway.

This inner part would wake me in the middle of the night as it sensed his presence in the room approaching the side of the bed. I could not make my body small enough to hide under the covers as far back in the corner of the bed. Frozen with fear as my eyes searched in the darkness for an escape route only to realize I was trapped in the corner of the room. *"Please God, wake me if this is a nightmare; bring Grandma."* My voice was frozen and my chest tight.

As I struggled more with this violation and discomfort, I splintered into more inner parts as I grew into a teenager that became more firefighter parts. Being in a state of fight or flight was the one state I worked best in eventually. Of course, I had no idea what I was running from over the years of building a professional career. Situations or companies I ran from were because of their issues, not mine. They were the problem, not me. Unfortunately, to protect the runaway, my anger grew to be a powerful controlling part.

These reactions were not describing split personalities because I was conscious throughout my life but not aware of why my feelings were driving me in these ways. Self-awareness began when I stepped into the role of Mom's essential caregiver.

As a dominant perfectionist, there was no such thing as being broken. There was only surviving perfectly or what was perfect to me. Since I have been able to break apart the onion in my heart, I have found healing and love. I can finally see the past from a new perspective.

I can truly feel my way through the memories to forgive. Part of feeling like I was always on autopilot for so long, neglecting my health and avoiding people, was because these parts were always on. I could stay in my head and be the accountant I had become because it was an easier function by analyzing trends rather than working with people and risking harm to my heart or being judged by them.

In the beginning, my anger towards Mom was from her resistance to living healthier to remain independent longer. As I observed later, it was because she adamantly refused therapy and any attempts towards healthy changes.

The woman that raised me was such a fighter. She pushed me to excel no matter what. Mom said, *"Life is what you make it,"* and she was right. I made messes and tried to hide from them rather than learn from each one. This advice came from her teacher part, but my runaway part could not appreciate her wisdom. When I needed her to be a fighter once again, she was content with merely existing.

I used to think this was because Mom's generation did not consider therapy as a form of self-care for mental and physical health. However, during Mom's birthday lunch with me years ago, I was given a glimpse into Mom's wounded inner child when she shared about her sexual trauma from childhood.

Therapy would uncover and heal a time when Mom had been told as a teenager, *"It didn't happen. You're lying."*

If her own family reacted this way, how could she ever trust a therapist, a total stranger? This shed light on her attitude in life of *"why does it matter?"*

When Mom was a young teenager at roughly 14 years old, she experienced sexual abuse by her oldest sibling. This experience was the first source of post-traumatic stress disorder (PTSD). The second shocking offense came when she ran to her father, as Daddy's little girl, for help and told him of the horrible deed. He did not believe her, so he beat her for lying instead. Her proverbial heart was broken. Hanging onto her self-worth set poor lifestyle habits in motion.

Dad had mentioned her protective side but not how deep or damaged her heart had been. Her worth as a child was not valued, so she learned not to value herself either.

Mom only knew to cover it up and run away with me when something similar happened to me. She took me away from all extended family on both Mom and Dad's side of the family. Mom had an inner runaway too. Of all things to bond over, sexually abused yet surviving to become the women we are today. Only now do I get to break the cycle and stop running.

Finding the courage to attend therapy allowed me to learn what gave birth to my inner parts and how deep my old programming went. I was blessed with divine guidance that lit up a path to two powerful therapists to help set me free from the prison of my past.

With this new gift of time to care for Mom, I had a renewed sense of awareness that gave me the will to peel back the layers of an onion which had been guarding my heart for far too long, just like Mom.

Going back in time to identify the layers was not easy, but it had to be done. I could cleanse the source of my bad food cravings, nightmares, and anger towards Mom. I was learning about each of my inner parts and why they were reacting to Mom's parts. I know Mom did what she had to do to protect her daughters, but we never knew of her trauma or sacrifices to walk away from family to protect us.

I also was able to gain insight into why Mom always said, *"You know I don't get attached to things."*

Yet over time, as Dementia progressed, she became a hoarder. Keeping the pain locked inside her mind, riddled throughout the tissue in her body, kept her emotionally stuck. I could not hug her or try to get close to her until she was willing to reveal her wounded inner child to me. A lifetime of poor lifestyle habits had already taken a toll on her. Setting her free from the past was not going to happen.

My emotional issues were slowly resolved through therapy, support groups, meditation, and self-expression. Before reaching out for therapy, I was so afraid of speaking about my feelings. I feared retaliation, ridicule, and a variety of family fall out. By holding back from expressing my emotions, I created worse situations by allowing my emotions to bottle up and explode later or not allowing others to get close to me.

The more progress I made in my therapy sessions, the more Mom would come to mind. Then the realization hit regarding Dementia and how those living with it revert in time which causes some irrational responses. I worried if Mom would revert to the time as a teenager to relive those memories since she never allowed herself to go through a healing process. I can only pray that her memories of that period are not still intact.

Although the human psyche cannot be explained with a simple answer, we can bring light to these issues to bring about resolutions. The concept of healing the heart to heal the mind is a psychological issue and a medical issue.

The psychological perspective feeds the garbage in, garbage out cycle when we don't even realize it. Our society is still struggling to understand the difference between mental health and physical wellbeing.

Not knowing how to deal with a broken heart or being ashamed of the hardened heart leads many of us to self-medicate. Not knowing how to deal with issues that cause us pain creates a problem when we avoid or try to numb the pain with medication like pain killers, alcohol, smoking, or other substance abuse.

These are obvious dangers to a healthy heart, yet those are not the real problems because they are the reactive negative solutions. We cannot live life in a bubble or be in complete control to avoid broken hearts or angry hearts because life was not intended to be lived in a fog. Stuff happens! How else would we learn to grow? Not dealing with life could give rise to the onion in your chest, layers upon layers of stinky emotions blocking your heart.

The mechanical parts of your heart will get gummed up from life's sticky situations like scar tissue. This psychological scar tissue is what holds our wounded inner child hostage in the first place. The longer we let our wounded inner child stay in pain or avoid the pain, the more we block ourselves from making better decisions to lead a healthier and happier life.

You can tell if feelings of loneliness and shyness emotionally block your heart. Thinking with our head instead of our heart is the protective yet reactive response to an emotionally blocked heart. The mind, or "ego," will have you fight for control to avoid the pain and silence the wounded inner child. It will also create codependency, jealousy, or a harsh, judgmental frame of mind towards others with the intent to protect and control.

As a caregiver, cleansing these emotions by digging into your onion layers can be the beginning of a simple resolution to release repressed memories or old grudges. The process may not be as simple because those layers may have formed throughout childhood by the same parent you are now responsible for caring for. It is very difficult to care for a loved one aging with Dementia, but when you have an unresolved past that blocks your heart, caregiving can feel impossible. The lack of choice brings on emotional stress, which is piled on by the added physical stress.

Being open with your emotions is the first step. I often avoided people or situations who remind me of past situations because they pulled those unwanted memories into my present. When you begin avoiding your loved one because of the past while they desperately need you in their present, you might indirectly create a senior neglect scenario or lose the compassion required to be a successful caregiver.

It might seem unfair when your focus is how much they hurt you in the past, therefore it is important to resolve. An old painful emotion your inner child is holding onto is not poisoning your loved one. The memory is holding you back. Your loved one is struggling to remember their day-to-day routines, not what they did to you when you were a child. The more you try to self-medicate, the more you damage your own heart in addition to other organs. If you cannot take care of yourself, you cannot take care of your loved one.

We cannot change the past, but we can be open about it to understand it better. If your loved one has enough cognitive ability to carry on a conversation about these issues, then it is worth the try. Do not expect them to remember the situations or even understand your pain because it may add more stress.

If the person who created your wounded inner child is deceased, consider writing them a letter about what you would have said if given a chance. Then you can read it out loud, burn it, or shred it. Expression of the pain is still very beneficial.

When I attempted this conversation with Mom, she was only concerned with why I wanted to talk about it and seemed more defensive than I was. I did not consider what period she might have been in when I started to ask about our family vacations to Puerto Rico. Her responses let me know right away I would not find the answers I was looking for to fill in the gaps.

Seeking therapy and finding a way to forgive them or whoever is causing the emotional blockage will heal you and give back a healthier heart long term. Finding a clean slate may help you genuinely care for and love them while you still have them.

Forgiveness is one of the most powerful forms of love anyone can give and receive. It is yet another choice to make throughout your caregiver journey. Once you arrive at this point in your journey, you will be able to heal your inner child and give love more freely to your loved one in the form of care.

It would be beneficial to make an honest effort to go out into nature throughout this emotional cleansing. Finding time to meditate can be difficult in our busy work, school, or caregiving days. Step outside during your busy day for 10-15 minutes to close your eyes and breathe in the air. Enjoy the breeze on your face with the sun or hear the birds sing. Set a timer on your phone to remind yourself when it is time for a mental break.

Write down what comes to mind or speak it aloud to the universe all around you. Your energy will begin to shift if you allow space for it to flow freely. As the months went by, my stress level went down, and my sleep cycle returned to deep restorative rest.

My heart gradually healed by making different choices to change my eating habits and limit self-medication by replacing it with meditation and therapy. I gradually accepted the past and finally understood why Mom's actions were an automatic response for her and how she could not be empathetic to our needs.

I finally began to understand who she was and who I was. Now I can express my feelings, let go of old grudges, fears, and bad habits of worst-case scenario worrying or anxiety-driven planning. I finally began to trust others enough to get close to me. Something Mom still struggles to do. I acknowledged that my worry came from a lack of knowledge and not trusting God to see me through this journey.

I now felt more compassion for Mom and Dad as individuals and their stories together.

Her behavior before and after Dementia symptoms began to make more sense. I could gradually see her as a person living with Dementia with all the challenges and stress this way of life caused her. Once again, God found a way to bring to my attention how this journey was not about me.

Mom was already living with depression when she met Dad. He became her prince in shining armor to whisk her away. Back in their day, going to therapy was more of a show of weakness. Healing her inner child was never a thought. She entered and lived the rest of the marriage with a broken heart.

So many people are dismissed in society as people living with Dementia or a broken heart. Trying to convince Mom how beneficial therapy is in present times is still a struggle. She attends her appointments and tells her Neurologist every appointment she is fine and does not need to be there. Her actions speak much louder than her words. I have come to accept this is her automatic defensive response which means *"Leave me alone. I want to hurt in private."*

Even if you feel therapy is not needed, changing eating habits will certainly help your heart. Many processed foods or junk foods cause mood swings or anxiety along with weight gain or insulin resistance.

Author Sharon Feiereisen from *"Eat This, Not That!"* published an article on 20 Foods That Put You in a Bad Mood. She describes how supermarket cookies and extra cheese pizzas are doing a lot more damage than simply expanding our waistline. Below is her list of mood-altering foods

1. Soda Drinks (especially diet, aspartame)
2. High sugar juices
3. Cocktail Mixers
4. Bagels
5. Agave Nectar
6. Vegetable Shortening (High omega 6)
7. Cold cuts (packaged meats like ham, bologna, hot dogs, and even turkey)
8. Packaged, processed Seeds (Salted Sunflower)
9. Salted Peanuts (Sodium/MSG)
10. Baked Goods (Refined sugars/saturated oils)
11. Margarine (Saturated Fats)
12. French Fries (refined carbs/Salt)
13. Canned Foods (should be BPA Free)
14. Processed Foods (shelf life)
15. Coffee (excessively)
16. Cereal (refining process)
17. Wheat (Gluten)
18. Dried Fruit (additive/preservatives)
19. Alcohol (in excess is a depressant)
20. Potato Chips (saturated fats)

Chapter 7
One Hot Mess

2 Corinthians 5:13 (NLT)
If it seems we are crazy, it is to bring glory to God. And if we are in our right minds, it is for your benefit.

We began to call Mom Queen Bee as she lay in bed from exhaustion, completely withdrawn from our lives. We watched Dad cook and bring trays of food to her on the couch or in bed to make sure she took her medicines as well. Most of what Dad explained about Mom's mood swings was connected to chemical imbalances. One seemed to make her tired most of the time and short on patience the rest of the time. He accepted her as she was and did not love her any less.

During my teenage years, it seemed as if Mom was living purposefully as a teacher. She was driven to educate her ESL students and protect them from the world's cruelty for not speaking English. That same fierce drive would appear like more of an autopilot as the seasons changed.

Rising with the alarm clock to shower and dress, take her meds when Dad offered them to her with a cup of coffee and toast, then out the door to hopefully beat morning rush hour traffic. The 6 to 8 class teaching periods, grading papers, and later lesson planning were a defined routine. She had a daily routine to keep her on time, leaving the house and returning after a long day.

We were all living very monotonous routines between work and school. So how do we live a life of purpose when we are not sure what our purpose is? When we live in a comfort zone with as little chaos as possible, are we living in our purpose and don't even know it? Or are we stuck on autopilot with a routine helping us like bumper pads in the bowling lane for the inexperience?

Autopilot was the mindset Mom was operating within. She was comfortable with not being present in our lives to raise us or steer us as she was doing so with her students. She was comfortable being the silly "cool" teacher for her students that covered her desk in thank you notes and letters of appreciation.

Her routine was thrown off when she finally fell asleep. Sleeping past her alarm clock would start her day sluggish and in somewhat of the fight or flight mode. Her students learned to cover for her when she was tardy past the first bell. None of them knew why but they knew to cover for her, and they would be rewarded. Dad eventually said, "Come on, Baby, you can't keep doing this."

Instead of coming home exhausted, ready for the couch, as usual, she would surprisingly still be full of energy as she chatted about her day in the classroom. The day's stress triggered the manic moments of high energy or what I called her nesting time.

With her irritability looming around her, she walked into my room and demanded it cleaned up before I went to bed. In my adolescent years, I thought I was clever by shoving everything under the bed as far back as possible with the rest into the closet. She walked away long enough to brush her teeth and put on some pajamas, then came in and crouched down on the floor to reach under my bed to pull every last bit of junk to the center of the room. She turned back to the closet, ducking under blouses hanging up to do the same thing by tossing what she found out of place onto the growing pile in the middle of the room.

Mind you, if I walked into her room at the time, it had clothes all over it, both clean clothes waiting to be put away or hung up and dirty clothes piled at the foot of her bed. Do as I say, not as I do.

She spent many hours in her office room with that same irritable cloud still looming to continue working on lesson plans. Once she finished with the lesson plans, she played computer games or picked up a book to read. She lost track of time easily without feeling the fatigue then worked or played games through the night because she could not sleep.

Dad asked her to come to bed several times, but she kept tinkering away with whatever kept her from boredom. From my room down the hall, I watched as he rubbed his face in confusion and slowly pulled her office door closed. I eventually went to bed along with my sisters. The next morning Dad always made sure she had coffee with her medicines before she left the house to do it all over again.

Mom's craziness or silliness became more than episodes of highs and lows as the months and years went by. Events started to occur where details did not make sense anymore with Mom's explanation of time slippage or poor judgment calls. Her actions spoke much louder than her words, but we could not translate the meaning. Even on the days she left on time for her morning commute, she began to return home later and later.

Why was a middle school teacher returning home from the school day at 9 or 10 PM? In previous years she remained after school to tutor students and, in some cases, to provide a safe ride home. Some weekends, I even recall meeting up at the school to redecorate her classroom for seasonal changes with some of her devoted students. Afterward, she took them out to eat or shopping for shoes to thank them. Weekend driving was during daylight hours. Returning after 9 or 10 PM during the week seemed a bit more concerning later down the road.

Where had she been all this time? How much longer would she be? Why did she not think to contact us, let us know she was alright?

Mom did not have a cellphone during these early years of decline, but her classroom had a phone. As soon as she walked in through the door, Dad was ready with a barrage of questions. Where have you been all this time? Why didn't you call? Didn't you stop to think we would be worried? Why couldn't 'whatever it was' wait until tomorrow? Are you hungry? What have you had to eat in the last couple of hours?

Mom sighed and said, *"I forgot."*

He fired right back, *"forgot that you had to come home?"*

Mom's response then and more often after was, *"No, I forgot what time it was."* He would look back at her with squinted eyes, like something smells fishy, but would drop it as soon as he said, *"You're crazy, you know that?"*

She was finally home, and he was tired. He wanted to make sure she ate so he could go to bed. He looked angry, but deep down, he was hurt because he was worried. He did not want to think about the worst-case scenario or start a bigger fight right before bed for us to hear. The pattern was emerging, and her routine was evolving.

These behaviors and slippage of time were spelling out more than her Bipolar manic-depressive tendencies. We could not predict a cycle as easily, which was more than the craziness that we grew to accept from her. Before, we usually had a reason why we could dismiss the oddities or temperamental outbursts. Eventually, we had to face the facts. Her strange behaviors or poor habits were no longer about mood swings and soon about her safety.

We normalized Mom's insomnia and did not have the smallest clue because we knew she would sleep on the couch as soon as she came home from work early. It was her routine. She got up early Saturdays to work in her flower beds or build doll houses. Then she only stopped to take a nap or get a sweet snack.

Eventually, her lack of sleep became our reason to dismiss her outbursts. She may not have been crazy, but she certainly was crankier than normal. We assumed she knew what she was doing and let her be, time and time again. Until the phone call in the middle of the night for Dad to come to get her, she began to sleepwalk or sleep drive.

Big Sis was the first to get married and moved into a house three blocks down the road with her husband. She had a black poodle that our cocoa-colored poodle would run away to visit. It was funny when he did it a time or two. How remarkable that this dog could find her by scent, knowing exactly which house to find her in.

It was funny until Mom had begun to do something similar in the middle of the night. She had walked down to Big Sis' house, three blocks away in a drunken stupor with no awareness of how she got there. She knocked on their door with a deer in the headlights vacant smile. They called Dad right away to alert him that Mom had wandered over to their house.

Dad answered the phone, saying, *"How the hell did she do that? I'll be right there."* After living through the Vietnam war, Dad was never a heavy sleeper. He would catch us every time as teenagers trying to sneak out of the house or upon returning as if he had a sixth sense. Eventually, he accepted that if Mom was not in bed next to him during the middle of the night, she was either in her office room or asleep on the couch.

The house was locked up, dark, and silent until he slammed down the phone and rushed down the stairs to grab his keys to go pick her up. He pulled up curbside and walked up to her, saying, *"You're killing me, Baby. Come on, let's go home. You're crazy; you know that?"*

On another occasion, she was wide awake but left the house to get Dunkin' Donuts at 4 a.m. but could not find her way back home. She was gone for 2.5 hours after finding her way to the highway heading south towards San Antonio from Austin. No Google Maps or Waze to use back then either. She drove until she had the sense to turn around.

When she finally pulled back into the driveway, Dad peeked out of the front living room window, hiding behind a curtain. She eventually walked up to the front door to find the doors locked. She leaned into the door while she attempted to hold her coffee and donuts to unlock the door. Dad unlocked it from the inside and pulled it open slowly, standing in the doorway, face to face, with the look of surprise and worry. Not quite a terror because once again, she found her way home in one piece.

He eventually asked her, *"What were you thinking? Come on, Baby."* With pleading eyes saying, give me a break already, as he rubbed his face with his hands and over the sides of his head. All he could get in response from her was a giggly response of *"I was going out quick for donuts but got lost. It's no big deal. I'm Okay."* The first of her many dismissive responses to getting a little turned around. Never mind, we had lived in the area for almost two decades.

Moments like that and many more were often blamed on her exhaustion. She was always so tired but rarely got good restorative sleep. If she could not sleep, then she would find something else to do, even if it meant leaving the house in the middle of the night or early morning hours while everyone else slept.

Growing up in Austin, we had lost touch with our aunts and uncles or Mom's brothers and sisters over these years, so we did not think about family history. Even if we had, this was our *"dirty laundry"* to keep in the family. We did not talk about this with the extended family or neighbors. It would have invited too much scrutiny, so we thought.

If we watched any sitcom which portrayed this way of living, we laughed at it and then called each other the character's name. Dad sometimes referred to himself as the 1970s All in the Family Archie Bunker character, the World War 2 veteran, blue-collar worker, and family man. Then Mom as Edith, the ditzy and kindhearted wife who Archy would tell *"stifle"* herself and often called a dingbat for doing silly stuff. It was our translation of a normal funny reality with no serious consequences to stress over this way. It was a way to deflect any serious or real worries as long as we found the humor in her issues or events.

Mom was too young to consider Alzheimer's in her mid-to-late 40s. However, depression and poor lifestyle habits did lead to a bad heart, or what doctors later diagnosed as Congestive heart Failure with Atrial Fibrillation (A-Fib) and Long QT Syndrome (LQT).

Mom had a routine with purpose while teaching. She remained the high functioning individual to live with Bipolar tendencies. Her students became her motivation and reason to live, not her children. Running on fumes or not getting enough sleep so she could lesson plan overnight was what she considered being a survivor and sacrifice for the sake of her career.

Traditional living passed down from past generations taught her survival but not how best to survive or what we now know as heart-healthy survival. At no fault of their own, they too survived on all they had and as they had been taught. The cycle continued down through the generations.

Then one day, in her mid-50's Mom almost fainted at school as she was about to leave for the day. An emergency after-hours appointment resulted in having a dual pacemaker with a defibrillator installed. Mom became even more depressed and less active than she was before.

Instead of being thankful to be alive, she fell further into a dark void of existence. She hid her emotions behind fake cheesy smiles while the physical scars on her chest from the procedure made her feel damaged, unattractive, and hopeless.

For someone who never cared about her appearance or wellbeing, from hair and make-up to wardrobe or fitness, I could not understand why this was not the vital turning point for her to change lifestyle habits. Instead, she remained on the couch, sleeping whenever she could, even over the weekends. She withdrew from life even further when she was not in the classroom. Her creative space for her dollhouses was boxed up, and the house itself became dusty and brittle. The flower beds were neglected and overrun with weeds or died altogether. Her passion for creating slipped away, yet she would still claim to be a survivor.

As my sisters and I began having children of our own, she seemed to come back to life with the birth of each grandchild. The cameras were out! She had a reason to purchase more cameras, a computer, and a color desktop printer. Thanks to each new addition to the family, they sparked joy in her life. In an instant, it seemed, she snapped into a proud grandparent, snapping so many pictures to show off to family and friends. The trip to the store was once again the momentary high or temporary therapy.

Photo albums were started again, even though our very own baby albums were boxes filled with pictures. Flower beds were revived, which meant car rides with the grandchildren to Lowes or Home Depot. A couple of different dollhouses were purchased with multiple bags of miniatures from Hobby Lobby and Michaels to fill them as the grandchildren eagerly helped build a very detailed mini world. Baking in the kitchen became an interest again. Anything to enjoy the grandchildren as they got older.

As the years continued, purchases became larger and larger ticket items. Mom wanted whatever technology she could get her hands on. Computers, jewelry, cars, furniture, appliances, and kitchen wares were purchased without regard to household finances. Mom bought more and more yet refused to get rid of anything.

She was once quite the organizer and quick to hold a garage sale to let go of extra stuff before slowly becoming a hoarder. Her continual rebuttal was, *"you never know when you might need it."* Broken or not, it was put into the garage, or she made space to tuck the item away in a closet. More moments when Dad would shake his head while saying, *"You're crazy."*

She was hanging on to junk! Items we all knew would never be used again or needed. Now I know what might be junk to me could be a treasure to you, but when I found a mason jar filled with 13 used toothbrushes under her bathroom sink, I called it junk.

Again, the dismissal of her *crazy* state of mind meant we overlooked the hoarding as another symptom. Judgment or the ability to rationale was certainly missing, but she was still Edith to Dad, and he was still Archy Bunker. Even though it was getting harder to laugh at the craziness of her actions, we had nothing else to compare it to when Dementia was not understood back then.

Dad's escape from reality was to travel for work. The problem with his escape was that if Dad was traveling for work, she had to take medicines independently, which she would not do. As the week progressed, she would gravitate down to a low mood swing. Several impulse purchases would bring her back up momentarily to a high mood swing. Spending time with the grandchildren later seemed to give her the same high mood swing, but this eventually faded. Mom remained in low states longer and longer with less high states.

As the grandchildren grew older, their interests changed. Not unusual, but this meant the indoor activities became more outdoor activities. Swimming in the backyard pool was a great way to entertain them while getting a little bit of exercise herself, back to the stores for water toys, floaties, and beach towels. After several hours in the pool, sleep should have been the natural end of the day, but it did not happen as easily. Sometimes Mom was overstimulated and still could not reach deep restorative sleep.

Eventually, she would start to turn away from being able to spend time with the grandchildren. It was more effort than she was willing to put in, so she opted to sleep on the couch instead or read a book. She started to remind me that she had raised her kids already, and she was done raising anymore. As hurtful as it sounded at the time, I understood her point of view. At first, this new side to her seemed like a normal assertive request for some alone time or to enjoy a quiet space. Her alone time became more of a gradual withdrawal.

This high-functioning Bipolar petite yet feisty woman was not crazy at all. Since this *"craziness"* was connected to behavior related to judgment or lack of empathy rather than memory for quite some time, Dementia was not considered until much later. Mom's symptoms did not start to be more prevalent until after she retired at 55. Her daily routine, which was helping to keep her focused enough or functioning somewhat, was gone.

Since Dad did not know what was happening to Mom or how to help her truly, this kept them bickering and fighting more often than usual. We could not reason with insanity. She eventually became intimidated by his frustrations. No matter what he tried to do, for better or worse, she inevitably pushed him away in sickness and health.

Eventually, this led to her pushing him out of the home on three separate occasions before she filed for divorce after 37 years of marriage. Mom was showing Dad she did not need him or the medicines to survive. She was going to be strong no matter what he tried. Only she missed the entire point because he was not the enemy. Being a true survivor is fighting for life, not merely existing. Reasoning, common sense, and judgment seemed to be gone.

Once Dad left the house for the third and final time, Mom's decline was more than obvious. The high functioning Bipolar tendencies became total depression. She tried to hold the survivor façade but to no avail. Shortly after their divorce, Mom retired from teaching without a plan to live life purposefully. She fell apart over the next couple of years.

We saw what we wanted to see for some time because the truth would have invaded our lives, far more than we were willing to accept or cope with this new reality. My sisters and I lived with families of our own by this point.

Our high functioning Bipolar Mother was depressed and in denial, resulting in insomnia, time loss, poor judgment, lack of empathy, and eventually memory loss. It was time to go to the specialists since she would not go to a psychiatric doctor or neurologist by choice. We had dismissed her mood swings and odd behaviors long enough. There was something wrong that was not going to just go away by living for her.

Chapter 8
Steps to Take Before and
After Diagnosis

Galatians 6:9 (ESV)
And let us not grow weary of doing good, for in due season we will reap,
if we do not give up.

As I became consumed with Mom's care, I started to fill with fear for various reasons. I also started to pull away from my life to take control of hers. Mom used to hide behind humor, in the beginning, to appear strong and in control, but once I stepped into her world, it was more than clear who needed to be in control.

She used to say, *"Well, you know how the saying goes - Here today gone tomorrow."* This phrase became my motto for the little progress she made. It also refers to more than her physical presence because the lessons I tried to model today must be repeated tomorrow and every day after that as she progresses in stages. The caregiver must become the model of healthy living to reaffirm their need for it and their own need for sustainable energy.

Trying to balance every little detail only contributed to more stress and put me on an emotional rollercoaster. I stepped in where Mom left off and had to find my way through a laundry list of changes that needed to be made. Part of this helped me to stay busy and distracted, but most of it made me fall apart on the inside.

I began to forget eating my meals after being on the run. My Body was drawing energy from a poor diet aside from restless sleep. Even though I found a better lifestyle now, these months and years spent before diagnosis kept me in a constant state of fight or flight mode, which kept levels of stress high and energy levels low.

When I cared for her part-time, I left work at the end of a long sedentary workday feeling too physically drained to consider exercise later outside of work. A body at rest tends to stay at rest rather than the body in motion remaining active. An Active person has a better chance of reducing depression, but it is difficult to recognize situational depression.

Caregiving becomes the unintended excuse to neglect ourselves. I know I had trivial reasons to postpone my appointments, time with friends, or engage in my self-care because I put Mom's needs above everyone else's. I slowly realized I had to remain active by finding new ways to adapt to my routine. It will not help you or your loved one, no matter how you attempt to justify skipping the gym or even taking a walk. Learning to be flexible is key.

As my workdays became longer, I experienced even more fatigue and back pain. I used to think it was solely stress-related or basic aging, yet a blood test would quickly reveal extremely low Vitamin D levels. Being active outdoors lifted my spirits along with my vitamin D levels. A vitamin supplement may not be everyone's simple answer, but it is certainly important enough to get natural Vitamin D regularly.

Especially if your diet is poor and you typically spend the bulk of your week indoors under fluorescent lights. Without Vitamin D, our body cannot truly absorb other nutrients. I had to find better ways to prepare my body and mind for this journey, and you will need to as well.

Being prepared may seem ridiculous when you have no idea where this journey leads or what type of diagnosis your loved one may receive, but there are some things you can do while you wait on a diagnosis. Waiting could take months or years when it comes to diagnosing Dementia. I wish someone would have told me when I started this journey years ago how to be prepared. The proactive preparation would have lessened my anxieties and worries about what life was about to become for our family.

Preparation starts with research. You can research just about everything on the internet, but you can also narrow down your search with tools such as Scholar.google.com. This search engine is a freely accessible web search engine that indexes scholarly literature's full text or metadata across various publishing formats and disciplines.

I read many different medical journals from doctors and scientists published through the Mayo Clinic, which covered published journals worldwide. It was fascinating to see how advanced science had become to understand the brain. Yet, our capitalistic society in the US seems to find ways to profit from the information rather than help society learn.

This information made me grateful to know better and skeptical of every *"walk for a cure"* approach because it did not match the science. The UK and Australia seemed to be so much further ahead in knowledge and compassion for those living with Dementia.

Much of the information I discovered was confusing at first, and then it made me angry. Angry at the world we live in regarding how children are taught in school about health and fitness. Angry at the causes of Dementia that stare us in the face every time we turn the tv on with endless ads to buy junk food as cheap and fast as it can be made.

When I began to turn that anger towards Mom, I had to dig deep to understand a higher power greater than I was ready to handle. The concept of prayer was foreign at first, and then it became my go-to response. I believe the next preparation level continues with prayer.

Prayer encourages us to look outside of ourselves and appreciate a different perspective, a divine perspective. Growing up, our family seemed to only pray in times of crisis or grieving. Now I know I can pray whenever I feel the need, no matter the issue. Where science runs out of answers, God takes on the rest. He can handle your anger, frustrations, and fears better than you may realize.

I began to pray every morning to thank God for the air that filled my lungs. I thanked him for the time he had given me with Mom, even when

I wished it was with better circumstances. Some mornings I would pray for forgiveness when my frustrations got the worst of me with Mom.

Other days when I could go for a drive, I turned the radio off to have a 'come to Jesus' meeting because I could not understand why or how our family was falling apart. I had moments when my faith waned. I did not want to talk to God at all during those moments.

I could not understand why He would put us through the turmoil, so I turned my back on Him. The Spirit would not let me go and kept filling me with hope and dreams with visions to bring me back.

The curiosity of life after death seemed to come to mind more like seeds planted by the Spirit. I worried about having the strength to endure this journey. This curiosity gradually started to turn me back to God with more questions.

I realized I would rather live my life as if He was there all along and die to find out He was not than to live my life as if He was never there for me and die to find Him waiting to bring me home. The thing is, prayer helped me lift pieces of my burden. Learning to be open to His ways gave me enough relief from handing my struggles over to Him to trust that He knows better.

His way, not mine. His will, not mine. His love, not my fear. His grace, not my worries and anxiety.

The more I accepted these thoughts in prayer, the more I could accept I was not in control in the way I thought I was. This journey was not about me when it felt like it was all about me. My soul purpose is His plan that I was called to fulfill. I could choose to fight it every step of the way, or I could choose to surrender. I still try to find those moments or issues that I can control, but it comes from awareness and being in the present moment. Surrender is a process because it does not happen overnight.

My anger, fear, worry, and anxiety came from being stuck in another place and time. Worrying about a future that had yet to occur or feeling stuck in a resentful past was nothing more than a distraction from the present gift of time with Mom. As I learned to surrender my past burdens, God answered my questions and guided me when I felt stuck.

The diagnosis was not going to change what we suspected or fix her in any way. It was more of a process of acceptance for me. This journey has become more of a transformation for me than it was for her. Even though we are both transforming towards our journey home, it has been on two entirely different levels.

Early Diagnosis allows people living with Dementia and their families the time to plan for the immediate future. Catch your breath and then plan for the revised future, which includes the end.

Proactive approaches provide an opportunity for your loved one to participate in decisions for care which include living options, possibly avoid financial burdens, and prepare legal matters. They will benefit from treatment and support services for possible reversal. They might even delay the process, significantly reducing healthcare costs by delaying placement in an assisted living or nursing home.

You will benefit from the following pointers of what to do before and after a diagnosis.

1) *Become educated in the form of Dementia you are seeking a diagnosis for and ask doctors about their prognosis*

An early diagnosis gives everyone involved precious time to become more educated. This knowledge will feel like learning a new language or being hooked up to a fire hose, so try to take it in small bites. Finding out what you can do will help provide you with a sense of control after this potential diagnosis may initially make you feel out of control.

The education will provide details about what area of their brain is experiencing shrinkage, deterioration, and disconnect to give you an idea of emotional, behavioral, physical, and cognitive changes to expect. This education will also remove more fear to replace it with medical reasoning. Then as time passes, ask the doctors about your loved one's prognosis at future appointments. This information will help line up financial planning and how much time they will need their funds to stretch before filing for Medicaid.

I know this was a hard question for me to ask at first because I did not want to know when I would lose her, and then I did want to know when I accepted her journey home was inevitable. I wanted to be more prepared. It came across as insensitive to my family. Still, when you objectively and proactively plan, then you will be prepared even as you grieve along the way.

2) *Remain Positive and Hopeful*

Hope may not be the first response, but it needs to remain in focus. While you gain more knowledge of what is happening to your loved one and what to expect going forward, begin to build a game plan.

Having something positive to focus on instead of stewing in the heavy details makes a world of difference. Positive thinking alone has proven to be beneficial for health and well-being. Even if you are trying to be positive for your loved one, it can become the pivotal point for change in both of your lives. If you struggle with your thoughts, create a gratitude journal and find one thing that makes you grateful. Sometimes I was grateful I did not have a meltdown.

3) Get the family on the same page or establish your page

The sooner everyone involved is aware of a potential diagnosis and what it means for your loved one, the family will worry less about the future. You do not need added stress from trying to keep a secret. This type of journey will need all hands on deck or respectfully stepping aside. Being honest may create issues, but time is of the essence. Understanding what everyone's role will be throughout the process is helpful. Not everyone needs a role to support their loved ones. Sharing the roles as much as possible to avoid placing the burden on one family member is important.

If this is too much to handle for any family members due to age or experience, that needs to be openly discussed so there are no hurt feelings or unfulfilled expectations. Be mindful of the maturity of children before expecting any responsibility or care from them. If you have no other choice, check in with them often to see how they handle the burden of care. It is important to monitor their mood changes because they will be just as susceptible to depression as we are. There is a big difference between their willingness to help and their responsibility to care, which adds pressure.

Family drama can flare up over misunderstandings and lack of knowledge which makes this process stressful for you and your loved one. Once everyone is on the same page, a real game plan for doctors, finances, living arrangements, daily routines, and supporting services must be defined as quickly as possible. Coordination will help remove as many assumptions as possible or opportunities for miscommunication.

4) Begin drawing up a game plan (Financial and Estate planning)

Diagnosis may not be a clear understanding as to what stage your loved one is experiencing. Stages with cancer do not apply to forms of Dementia. Applying a stage was my way of coping with the loss of time and the anticipation of the end time. Care becomes more expensive as they progress in stages 4 to 5, as discussed in chapter 3 under the Stages of Dementia.

Estate planning may seem like it is too soon or you have time, but in reality, you need as much of their input as possible. So again, time is of the essence. Start asking family or friends for recommendations of Elder

Law Attorneys and start a consultation. Begin taking inventory of your loved one's assets to better understand their financial status and access to resources.

Maximizing Mom's retirement income and any nest egg savings became an immediate plan. Knowing what she could afford helped for long-term planning from in-home care to memory care communities. Plus, we must also consider the potential for end-stage special nursing skill expenses. Part of this type of planning will require Caregiver Compliance documents, also discussed in more detail in chapter 16 Caregiver Compliance.

5) Schedule time for your therapy sessions.

Even before a diagnosis is received, you will undoubtedly feel all sorts of emotions and even possibly ponder the meaning of life altogether. Talking to friends and family may be helpful at first, but they may not consistently have their own mental or emotional capacity. I fluctuated with mood swings between medical understanding and feeling overwhelmed, which my friends could not handle.

I came to this journey very angry which unfortunately came before compassion. Most of my anger was directly related to unresolved childhood resentment towards Mom that kept me from seeing her as a person in need. Therapy helped me to understand the past, present and no longer fear the pending future decisions.

Therapy also helped me cope with the present as our family struggled to find and stay on the same page. Eventually, the page was torn in half, a wedge was inserted between my siblings and honoring Mom. I worked through family drama in therapy to help find acceptance and surrender.

6) Make time for yourself.

In the beginning, the time I had for myself was forced by my inner child running away. I did not allow time for myself other than maybe crying in the shower. The weight of this journey was sinking in faster than I knew how to respond. I had not recognized the changes taking place as the beginning of my transformation.

Therefore, time spent away from Mom started with guilt. Over time I began to acknowledge the transformation and allowed the curiosity to build. As I made time to meditate on God's words, exercise, or go on nature walks, time away from Mom began to hold less guilt and provide more energy. Later I included time for manicures, pedicures, massages, or catching up with a friend.

During my time away, I attended a study that introduced me to Enneagrams. This tool helped me to understand my motivations and reactions to others. Once I discovered that I am an Enneagram One with a Two wing (1-2), I began to have one epiphany after the other. The Enneagram is designed around a scale from 1-9, which determines what motivates us. The 1-2 wing means I am classified as "The Advocate." I no longer felt bad about what I was doing for Mom and what my family could not understand.

Ones are teachers, crusaders, and advocates for change with an Achilles heel for perfectionism & criticism. As a 1-2, We are afraid to make mistakes and be judged harshly. The journey began to have new meaning and understanding why we experienced so much family drama. My family's motivations were quite different. This journey brings about the best and worst of us by default. I encourage you to figure out what your enneagram number is at www.enneagraminstitute.com/type-descriptions.

7) Fuel up for the journey

Once you begin to feel like your world is not spinning out of control, you have begun to accept this caregiver journey which means you will need provisions. If we were planning to go on a hike, we would pack essentials like water and snacks. We must fuel up and pack plenty of hope to sustain us during the peaks and valleys ahead on a caregiver's journey. I have found my energy is more sustainable when I follow proactive measures to maintain my blood sugar and metabolic rates before stress has the opportunity to drain my energy.

Feelings of depression will lend to fatigue, but when I binged on comfort foods, I created a cycle of defeat and depression similar to Mom's highs and lows. Don't pick a diet or trendy time-saver; pick a lifestyle change to sustain you and protect your health for the long run, as explained in Chapter 12 Proactive Measures. Flexibility may be key, but sustainable energy lends to survival before and well after diagnosis.

8) Begin to prepare for downsizing

While you create compliance documents and proceed with estate planning, you will be well aware of what you have available at their disposal to cover the cost of care. We tried to fulfill Mom's wishes by keeping her in her home, but the time came for her to downsize and then again to move in with us three years later when she needed more

24/7 care. This move helped to buy more time to avoid assisted living expenses, but we had to shift again to a memory care community within three more years.

Downsizing is a very difficult process emotionally and physically. If you happen to be financially stable, you may avoid downsizing before your loved one needs professional care 24/7 or hospice care. Your loved one's home will eventually become part of an estate, and the need for liquidation will arise again.

Planning for this in advance will benefit you greatly. Even if it is years before you downsize or rightsize, it is better to go at your own pace than to find yourself in a state of financial panic or medical emergency. Just as you prepare for the beginning of a journey, there is also an end. Author Kim Stanley has two books to consider reading - *"How to Make a Downsize Move"* and *"Step by Step to Right Sizing."*

9) Make doctors, dentist, Self-Care, and friend lunch/dinner appointments well in advance

Caregivers neglect their own needs making them vulnerable to illness before and immediately after their loved one passes. I became more familiar with Mom's doctors than any of my own. It became too easy to say *"it can wait"* as if I was no longer important. She became my child. I could argue that I did not have the time, but that doesn't hold up because I was not making the time for my needs at first. By not making my needs a priority, I was contributing to more resentment and anger.

I was doing what I felt was right for her best interests and absent-mindedly neglecting my own needs. I did not realize this until I began to feel so lonely. I thought I was sparing my friends from hearing the sad details, but it was too hard to talk about my feelings. I could not help comparing my overwhelming life to their less complicated life. I often assumed they would not understand, so I did them a favor by keeping it simple by saying *"I'm fine"* or *"I don't have the time for lunch or a happy hour."*

I found myself talking to my dental hygienist more or massage therapist, wishing I could have a drink with them to feel normal again. They understood the pressure points our bodies go through on this journey. I needed something and someone to look forward to aside from my husband. I love him, but this journey affected our relationship in other ways. I needed the girlfriend chat or a different level of connection to feel normal.

10) Learn to work the calendar

Staying organized helped me manage Mom's life, but it also helped me download all the little details that would keep me from falling asleep. Brain dump as much as you can onto your calendar. Whether you have a smartphone or carry a printed organizer - use it. I put all my scheduled care days with Mom as far in advance as I could before she moved in with us. I could plan for her appointments, kid's events, my appointments, and any other details I could squeeze into the notes section.

I placed 4 or 5 calendars throughout the house for Mom to see and mark off the passing days before her to give some sense of reality. Homemade photo album calendars are great. The sillier or cuter the pictures, the better because they might spark memories. The calendar in her room was to help avoid arguments over shower days, blood sugar checks and help her see who and when her next doctor appointments would be.

Even when we did not argue, the calendar insight did help to spark up some conversation other than the typical weather for the day. I could use the month to encourage her to keep up with an activity to see the difference in her weight and blood sugar checks. I was also able to encourage more fluids when she could see the number of days from her last bowel movement.

Her grandchildren's birthdays were also written on her calendar to keep it fresh in her mind or have a quick reminder as the calendar months changed.

Chapter 9
Sibling Rivalry:
All is NOT Well

James 4:2-3 (NIV)
You desire but do not have, so you kill. You covet, but you cannot get what you want, so you quarrel and fight. You do not have because you do not ask God. When you ask, you do not receive, because you ask with wrong motives, that you may spend what you get on your pleasures.

Caregiving may come naturally for some people, but to others, it may be a real struggle to engage compassionately. Home Health companies provide care in a variety of ways to fit the needs of strangers. They know to step into a home with caution and respect for the care recipient. Sometimes, approaching with respect and compassion is as challenging as emotionally adapting to change from a diagnosis to family.

Some cultures expect children to care for their parents, regardless of economic struggles or geographical barriers. Our family had mixed opinions on who was responsible for Mom's care. I have two sisters that I love dearly and pray for every day even though we are estranged. Not being on the same page with Mom's diagnosis and plan for care proved too much of a burden on our relationship.

I could sum our struggles up to be a difference of opinion, but it goes deeper than that. Our opinions came from a place of brokenness. Just as Mom entered her marriage to Dad with a broken heart, we entered our caregiver journey with broken hearts. Even though my sisters and I were raising our own families, the burden of taking care of our Mother fell on our shoulders after Mom and Dad's divorce.

Between the three of us, it seemed logical and fair to share in the care equitably. When I tried to delegate days and times for caregiving, I was not taking into account where they were in their own heart space. I did not understand the matters of the heart could be so deep and delicate until later on in my journey. Being aware of my many parts did not happen until after we became estranged. Understanding where my deeply rooted jealously originated took time.

Each of us managed our emotional pain in different ways. I assumed caring for Mom came from a place of love more than a place of struggle or obligation because it did for me. We all lived in the same city within a reasonable distance from Mom. It was supposed to be easy enough to divide and conquer. It did not have to be a burden for any one of us alone.

I was sadly mistaken.

Our personal needs came first. Our families came next. Mom was not the immediate priority and sometimes came last in our hectic life schedules. School routines for our children with after-school practice, games, choir, or band schedules on top of homework and dinner meant Mom had to wait most of the time.

Mom declined well over a decade. By the time we accepted where this situation was headed, it had already consumed our lives. The sibling rivalry from childhood continued to grow on a much bigger scale. As grown adults, we had an inner child desperately wanting to be acknowledged and feel worthy. We each needed to be heard now. Reacting to Mom's needs brought back the past when we were not heard or even treated as if our feelings mattered.

We were grieving and coping poorly with each other and still expecting Mom to be the referee to an extent. Mom's way of handling issues when we were growing up or showing us who was in control was through money. We had behavioral awards linked to money and consequences paid from the money we earned. Our childhood mindset of Mom's love currency haunted us throughout our journey in the beginning. If one received more money than the others, jealousy was created rather than celebrating each other's achievements.

Appreciation for care was also shown through money early in our caregiving journeys which I did not like. Each time Mom offered me money, I told her she could pay me by taking better care of herself. That was too expensive of a response for Mom. We may have been aware of Mom's poor judgment and lack of reasoning, but entitlement also carried a price tag.

An outside professional caregiver would be paid an hourly wage at the going market rate. They typically have a set list of activities of daily living (ADLs) routine to assist with eating, bathing, dressing, toileting, transferring, and continence. No one was taking them to Disney World or the Mall for shopping trips. None of them were asked to hold out a hand and tell her to stop piling on twenty-dollar bills when they felt it was enough. Lack of judgment was a blind spot for Mom and allowed for old family drama to resurface.

Mom needed help with daily tasks without any strings attached. Since she stopped driving, groceries had to be purchased for her, or one of us had to drive her to the grocery store. We did not have the convenience of grocery curbside or delivery services yet.

We had to coordinate routines to make sure someone was managing her medications, preparing meals, managing her household and finances. Without drawing straws to see who accompanied Mom to a doctor's appointment, we also had to consider communicating her needs to each doctor. See a need, fill a need - without expecting a reward for sacrificing time.

My Big Sis was my nurturing surrogate mother. Even though she was the one to terrorize me into hysterics by sitting on me while popping my toes, she was also the one who fearlessly protected me from any bullying in school. She had the first-born grandchild, while my first and 2nd grandchild would be six months later.

I was so scared of not knowing what to do when it came time for me to be a mother, but I watched her be the total opposite of Mom over my last two trimesters. My confidence built as I watched her be an incredible first-time mother. When I had questions or found myself in unknown territory, she was always the first call before calling the pediatrician.

She continued to have two more children while I went back to the corporate world. I wanted to be a career Mom, but she was more of a home engineer. Caring for babies while managing a household came so naturally to her.

My Little Sis was my partner in crime. Although she is four years younger, it did not stop me from including her in everything I could. We often went downtown Austin to the district known as 6th street, lined with bars and dance clubs. Then hang out past curfew at times, eating junk food and chatting through the night. We picked up exactly where we left off the next morning.

Little Sis was a tall and slender ballerina dancer with a graceful range of motion. An artist and Yogi at heart that introduced me to mindful meditation. Someone willing and open to venturing out in search of spiritual awareness beyond our childhood Catholic religion. At the time, we balanced each other between the far left and right brain mentality to keep each other grounded.

Growing up, we did not learn resolution skills. We pointed the blame finger at each other before any questions were asked. If either of us did something that we knew would get us in trouble, then we stayed silent. Dad swore a fourth kid lived in the house with us called the 'I-don't-know-kid.'

We united fronts when it served our personal goal but held no valid code of honor. We covered for each other through thick and thin until our privileges were taken away. Dad knew we would eventually break under pressure. Just like Mom and I were reacting to each other, my sisters and I reacted in ways we did not know how to handle aside from fighting.

We had each other's backs no matter what. And yet, we did not hesitate to turn on the other either. A dysfunctional family loyalty came from our understanding of Mom's bipolar cycles and Dad's need to keep the peace under our roof. I learned the feeling of betrayal was subjective, and keeping the peace meant pleasing everyone.

Not knowing what this brokenness was for each of us because we did not talk openly about these feelings left many unresolved arguments and hurt feelings. We went from periods of silence or avoidance to attempts to take control. It was easier to take control of Mom's life than manage the points of pain in our own lives. We were stuck in an emotional state of flight or fight to avoid uncomfortable feelings.

As the years passed, the tension between us grew, and the will to care for Mom waned. Big Sis froze, Little Sis fled, and I stood on shaky grounds to fight for Mom. Thankfully, Big Sis eventually came back around to join me in the fight to protect Mom while caring for her as well for several more years.

My sisters and I tried to be a team, but we reached a point that we could not sit in the same room. I desperately tried to understand how this journey became so incredibly emotionally charged. I had to figure out how I went from being best friends with my sisters to barely acquaintances and later estranged.

The more we did for Mom, the less she would do for herself no matter the task. We eventually talked enough to understand that Mom was pitting us against each other to get whatever she wanted at the time and tried to stay mindful of how or when she was manipulating us.

As soon as I stepped in to handle the financial, legal, and medical areas, I suddenly became the overbearing 'know it all' sister. Only this time, I owned up to that label. I felt there was no other choice because it became clear that Mom's care needed to be more tailored to her changing needs, and the level of protection for her assets also needed to be put in place. Without any long-term care insurance to depend on, she could no longer afford to be irresponsible with her money.

I could not help but approach this from a place of logistics. This approach was helpful to me, but the logistical perspective left very little room for emotional consideration. Our journey was dominated by family feuding, which made adapting to change painfully difficult. Mom needed more routine care over time which was clouded with our arguments over differences of opinion.

Being proactive and removing opportunities for fighting at this point meant decisions had to be made while Mom was still coherent enough to sign for her wishes. The undetermined future regarding how quickly she might decline and need special care or downsizing to a memory care community was out of our control. Decisions had to be made no matter the grievances between us siblings. Taking this step helped me keep caring about Mom's needs and well-being priority over our petty or emotional challenges.

The three of us were doing the best we knew how to do within our daily time restraints to balance our lives within our emotional limitations. Routine visits to Mom on designated days became our strategy once the fighting became a knee-jerk response. It was both an acceptable way to cover her daily routine needs and a blessing to avoid each other. Big Sis spent Fridays cleaning the entire house. Then I spent Mondays, Wednesdays, and Saturdays with Mom. Little Sis spent Tuesdays,

Thursdays, and Sundays with Mom.

Our schedule seemed reasonable, and it should have been an easy schedule to maintain. Still, Little Sis needed more days to work as a single parent, and the underlying energy between Little and Big sister started to brew a heavier cloud of bad energy. This cloud grew and pushed them further apart as the months passed until Big Sis decided she could no longer deal with this schedule. Feeling unappreciated and unwilling to fight any longer, she stepped away for a couple of years, leaving Little Sis and me to balance the load.

Little Sis and I attempted to be there for Mom while maintaining space for each other. We also had some bad energy brewing too but still needed each other for moral support. Even though we continued to react from our inner wounded child, we learned how to tolerate the other if it meant meeting Mom's needs. It seemed like the happy medium, but nothing was resolved, so the fighting became more personal defensive attacks.

We were emotionally stuck in the inner wounded child or *"wound-ology"* as referred to by the Author of Anatomy of the Spirit, Dr. Caroline Myss. Being trapped in our own mental and emotional status clouded our judgment, making it impossible to approach this journey with grace and mercy towards each other.

Our difference of opinion went from respectful disagreements to serious physical fights, which only caused Mom more unnecessary stress by being caught in the middle. Being able to assess current situations rather than living in the past was difficult.

We dismissed each other's point of view because it was not about Mom's needs or current status; it was about something entirely different. Something at the time I could only understand as selfishness rather than recognizing their inner parts. We were not capable of making simple decisions when our minds came from old feelings or grudges. Mom's judgment was lacking altogether, while ours was clouded with shame, unworthiness, and entitlement. The wide range of unknown territory within the frame of reference of living with Dementia added to our mixed opinions.

I could tell Mom was trying to cope with frustrations over the loss of independence and abnormally aging, but continuing to be the referee as she once was when we were younger only added to her stress. If we had a chance to be in one room altogether to discuss Mom's needs, Mom sat quietly, withdrawn from us or the situation. She was unwilling to face the truth and incapable of comprehending the situations at hand.

We attempted to talk about her appointments, the results of tests with our expectations, or the next steps to take. I dictated what needed to be done from a medical and psychological approach, while Little Sis argued from a holistic approach. I felt Mom needed anti-depressants, where Little Sis was entirely against them. Big Sis tried to point out why we were both wrong yet not offering any particular approach. Mom sat there shrugging her shoulders, saying, *"I don't know."*

Yet once each of us was alone with her, she would speak freely about what she wanted or negatively about the other. She was playing us to get what she wanted. More often than not, what Mom wanted was to be left alone to exist in her world of denial so she could die in her sleep. Neither of us was willing to fulfill those wishes, but finding a compromise was impossible for us.

I begged Mom to be more open with me because I could not help her if I did not know the issue at hand from one day to the next. Continually playing a detective researching her past and present actions or behaviors caused me to become a disciplinary parent to Mom.

At the same time, Little Sis was becoming a friend parent in the hopes of maintaining Mom's financial assistance. Big Sis tried to stay out of it entirely as much as possible even though we continued to try to have family meetings. The only time we could do this successfully was in the doctor's office or the hospital for another outpatient procedure. In those moments, we had a medical referee to help us get on the same page without arguing, if only for the moment.

Ironically, Little Sis kept encouraging me to meditate to find a sense of inner peace as she had been doing. The three of us needed to find inner peace and balance with each other.

We were taught the same sets of morals and values. And yet, our life experiences with Mom had been different enough to give each of us a different view. Neither of us expected Mom and Dad to divorce any more than we expected Mom to be living with Dementia. We were too stuck in our emotional pain to appreciate each other's pain.

Dr. Carolyn Myss wrote about being emotionally stunted throughout life which covered seven stages of power and healing. The fourth stage concerns matters of the heart and where this wounded child resided within each of us.

"As children, we react to our circumstances with a range of emotions: love, compassion, confidence, hope, despair, hate, envy, and fear. As adults, we are challenged to generate within ourselves an emotional climate and steadiness from which to act consciously and with compassion."

"By releasing our emotional pain, by letting go of our need to know why things have happened as they have, we reach a state of tranquility. To achieve that inner peace, however, we have to embrace the healing

energy of forgiveness and release our lesser need for human self-determined justice."

So that's what I unknowingly had been doing all these years. Seeking justice for Mom but coming from a broken heart made it difficult to trust in the Spirit's guidance or have compassion for my sisters along this journey. My inner child was not ready to trust anyone, which meant I needed to stay in control instead of learning how to let go and forgive.

Sometimes I think we lost track of what we were arguing over. The resentment coupled with an overwhelming feeling of the burden of care left no room to even think about forgiving the other. I could not even forgive myself for not looking into my past for areas of healing.

Years later, no longer in the eye of the sibling storm, I can finally see where many of those childhood experiences were designed to challenge me. We all have at least one moment that leads us to intense grief. Those moments are divinely designed to force us to grow beyond our comfort zone. If life were easy, we would not learn valuable lessons or connect with others who share our grief.

In this case, the heart without growth is blocked like a shoe with gum stuck on its bottom, and growth remains stagnant. Mom's needs were forcing us to grow, but our broken hearts kept us stagnant. The sticky residue is visible to me now because I have taken time to reflect, but I was so lost in the moment. Reflecting on past relationships may help you to find your areas of stagnation.

Even though I have grown up into an adult sharing this story with you now, I did not recognize how stuck my heart energy truly was until I became a caregiver. Forced to grow beyond my comfort zone and feel my way through life instead of analyzing to avoid difficult moments was never something I ever considered doing.

After I stepped away from the corporate world, I did not leave it behind entirely. It was old energy that shaped my current identity. I was not ready to let it go, nor did I understand if I was supposed to let it go completely. The struggle here was acknowledging the old energy. The heart keeps an emotional record as we live life, like a database that needs purging now and then for more space. The heart in this stage is also known as the fourth chakra.

There are seven chakras, or energy wheels, in the body. You can read more about chakras on your own as you are guided. I introduce this now because the heart chakra (fourth chakra) led our family on this journey and sent us on splintered paths away from each other.

According to Dr. Myss, the loss of fourth chakra energy can lead to jealousy, bitterness, anger, hatred, and an inability to forgive others and ourselves. We are not born fluent in love but spend our lifetime learning about it. As we learn, each stage presents a lesson in love's intensity and forms such as forgiveness, compassion, generosity, kindness, caring for ourselves and others.

Dr. Myss further explains how compassion is a learned skill because the wounded child within each of us contains the damaged or stunted emotional patterns of our youth, patterns of painful memories, negative attitudes, and dysfunctional self-images.

Do you recognize the sticky gum around your heart still needing to be cleansed?

A heart left with wounds unhealed or unresolved will keep us living in the past. Even though you are in the present moment with your loved one learning to live with their current state of Dementia, the decisions you might be presented with could become the triggers to unlocking the flood gates for all those unresolved issues.

Trying to resolve them while they are in this state of Dementia may not bring resolution or peace to your caregiving journey. Being able to resolve issues with your siblings, spouse, friends, or even co-workers may bring you peace and purpose. Once we stop running from our past, our present finally feels like the gift intended to be. As the present begins to feel more of a gift, appreciating others and where they are on their journeys will teach us about compassion and respect.

In the beginning, I carried my wounds into my new caregiving role. No matter how hard we tried as adults to have rational conversations and discuss matters, we could not make feasible preparations to share the burden because it usually ended in an argument or passive-aggressive responses. We were living a real-life version of the Lord of the Flies novel by British author William Golding. Only our island was Mom, with disastrous attempts to govern her needs.

I know our parents did everything they could to the best of their knowledge and abilities at the time so that nothing could be changed, nor should it. It is all part of a greater plan. We can understand why we act or react the way we do to learn from it and move on in life. Learning from it allows for continued growth instead of remaining emotionally stunted.

At some point in our lives, we must cleanse the old so new may rise. At some point in our lives, we must take responsibility for our actions. Hanging on to childhood grudges is holding onto poison for your heart and released in small doses every time it is brought up again or thrown in the other's face.

Finding my seeds of jealousy and attempting to pull them out by the roots took facing the past, picking it apart, understanding it, and then releasing it. What we did not see as children was the constant competition to acknowledge who we were as individuals. We could not see as adults that this competition was ongoing, which kept us from seeing the other's true self throughout our sibling rivalry.

Our present-day arguments eventually started with *"You always do this...."* or *"It's all about you...."* and *"You're not hearing me...."* The past crept into present-day attempts to care for Mom, which altogether turned our wounds into mental blocks. Resentment and jealousy surfaced with anger and judgment before any inkling of forgiveness to bury the hatchet. We were more concerned with assigning responsibility and holding the others accountable. We could not forgive, forget, and restore order. Not even for Mom's sake.

We retreated to our own families for support, leaving Mom alone again without support for some time. Eventually, the conversation was no longer in person or over the phone and completely through text message. Avoiding the face-to-face chats was great, but later even texting made things worse because you cannot hear a tone in a text no matter how sincere you intended it to be received. Besides, the underlying issues remained unresolved, so the form of communication did not seem to matter anymore.

"Stop telling me what to do. I am a grown adult. I'm not stupid, you know?!" This repetitive attitude expanded the mental block. We could not focus on Mom's needs without getting sucked into our need to be validated. This seed of jealousy grew into an ugly vine choking our love for each other and distorting the image of each other into a monstrous offender or bully.

My turning point began to evolve. Understanding Mom's needs were very important, but not to the extent of denying our own needs. We all tried to work well within the chaos. We all needed to feel significant on this journey. We all felt out of control, and we all tried to stay in control. Neither of us could hold the powerful lightning bolt of change this journey forced upon us.

I reached the point of no return and grabbed the bull by the horns just as my Aunt Vilma warned me would come to for Mom's sake. I stepped in without regard for either of my siblings' feelings because it became incredibly clear how much our fighting was not helping anyone and only hurting Mom and each other. Decisions and preparations had to be made that would not please everyone.

So, if after reading this chapter and it hit a few pain points for you, then consider the following as you attempt to mend the frayed edges from your sibling rivalry.

1) Go down memory lane.

Be brave and take the time to think back to when you and your siblings were kids with these questions in mind. What were you like? What were they like? What were your interests? What were their interests? How did your parents respond to each of you? How did your siblings make you feel? What moment caused those feelings? Did you grow closer or further apart because of a moment?

Dad may have raised us to be strong independent women, but we certainly were not prepared for the demands of what living with Dementia brings. Instead of being strong for each other, we were strong against each other. Responding defensively rather than compassionately made this journey difficult to navigate. Our unresolved childhood arguments created expectations that could not be fulfilled now.

As you answer those questions, it may uncover your onion layers, but it is only the beginning of identifying the top layers. These top layers typically cause our reactions to protect the deep-seated parts connected to our desires, outward actions, motivations or impulses, and behavior patterns.

You should begin to recognize those old feelings tied to old moments and hopefully see how your knee-jerk responses in the present time stem from that inner child. Saying *"oh, that's just how they are"* is not understanding *"why"* you or they are that way. Distinctive thoughts, feelings, and character traits have their own stories that fall into three groups. Managers, firefighters, and exile parts become our subconscious protectors.

Managers are the controllers, perfectionists, people-pleasers, analyzers, worriers, striving, caretakers, and inner critics.

Firefighters are addictions, overeating, alcohol, obsession, distraction, excessive behaviors, and anger or violence.

Exiles are deep inside that harbor fear, shame, worthlessness, sadness, helplessness, and loneliness.

Keep in mind every action has a reaction. Sometimes those reactions today are delayed responses to actions, even trauma, from long ago.

2) Accept each other as individuals.

You may have more inner parts than you think. Each one is part of us as they are a part of them. If you reacted with painful emotions as a child from a moment with your sibling or parent, then you can only imagine how they may have reacted. Your pain, resentment, anger, and fears are valid. Theirs is too. Therapy helps because you can be guided through those moments to take a different look. When you can gain a fresh new perspective, then this is where forgiveness and healing begin. Stop denying, ignoring, judging, hating, or wanting to rid your parts or siblings.

I used the power of prayer to ask God to show me how He sees them. Remember, His will not mine. Once I did, I was shown images in my mind's eye of Little Sis when she was a little girl, about seven years old. I saw a lost and scared little girl desperately trying to stand up to my inner angry child. I gained a new perspective by asking for it, which changed my actions and intent going forward.

3) Define what self-care is to you.

I used to have dreams of being cast out at sea on a troubled vessel. As the vessel was going down, I was faced with being able to save only one person. It was my Dad on one arm, and on the other, it was my first-born son. I struggled to let go of Dad, but he eventually told me to. He knew his weight was too great for me to bear. Then I struggled to get my son to the surface until I motioned for him to push for the surface on his own. I had to free myself of emotional baggage before I could return to the surface, and certainly before I could help myself guilt-free.

This concept in itself seemed to be at the core of our arguments. The lesson here is saving yourself in this capacity is far from selfish. For each of us to maintain our own families and Mom's needs, we would have to exert an amount of selfishness through self-care. The level of care and attention for Mom proved to be too great for Little Sis. She went on a separate journey of her own, taking the anger and hatred with her. Big Sis tried to hang in as long as she could at the expense of her health. I could see she was not willing to admit to burnout or safeguard her health.

Self-care can mean many different things to your siblings. Acknowledge the need and create a routine that allows you to meet your needs and respect that they need to do the same.

4) Practice open communication with an open heart in a judgment-free zone.

Mom and I became an island in my mind. I held the conch and was no longer afraid of using the power, but I also felt more alone on this journey without my sisters. The fighting had gone on for far too long. Nothing was changing or getting resolved. The only change seemed to be Mom's decline. I chose to swallow the tears and choke down the guilt of standing my ground to protect Mom and provide her with the best quality of life until her last breath.

Every breath we release in the form of words to our loved ones and siblings has the power to heal, express love, or inflict pain. When I wasn't consumed with anger, I could remember the golden rule - Do unto others as you would have done unto you.

Finding the delicate boundaries between when to avoid, when to be silent, and when to express feelings became a practice in humility. I continually thought, "how would I want to be treated?" and then tried to be that person before judging either of my sisters. No one is perfect, but the ole' saying does apply here - practice makes perfect. Perfection is found within the intent to keep an open heart so that every breath, every word is not wasted or used as a weapon.

5) Allow the Spirit to guide you.

When I reflect on past dreams, I can see that the Holy Spirit guided me. Although we started with good intentions for Mom, we could not help her until we helped ourselves. We were never truly going to save her from Dementia. Her journey has a defined path now, with each one of ours leading us in different directions.

Through this process of letting go, I gained more of an appreciation for what it means to lay down your life for your friends (family). I now believe caregivers are chosen. God knows us well before we are born and puts solutions to our problems in place long before we ever experience the problem. Our reactions to the problems create turmoil when we are not well equipped to handle them emotionally. Our lives are structured in such a way to provide opportunities to learn along the way. Some people are placed in our lives as we need them; others are taken when they are done serving their purpose.

6) Accept this journey will present tough decisions to make.

The deterioration of the brain creates more of a loss than anyone can imagine and often more than many are prepared to lose. Difficult choices surround this journey, even when you feel like you do not have a choice at times because it is often the uncomfortable choice that must be made. I chose to do what I was guided to and honor Mom to the best abilities as her fiduciary and daughter.

I also chose to seek therapy to heal my inner child to be a better caregiver to Mom, better wife to my husband, and better mother to my sons. I did not want to spend our remaining time with Mom in resentment. I wanted to stop saying *"I should have..."* or *"I could have...."*

I did.

I gained peace of mind at a cost. I learned not to feel guilty about making hard choices and even the average day-to-day choices to protect those I love. In these cases, it must be done so life can continue to move forward with as much peace and harmony as possible.

The more I accepted my life purpose for Mom and to teach others, the more I accepted that I might never speak to my sisters again. If I truly honor thy parent, then I had to separate her care from the family drama. Only time will tell what will come of our relationships. Not a day goes by without prayers for Little Sis to find peace and hopefully someday find true forgiveness in their heart as I have. Not a day goes by without wishing things could have happened differently.

Chapter 10
When We Know Better, We Do Better

Hebrews 4:12-13 (MSG)
God means what he says. What he says goes. His powerful Word is
sharp as a surgeon's scalpel, cutting through everything, whether doubt
or defense, laying us open to listen and obey. Nothing and no one is
impervious to God's Word. We can't get away from it – no matter what.

I am doing better now because I know better. My family needed to know what to look for if I went off the deep end and became the *"Crazy"* woman I grew up hiding from or avoiding. Maybe it is just me worrying about nothing, but they seemed to think all is well now, so why bother. This response is what too many do until they find themselves in a crisis.

I did not fear death when I stepped into Mom's world. No. It was the fear of losing control over my own life and health. Compassion and acceptance have replaced the fear that was in my heart. Compassion is a learned skill.

IT SCARES ME when I think about becoming this kind of burden on my family or our sons fighting over my care. I know I can be proactive rather than allowing them to be reactive while educating them along the way. I never stopped being the analytical accountant trending the details. I believe that is the part of me God was counting on to help me find my way through this journey to Him.

God is in everything should we choose to seek Him. He is even in the numbers or the analytical data I am drawn to as an accountant.

Part of my acceptance of becoming Mom's essential caregiver comes from knowing God takes our strengths and weaknesses to use in His plans. Instead of analyzing financial accounts in the corporate world, I have settled into comparing the matters of the brain with the heart and gut.

According to Nicole M. Gage and Bernard J. Baars, as published in Fundamentals of Cognitive Neuroscience (Second Edition), 2018, *"The frontal lobes seem to be the bottleneck – the point of convergence of the effects of damage virtually anywhere in the brain. There is a reciprocal relationship between the frontal and other brain injuries."* Although Mom did not have a brain injury as some might experience from falling or perhaps a car accident, her brain was injured by mini-seizures or mini-strokes unbeknownst to us.

Vascular Dementia symptoms may be most clear-cut following a stroke, but mini-strokes or transient ischemic attacks (TIAs) only last a few minutes. The clot then gets pushed along, like a temporary clog in the line. Vascular Dementia occurs over time as 'silent' strokes occur more often and become noticeable when the symptoms create a more significant disability. Chemicals in the body quickly break them down for normal blood flow to return before any lasting problems set in. TIAs can happen and leave no obvious symptom, unlike a stroke with long-lasting effects or life-threatening.

Aside from mini-strokes, Vascular Dementia is typically a result of diabetes, high blood pressure, smoking, and high cholesterol. Although Vascular Dementia is not reversible, it can be treated by managing the root causes to slow the progression if diagnosed early. Rather than waiting for an early diagnosis, we can also slow the progression through lifestyle changes.

Behaviors associated with Vascular Dementia:

1) Confusion
2) Trouble with paying attention and concentrating
3) Reduced ability to organize thoughts or actions
4) Inability to analyze a situation, develop an effective plan, and communicate that plan to others
5) Difficulty deciding what to do next
6) Problems with memory
7) Restlessness and agitation
8) Unsteady gait (pace in stride)
9) Sudden or frequent urge to urinate or inability to control passing urine
10) Depression or apathy

When Mom and Dad were both in their 50s, they were accustomed to eating poorly and dealing with stress in unhealthy ways. Their doctors ordered a cleanse and detox ASAP to avoid crossing the threshold into becoming diabetic. Mom used to say she was only doing whatever 'diet of the week' to help Dad stick to his. While Mom had dangerously low blood pressure, Dad had quite the opposite with dangerously high blood pressure.

Both Mom and Dad stubbornly avoided health warnings because *"well, we're all going to die someday from one thing or another."* Why not die happy doing what you love? Unfortunately, their glutenous love of highly processed junk and fast food or bar-be-que meats helped stack their deck. We were part of their retirement plan in place of Long-term Care insurance or Life insurance, so safeguarding their health was not a concern. They did not consider the effects of their choices on our livelihood.

Aside from Mom's clinical depression, much of the food she was eating had depressive-like reactions. The sugar spikes with the crashing blood sugar would make her seem depressed or irritable. That type of food was not only contributing to her mood swings, but it was also making her seem confused and sleepy most of the time. Empty carbs with no real nutrition will leave our bodies starved for energy and sustenance. Without sustainable energy, we drop into conservation mode, sluggish and sleepy.

The connection between poor diet habits causing diabetes is plain enough to see but what is not clear is how to avoid the poor habits. Many times, they chose to eat what they wanted out of simple pleasure, to die happy. Happiness usually comes in foods that spike blood sugar, like ice cream or dunking cookies in cow milk. This type of happiness was short-lived when the side effects of fatigue, heart palpitations, hair loss, or shortness of breath with cravings for more junk food followed. By seeking this type of happiness, they unknowingly created grounds for diabetes, Dementia, and mood swings that caused a marital strain.

When our blood thickens because of excess sugar, the blood becomes like molasses as the hemoglobin breaks down. Hemoglobin is the protein molecule in red blood cells that carries oxygen from the lungs to the body's tissues and returns carbon dioxide from the tissue to the lungs. Diabetes or high glucose levels damages blood vessels throughout our body. Damage in the brain blood vessels increases our risk for stroke and Vascular Dementia.

Tracking our A1C levels can aid us in preventing or mitigating Vascular Dementia. The causes of Vascular Dementia also include abnormal aging of blood vessels (atherosclerosis), high cholesterol, high blood pressure, diabetes, smoking, obesity, and atrial fibrillation (A-Fib).

Our A1C level helps indicate the average blood glucose levels over the past three months. It is also referred to as the hemoglobin A1C or glycated hemoglobin test. Aside from Mom experiencing TIAs in earlier years, her poor diet and lack of exercise raised her A1C levels, signaling prediabetes. Normal levels are between 5.7 and 6.4. Critical levels or red-light danger is an A1C of 9.0.

Mom's levels hovered between 6.7 and 7.0 before I stepped in as a caregiver, then dropped back to 6.0 to 6.4. When her daily nutrition and exercise were managed, the decline in A1C was possible without more medication.

Mom was required to have a dual pacemaker installed to aid her heart from A-Fib. I heard those terms many times back then but dismissed the information because the medical language was so confusing to understand. At best, we thought we had nothing to worry about because the dual pacemaker 'fixed' her heart. What it did not mean was she could keep going with the same lifestyle habits. The pacemaker was the emergency backup, not an autonomous maintenance system.

The issue with A-Fib is that it is caused by an abnormal heart rhythm in the upper chambers of our heart. The rhythm may beat rapidly or irregularly out of coordination with your heart's lower chambers. The pacemaker detects and paces the heart to correct the irregularity. A-Fib increases the risk of stroke because it causes blood clots to form in the heart, which can break off and go to the brain's blood vessels. Healthy blood pressure and preventing diabetes are paramount in combination with not smoking and getting physical exercise.

I was finally beginning to understand why Mom used to want to sleep all day and then was up throughout the night. It took every bit of energy she had to remain focused throughout her teaching day without proper fuel for her body to run on. We were all reacting to her mood swings caused by a combination of issues. Mom truly was surviving the best she knew how while we were dodging her highs and lows.

When Mom was in her prime, she taught junior high students various subjects and languages, including Spanish, French, and Latin. She loved building and working in flower beds during her time off and traveling over her summers with a fearless appetite for adventure to Japan as a parental guardian for an exchange program. The level of activity helped to balance spikes in her highs and lows.

Traveling during the summer was different. She went from routine schedules during the school year to the total opposite during the summer. We had a glimpse into what her retirement would lead to, but we were merely making sense moment by moment. There was always some reason to blame the erratic differences on, and if there was nothing, then the default was back to a dismissive thought to Mom is crazy.

When Mom retired after teaching for 32 years, her depression worsened. Depression was masking the initial symptoms of early-onset Dementia (also referred to as younger-onset) when she was in her early 50's. It is common for people living with Vascular Dementia to have Alzheimer's. Still, it more likely becomes Frontotemporal Dementia before Alzheimer's because of the pattern of deterioration in the frontal lobes.

Her neurologist treated depression and apathy with antidepressants, yet stronger narcotic anti-depressants carry side effects of death for someone living with dementia. Drugs that did work eventually needed to be adjusted up in dosage as her body fluctuated in weight or became accustomed to the dosage.

Therein lies yet another problem. Some drugs are effective early on, but once the body becomes accustomed to it or changes in weight occur, the drug becomes less effective. The dosage must be increased, or you have to switch to another one altogether. We are doubling down with problems because of more side effects or mood swings while the body readjusts.

The next problem with the medication is insurance. Mom is at the mercy of what insurance will cover under brand name versus generic. Finding what is also compatible with her existing list of medications yet still effective in treating her depression and apathy without causing additional agitation or other side effects can be tricky.

The break from her 32-year routine became the thread pull to unravel the rest of a greatly crafted life as an educator. Even she admitted about a year into her retirement that she should not have retired so soon. During her last year teaching, a violent outbreak in Mom's classroom scared her deeply, causing a loss of passion for teaching. A request for retirement mid-year felt like her only proper action to take at the time. Poor judgment or not, it led to a severe break in her survival routine.

The new routine was staying up all night and sleeping during the day. Then she ate junk food while watching tv all hours of the night. Her biorhythms dropped further out of sync. Flower beds were neglected, mail left unchecked, and days of the week began to slip away from her. She no longer had the desire for adventure in new places or new experiences. Sporadic day trips to splurge to feel better turned into spontaneous trips out of state without a plan or understanding of the consequence of poor or no planning.

One resulted in a car accident because she misread the intersection and misjudged the distance with oncoming traffic. The accident traumatized her enough to stop driving for a long time. Until she woke up one day and decided to drive to Florida to visit family, she unknowingly missed her Florida designated exit on the highway and ended up in South Carolina. The entire time was driving on very little sleep and nothing more than coffee to drink. With her ankles swollen, she finally became concerned enough to pull over and call for help.

Paramedics insisted on taking her into the hospital for more observation, but she insisted on being fine and just needed a break from driving. She had Dad's dog, Bonnie, with her and feared the dog would be sent to a shelter while she was in a hospital for observation. Our Aunt and Uncle had to pick her up and drive her car back to their house in Florida. Meanwhile, we had no idea where she was or how she was doing until my aunt told us she was safe at home with them.

We cannot make any assumptions anymore. We must learn about what real self-care is, how it looks and feels. We must have more compassion for others because what appears to be a crazy older person or what society sees on the news as a mental case could be another form of Dementia exposed in a negative light.

The painful fact is much of our society is living in a demented state of mind younger and younger. Depending on the type of Dementia, the

---

state of mind is quite different from one patient to the next. Younger-onset Alzheimer's is not attributed to genetics.

Behaviors Associated with Early-onset (Young-onset) Alzheimer's:

1) Memory Loss that Disrupts Daily Life (asking for the same information over and over, especially recently learned information, important dates, or events)
2) Challenges in planning or solving problems (paying monthly bills, developing, or following a plan; difficulty concentrating)
3) Difficulty completing familiar tasks at home, work, or at leisure (driving to a familiar location)
4) Confusion with time or place (lose track of dates, the passage of time; may forget where they are or how they got there)
5) Trouble understanding visual images and spatial relationships (reading or judging distance; difficulty determining color contrast)
6) New problems with words in speaking or writing (following or joining a conversation; struggle with familiar vocabulary; repeating themselves)
7) Misplacing things and losing the ability to retrace steps (may accuse others of stealing)
8) Decreased or Poor Judgment (dealing with money, pay less attention to hygiene or keeping clean, wearing dirty clothes for days at a time)
9) Withdrawal from work or social activities (loss of interest in hobbies, work, sports; avoid others because of the changes they are experiencing)
10) Changes in Mood and Personality (become confused, suspicious, depressed, fearful, anxious with friends or in places out of their comfort zone)

A correlation to the loss of memory is often the first response people make when Dementia is mentioned. Many understand this to be a disease of old age. It is hard to consider age while wondering how old is old anymore? Age is as much of a mindset as it is a chronological tracking number. 40 is the new 30, 50 is the new 40, 60 is the new 50, and so on. We strive to keep looking younger on the outside but cannot recognize our mental age on the inside at some point. Long after our mind goes, the rest of the body hangs on functioning even longer than we might want.

Before Mom's first outside caregiver friend, she did not want to exercise regularly and became very lazy long before presenting with congestive heart issues. Her body was not physically tired, so her mind was left with unresolved energy that manifested into anxiety, stress, and depression.

Insomnia would keep her up night after night, which would inevitably start the High's and Low's cycle until she crashed from exhaustion. This lack of sleep caused the foggy brain alone. We continued to dismiss the cues of confusion when driving, misplacing items, lack of memory, and withdrawing from her favorite hobbies. Again, we dismissed it all as her bipolar tendencies or exhaustion.

Mom often said she was a survivor, which we dismissed as her denial and stubbornness. She thought surviving was mental and emotional strength. The interesting thing here is I did not recognize this until I looked deeper into my past.

I used to view the ability to compartmentalize as emotional strength. That is until I was able to see how I was merely picking and choosing what I was willing to deal with over what I would rather avoid altogether.

Mom used this compartmentalizing with her daily school year routine to keep focused in her comfort zone. Eventually, this contributed to a state of mind which was not willing to accept she could not care for herself anymore. She compartmentalized for so long to keep the strong persona going she could no longer cry when the appropriate occasion presented, however sad or joyful.

When looking at your grown adult parent or spouse with frustration or even contempt for their behavior, stop and take a deep cleansing breath or two. Then visualize the image of the deteriorating brain in your mind as shown in the following image and remember they are not as capable or cognitively sharp as they once were.

Our loved one's rational thinking skills deteriorate as the brain deteriorates. In other words, they are not trying to make your life miserable on purpose. It felt like that many times when I cared for Mom on a part-time basis. Even after moving in with us, I still felt that she would do something solely to give me a hard time.

It was not until I went from part-time caregiving to full-time caregiver that I saw day-to-day behavior. This observation helped reaffirm her limitations, and even the time of day, she would be limited the most. I eventually determined what she could or could not physically do versus what she stubbornly did not want to do.

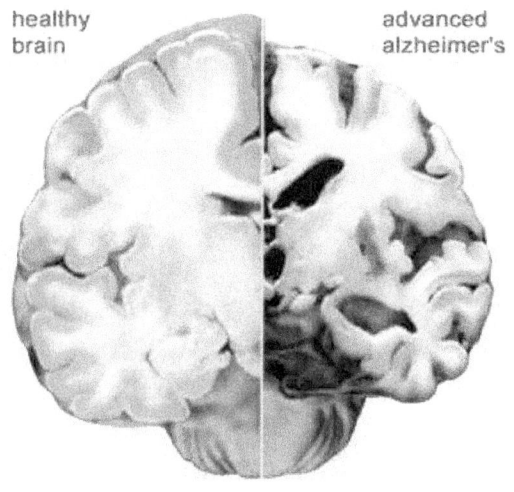

healthy brain

advanced alzheimer's

Brain Cross-Sections

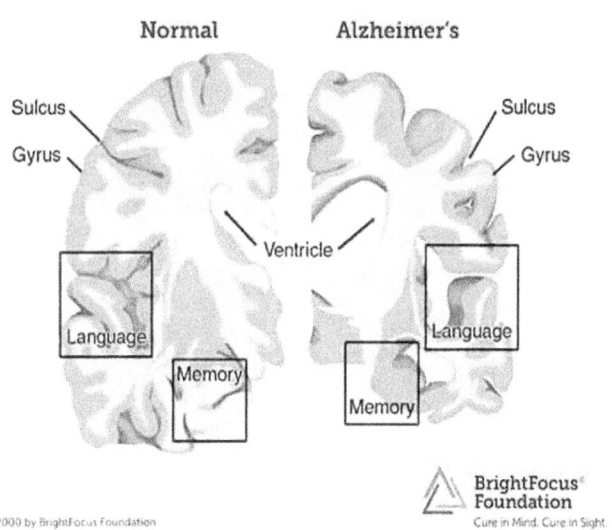

Normal

Alzheimer's

Sulcus

Gyrus

Sulcus

Gyrus

Ventricle

Language

Memory

Language

Memory

According to Dementia-related research on the brain, we typically lose the left-brain functions first. Losing the ability to keep self-control (left) combined with our feelings (right) can understandably explain earlier arguments that did not make sense

Lose on the Left, Retain on the Right	
Left Brain	**Right Brain**
Logic	Feeling
Facts	Imagination
Words	Symbols
Keeps control	Takes risks

before. Likewise, losing the ability to apply logic (left) with the impulse to take risks (right) creates unbalanced behavior in a mature adult that would not be normal.

Infrequent episodes of irrational behaviors make it difficult to spot if you are visiting your loved one now and then, especially if you are only calling to check in on them. If you live with them, a spouse perhaps, you would be able to identify shifts in behavior much sooner and more definitively. You must keep an attentive eye on them regularly to see subtle changes in behaviors or moods that indicate symptoms are present.

When Mom was teaching, she thrived in her classroom environment among the students and even faculty friends. Over the years, when I was still working, I called her during the day to check in on her because hearing her voice gave me peace of mind. She answered my questions about how she was doing like nothing was ever lacking or wrong. When I eventually visited her after church on Sundays to have lunch with her, I could see the obvious issues she did not mention over the phone. She was not fine even when she sounded like it.

Further down the road, Mom could no longer be calm and stable in environments with multiple people or pets. For example, during the period when Big Sis was helping, Mom lived between our houses. We both had Mom live with us for a month at a time. It gave all of us a big respite break and Mom a chance to be away from us too. By the end of every month, she eventually became irritated and more difficult than at the beginning of the month.

When she was at our house, she became accustomed to one quiet older dog with only our youngest son, my husband, and me around. I did have an additional caregiver twice a week to help when I had to work outside the home, but Mom liked having her around.

When Mom stayed with Big Sis, her house was not as peaceful for

Mom. They had three and sometimes four dogs whenever they were puppy sitting. They also had two exotic birds that squawked quite a bit at passing traffic. There was a family of five with Mom and occasionally a baby my sister helped care for another family.

Each time the baby's parent arrived to pick up the baby, the dogs and birds would sound the alarm. Mom was usually over-stimulated at her house by that environment which was shown by her acting out. My oldest niece had the opportunity to see Mom at our house one month to see the difference.

She quickly asked me, *"Is this how grandma is all the time with you?"*

I responded with a look of skepticism, *"Yeah, isn't she like this when she is with you guys?"*

She laughed and said, *"NO. Grandma is mean to us. She says ugly things and pinches too."*

At first, I thought this was because of my past family history. Then as the months passed and this became an issue, Big Sis began calling me to talk to Mom or asking me to talk to her in front of them at the monthly drop-off. I did not realize the subtle shift because I was not there to see it.

My sister's family thought Mom had a reason to be mean to them. Then I eventually heard what I assumed came from my sister's inner wounded child saying, *"You're her favorite. That's why she's nice to you."*

You can imagine the underlying resentment that built, but it had nothing to do with favorites and everything to do with her environment. When I later decided to transition Mom into a Memory Care community, the environment issue was confirmed.

The executive director shared with me how she learned what motivates Mom in the community activity-wise to help her engage and what activities trigger her to become agitated or mean to others. Mom responded better in 1-1 activities rather than six or more. The director pointed out that if you are paying close attention, you can almost see the switch flip in her eyes when she was ramping up to being overly stimulated to the point of lashing out.

Although the director could recognize Mom's trigger moments, she disagreed with me when I explained that Mom lived with FTD as part of the mixed Dementia. She explained the behaviors with Alzheimer's and dismissed what I explained regarding Mom's test results. I realized then the director was showing me a similar response as my sisters and even aunts to an extent. She had her professional experience related to mainly Alzheimer's without the benefit of seeing Mom's decline over the past ten years.

Many of these behavioral symptoms present with the top 4 forms of Dementia (Alzheimer's, Frontotemporal, Lewy Bodies, and Vascular) overlap, making it difficult to discern one type from the other. They may have two or three symptoms present at first but not all. If you doubt your loved one's symptoms, then reach out to their neurologist to explain what is happening. Your loved one does not have to know you shared the information. The information provided to the neurologist in advance will help save time and create a more productive doctor visit.

In the beginning, Mom was silly and somewhat crazy to us. As time passed, she became more crazy, illogical, with unreasonable personality changes. Denial, depression, loss of time, insomnia, extreme fatigue, mood swings, difficulty focusing, and poor judgment can make it difficult to get close to our loved ones.

The person we once loved disappeared into drastic mood swings with an even worse sense of judgment. Mom eventually became stuck in a moment, vulgar, apathetic, and lost interest in her hobbies. Self-care became a huge challenge and source of family drama.

When was allowing Mom to do what she wanted versus what she needed to be considered appropriate anymore? When is telling Mom to take a shower to deny her choice versus letting her choose to go a week without a shower appropriate?

I tried to include as much choice as possible initially, but as time passed, the choice was a source of frustration for both of us. If there were too many choices for Mom would get confused and respond with, *"I don't know, you choose!"* So, I made the choices going forward, and she went along with them.

Of course, this came across as telling Mom what to do all the time to my sisters. They even asked her why she would not speak up for herself anymore. Her response to them was, *"I don't know, it's just easier not to."* Back to the adage – Damned if you do, damned if you don't. What mattered more and more was what the doctors said rather than what my sisters said or thought about me.

Normal vs. Abnormal

Researching symptoms, behaviors, causes, and treatments with the keyword Dementia became my go-to before and after arguments or silence from my sisters at doctors' appointments. Either way, initial symptoms and learning to identify them are key factors to applying proactive measures instead of reactive fear-based plans. The more information you can provide to your loved one's doctor, the sooner you can help them beyond pharmaceuticals.

Once you begin to detect Alzheimer's or other forms of Dementia symptoms, you most likely want reassurance or clarity by obtaining a diagnosis. The unknown and scary life changes can be stressful, especially when deciphering normal versus mild, moderate, or severe stages.

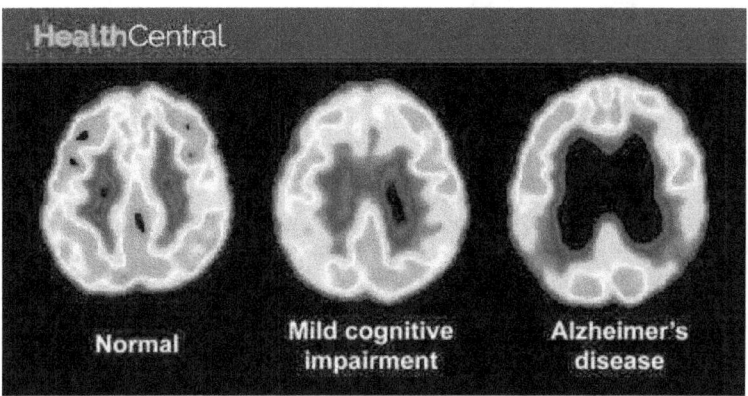

The problem with the deterioration of the brain is that definitive diagnosis comes from a brain autopsy postmortem. Anything else is done through a process of elimination through blood tests and brain imaging, physical and neurological exams, mental status and mood testing, and a thorough evaluation of medical history. This process may take many months before you have a general diagnosis for treatment planning.

Although Alzheimer's is the most common form of Dementia and easier to diagnose based on the types of tests and obvious symptoms, it takes longer to suspect since we are often in denial when we do suspect it. We dismissed symptoms over ten years because there usually was something to pinpoint or blame. We kept laughing through the silly things as she did, saying, *"oh how stupid, I can't believe I did that."*

It can take several years of observation of your loved one's behaviors (symptoms), physical exams, and neurological exams before finally having enough data to discern the type of Dementia. Unless, of course, you become more in tune with your loved one and pay closer attention to the details because time is the one precious commodity we cannot get back.

Your loved one may fear what this implies and may not be as honest with the doctor initially. Mom was so concerned about losing her driver's license or being seen as mentally unstable that she did not tell the doctor the truth even when she could remember.

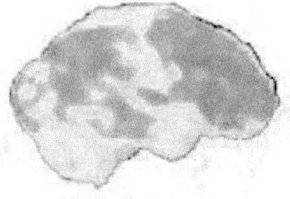

Normal   Alzheimer's disease

Alzheimer's is connected with the buildup of amyloid protein produced in our bone marrow and deposited in any tissue or organ. Lewy Body is connected with the depletion of the brain's chemical acetylcholine which allows the alpha-synuclein protein to build up in areas that regulate behavior, cognition, and movement. Two very different proteins, yet both affected by environmental factors more so than genetic biomarkers.

Vascular Dementia may not be related to protein build-up as Alzheimer's or Lewy Body but more indicative of stroke or damaged blood vessels and reduced circulation depriving the brain of vital oxygen and nutrients.

Behaviors associated with Lewy Body Dementia:

1) Impaired thinking
2) Problems with executive functions (planning, processing information)
3) Difficulty with visual information
4) Fluctuations in attention or alertness
5) Problems with movement, including tremors, stiffness, slowness, and walking
6) Hallucinations
7) Alterations in sleep and behavior

Having a magnetic resonance imaging (MRI), positron emission tomography (PET), or computerized tomography (CAT) scan of your brain is not exactly considered part of the annual wellness check. A full workup usually entails blood work, a visual observance with an OB check for women, a prostate check for men, and a urine sample. A healthy heart at the time of this type of visit does not release us from underlying causes of Dementia.

You can expect to hear about your body mass index (BMI) and blood work panel, which includes Cholesterol, Vitamin D or B12, or Potassium levels, for example, before they even consider asking cognitive questions if those questions are considered at all. Why would they?

Doctors do not spend as much time with you or your loved one outside of the 30-minute exam. Your concerns must be presented as clearly as possible for your loved one or even for yourself. Testing for Dementia will go beyond any wellness check. Most doctors know what tests should be performed. However, not all doctors are adequately trained in geriatric medicine.

Individuals living with Dementia place a high burden of care on health care systems and family members. "Neurologists, geriatricians, and psychiatrists are usually recognized as specialists in the management of patients with Dementia. However, it is also believed that general practitioners could diagnose the most common forms of Dementia since they act as gatekeepers to specialized care and are responsible for most of the encounters between patients and the healthcare system. Many doctors are not trained in Dementia since it is an optional elective in med school.

Mom's neurologist referred her to a Forensic Neurologist for testing because she felt the forensic testing would be better and more in-depth than what she was comfortable doing. The first round of tests was roughly 4 hours of Dementia rated tests, including cognitive functioning, attention, initiation/preservation, construction, conceptualization, and memory.

The second round of tests was 4 to 5 hours which included more Dementia rating scale-2 (DRS-2) along with geriatric depression scale, geriatric anxiety inventory, premorbid function (TOPF), Independent Living Scale (Health & Safety), Memory & Malingering, Behavior Rating Inventory of Executive Function, Instrumental Activities of Daily Living, and many others. Can you appreciate the complexity and see that Dementia is not solely memory loss?

Doctors concluded that Mom was living with Vascular Dementia first, then Early-onset Alzheimer's, and finally, Frontotemporal Dementia. She was living with mixed Dementia.

According to the FTD Association (AFTD), research shows that people generally live from 2 to 10 years after diagnosis, with an average of about 6 ½ to 7 years. The range of survival extends from as few as 18 months to over 20 years, so it is impossible to predict an individual's situation.

Trying to put a time frame to this myself drove me down a maddening path. My accountant's mind needed to forecast the multiple possibilities for her medical and living care necessities with her financial resources. I worried Mom could outlive her retirement much faster with the rising costs for her care.

Mom's diagnosis with FTD was both the relief to end the arguing with my sisters and the weight of reality. There was no reversing this diagnosis. There was only acceptance while continuing to find a way for all of us to have an acceptable quality of life.

I like to think we would have been more compassionate towards her needs back then if we understood what was happening or slowed the deterioration. Avoiding her eradicate behavior left us clueless, with Mom feeling unsupported. She did the best with what she knew back then to survive, which unfortunately closed us all out. She remained suicidal much of the time while we simply wanted to live a normal life.

What I may not make up from the past, I can make up now for her remaining years. The unknown is still the unknown when it comes to the time of death.

A diagnosis is not a death sentence. For us, it confirmed what we suspected later but was too afraid to address. It was no longer guessing about UTI infection, hormonal imbalances, or her bipolar depression.

Oddly, the diagnosis did give me peace of mind. I could finally put words to Mom's behavior and what felt like a lack of interest in our lives or unfair judging. Mom was not mean after all; she was a parent to the best of her abilities even after living with mixed Dementia.

Stubborn or not, she loved us in her way. For the sake of fate, her abilities declined as we got older, and we needed her more when she needed us even more than we could ever imagine.

I looked at my level of ability and compared it to hers. We wanted to feel comfortable with the changes we did not understand. We then continued to justify normal versus abnormal because it was heartbreaking to watch. Mom changed into someone we could not understand, control, or recognize anymore.

As she continued to decline, we had to continue to change with her and hang on to our identity. We struggled to live in silence as the fear of the unknown stared back through her vacant gaze from time to time. From stage to stage, we began to mourn while the challenges of the caregiving journey continued to rise.

Chapter 11
Medical Referees

Mark 5:26 (NLT)
She had suffered a great deal from many doctors, and over the years she had spent everything she had to pay them, but she had gotten no better. In fact, she had gotten worse.

At the beginning of our caregiving roles, it was all very convenient to care for Mom in her home. Trying to help her still feel independent was a challenge. Leaving her there to continue living alone would have hastened her death. Maybe I should have allowed for that by giving in to her mindless needs and desire to die in her sleep. She would have returned to be with Dad sooner.

I could not sit back and watch her waste away since there was no way of knowing when that would happen. Our society holds caregivers and those holding the rights through caregiver compliance responsible as fiduciaries of their estates and well-being.

I had more than a moral obligation as one particular nurse reminded me about senior neglect. I used the phrase 'waste away,' but rather, the Adult Protective Services or APS call it senior neglect.

Back in my early caregiver days, while I was still trying to balance work, home, and Mom, a nurse stopped to explain about senior neglect. All the while, she kept pointing out Mom's status as her example.

I had taken Mom in for yet another UTI during my lunch break. It was supposed to be a simple and swift pee-in-the-cup visit to get the antibiotics we knew she needed. I knew this nurse was doing more than her job when she told me how she saw this sort of thing all too often. It drove matters home to me when she said, "I know you think you're doing your best, but it's not good enough."

Boy did this trigger all sorts of resentment and anger inside of me. Mom's status was not my fault! Mom is a grown woman capable of taking care of herself. My sisters and I thought the same at some point, especially when it came time to do something for her we did not want to do. Little Sis assured me time and time again that everything was fine when I was not there with Mom.

Well, the devil is in the details, alright. I had to choose which master I served going forward. I wanted the blame to be pointed somewhere else, to someone else. Certainly not at me. I was working to help make ends meet in my household. I was pursuing my career just as Mom pursued her teaching career of 32 years. And yet, I was the one that was not doing good enough.

This caregiver role was already filled with various struggles, so I did not need to include the constant bickering and fighting or pretending things were fine when they were not. Now this outsider, not a sibling or family-related member at all, was pointing the finger at me! Having blame placed on my shoulders made it official in my mind.

If I was going to be the one held responsible for Mom's care, then it was time to take the bull by the horns. I was driven beyond self-preservation, denial, and the need to honor my parents. Now I needed to prove the nurse wrong to get her out from under my skin.

Even though Mom now has what she needs, our family is no longer the same. I no longer must fight to be the referee or feel like I was the only one fighting for Mom's needs. The doctors and nurses became the medical referees instead. I was more acquainted with Mom's panel of doctors than my own.

Mom's routine checkups exposed me to the basic questions and what was considered normal. Normal blood sugar (A1C), normal body mass index (BMI), normal cholesterol levels (LDLs or HDLs), normal creatinine levels, normal blood pressure with cardiovascular magnetic resonance (CMR). Only none of this felt normal to me.

I am not a nurse by any means. When I stepped into this journey as an accountant, my analytical skills did not serve me at first. I needed to become more of an observer. I was learning what questions to ask and which doctors to ask. I felt like I was back in school learning a new language. Connecting terms and data to what was considered normal with her level of activity or mental status helped me create my benchmark—no more relying on her mood swings from the past.

And still, sharing my research with my sisters only left me frustrated. They would not take the time to do their research because they would continually say she was fine from their brief moments with Mom. No mystery to solve as far as they were concerned. At that moment, she might have been fine, but Mom became quite the actress in front of doctors too. I was being treated as the *'know-it-all'* and dismissed like we dismissed Mom so many years ago. My inner child was triggered every time, saying, *"this is not fair!"*

I started to print out the information to share, attend support groups, forums, and caregiver workshops with hopes they would read the material to see for themselves what was happening to Mom. It was all starting to finally make sense to me of what was happening to Mom in previous years. A mental map emerged of her journey mixed with medical and psychological issues, which made me confident I knew what I was saying. It was an odd sense of achievement figuring out this jigsaw puzzle, but still frustrating because Mom was living with a mixed form of Dementia (Vascular, Alzheimer's, and FTD or behavioral variant.)

They did not agree because, for so long, we had only dealt with her bi-polar tendencies. They were not spending as much time with her either. Even when they did spend more time with her, Mom's inner performer began *'acting'* or showing off. Mom always loved to make people laugh and especially loved the shock factor certain actions or comments would bring. So, my sisters often said, *"See, Mom is fine; you don't know what you're talking about."*

No. No more pretending Mom is fine—no more allowing them to remain in denial. I had tried for so long to keep the peace and please both. Ironically, trying to keep the peace between them was tearing me up inside.

I changed her neurologist to get a second opinion to make Mom feel more comfortable because, with her background of sexual abuse and PTSD, Mom would never open up to the male doctor. Little Sis and her daughter sat in sessions with Mom and this neurologist, so Mom put on an act again. The doctor had the same response – Mom was fine.

This survival instinct that may have served Mom before was not helping the doctor or my sister see beyond her acting. No wonder Little Sis kept telling me Mom was fine. They could only see what was on the surface for that brief session and not how she had been living at home or barely existing. Actions speak louder than words when you pay close attention.

As soon as I found a female neurologist, Mom began to open up. She still did not like going to the doctor to see the 'shrink,' as she called the neurologist, but she opened up and spoke freely once we were there. She did not act as much around the female neurologist, but I still watched her go into her survivor's mode, which I later understood to be anosognosia.

A word composed of three Greek roots which combine to mean 'without knowledge of disease.' The condition that caused her to be unaware of her mental health condition, including Dementia. This condition often affects those with mental illness, traumatic brain injury, brain tumors, stroke, and other forms of Dementia. Knowing the difference will help you strategize care with this in mind to find workarounds to keep your loved one safe.

I stayed out of the sessions so Mom could get the most out of it and learn to trust the process. The doctor would eventually call me back with Mom to help her fill in the gaps of her inquiries. Mom still felt like I was snitching on her when I answered some questions. I reassured Mom that she was not in trouble and the doctor needed every bit of detail to help. Mom's childlike responses gave me a glimpse into her mental age before I was able to grasp the stages. These subtle changes became another observation for me to consider after a step down in stages.

Going to the doctors, especially the neurologist, became part of our monthly routines. Trips to the General Physician, Cardiologist, Gastroenterologist, Otolaryngologist (Ear, Nose, & Throat specialists), Ophthalmologist (Vision), Dentist, and physical therapists became our main outings.

Explaining the details of what brought us in or changes from the last visit allowed tension to build between Mom and me. I recollected similar arguments between Mom & Dad. An episode would happen that she quickly denied the need for an appointment with the attitude of wasting time and money on doctors.

I wanted to respect Mom's privacy, but at the same time, I wanted to stop reacting to the same passive-aggressive arguments in front of the doctors. Many times, we had already sat and waited for her appointment to finally be called back, only for her to tell the nurse or doctor she was fine. They would look at her and know right away this was not the case.

The nurses asked specific questions that Mom answered with childish or even flirtatious responses. As soon as they looked to me for answers, it started the same bickering. She would go so far as to tell the doctors I was lying and making stuff up. They knew better, thankfully, and smiled to play along. They collected samples, vitals and examined her to prove me wrong. Their smiles would eventually turn to looks of concern while they explained what they found.

As the years passed with this new way of life revolving around doctors' visits, something started to surface. Each time we stepped into any of these doctor's offices, I felt more anxiety.

These feelings were not coming from concern for Mom's health. Before the appointment, I had done enough research to understand more of the medical jargon to find a place of comfort while I watched the nurses do their jobs. I understood the terminology they used and what her results meant before Mom ever gave it a thought.

No, my anxiety came from wondering which nurse would hear Mom say I was lying and, in turn, tell me once again I was not doing enough.

The proactive response was to email or fax a letter to the doctors' offices at least two days before her next appointment describing any updates since Mom's last appointment. Changes in medicines and reactions to the changes. Any decline in abilities with events that may have caused the change in mental status overall.

The techs could file the email in her chart, so the doctor was prepared to ask more direct questions at her next appointment. It proved not only to be a time-saver for all of us, but it allowed the doctor to be the doctor in the room so I could be the supportive daughter at the appointment. I only had to fill in the blanks when she looked at me because she could not think of the word or phrase to explain her answer. It made the appointments so much easier to bear.

I needed my sisters with me on this journey. No matter how much we argued before when Mom lived alone, I still needed us to feel like a family, a united front. Blood was still thicker than water to me at this time. There was comfort in being side by side while caring for Mom simply because the fighting stopped in front of the nurses and doctors. If they were not going to listen to me, they could listen to the doctors and nurses instead.

I did not have to be right anymore if they would make an effort to be present, to hear it for themselves from the doctors. Hearing Mom's prognosis from the doctors eliminated an explanation from me, the 'know-it-all' sister. Coming straight from the doctor's mouth, they could deny, or protest matters with the doctor rather than me.

If we started to discuss matters in the doctor's office and began to disagree, the doctor was present to ask our questions. We could clear the air before we ever left the office and not allow any more arguments to be left unresolved. The doctors became our medical referees for some time.

The need for a referee or mediator is not unusual when a family is not on the same page, as we discussed earlier. We were definitely not on the same page because we were all lacking in medical information related to the multiple forms of Dementia. My sisters strongly disagreed with me because they could only consider the extremes or advanced stages of Dementia.

The limited knowledge available about early stages is how so many dismiss symptoms because we imagine a much older senior with extreme symptoms or in advanced stages. When we look into the eyes of our younger parents or spouse, declining before we ever expected the possibility of what a diagnosis changes is hard to accept.

The doctors and nurses may not have all the answers because Dementia is still incredibly misunderstood overall. Even if you cannot find common ground in your family before and after a diagnosis, the awareness is life-changing. The umbrella term Dementia is used because there are so many undetected changes in the brain that require close attention or monitoring.

Unfortunately, the devil in the details provides too many opportunities for disagreements when we are not a scientist. Understanding Frontotemporal Dementia (FTD) or Pick's disease is tricky. And yet, it is the most common form of Dementia diagnosed before the age of 60. Doctors are slowly understanding that FTD is a group of ailments affecting the same brain regions. These include behavioral variant FTD, primary progressive aphasia (PPA), corticobasal degeneration, progressive supranuclear palsy, ALS.

Each of these signs and symptoms looks different from one person to the next depending on what stage they are in, affecting behavior, personality, language, and physical abilities.

Behavior and personality changes:

1) Poor Judgement
2) Loss of empathy (being insensitive or rude; seeming cold and selfish)
3) Socially inappropriate behavior (hoarding)
4) Lack of inhibition
5) Repetitive, compulsive behavior (humming, hand-rubbing or finger flicking, foot-tapping)
6) Inability to concentrate or plan (judgment, organization, or understanding abstract ideas)
7) Frequent, abrupt mood changes
8) Speech difficulties (language problems)
9) Problems with balance or movement
10) Memory loss
11) Excessive craving for sweets (change in food preferences, poor table manners)
12) Seeming subdued (socially isolated and withdrawn)
13) Losing interest in people and things (hobbies or favorite past times)
14) Losing drive and motivation (become easily distracted)
15) Neglecting personal hygiene

Language problems:

1) Using words incorrectly
2) Loss of vocabulary
3) Repeating a limited number of phrases
4) Forgetting the meaning of common words
5) Slow, hesitant speech
6) Difficulty making the right sounds to say words
7) Getting words in the wrong order
8) Automatically repeating things other people have said

Physical problems in later stages:

1) Slow, stiff movements, similar to Parkinson's disease
2) Difficulty swallowing
3) Loss of bladder control
4) Loss of bowel control

As stages progress, the continued degeneration of the brain with FTD will overlap with other neurological (nerve or brain) functions creating problems, including:

- Motor neuron disease – causes increasing weakness, usually with muscle atrophy or wasting (Lou Gehrig's disease).
- Corticobasal degeneration – causes problems controlling limbs, loss of balance and coordination, slowness, and reduced mobility.
- Progressive Supranuclear palsy – causes problems with balance, movement, eye movements, and swallowing.

Symptoms may occur in clusters, while some may be more prevalent in the early or late stages. FTD tends to be the natural progression after Vascular Dementia. FTD causes cell damage in the brain's frontal lobe (behind the forehead) and temporal (behind the ears) lobes. It would be strange to say I was drawn to this knowledge. Once I understood this particular degeneration generally starts with personality and behavior changes and may eventually lead to severe memory loss, I knew this was what Mom was enduring.

FTD affects people between the ages of 45 and 65. According to the Association for Frontotemporal Dementia Degeneration (AFTD), this form can occur as early as age 21 or as late as 80. Memory tends to be a more prominent symptom in early Alzheimer's than in early FTD, although advanced FTD often causes memory loss. Behavior changes are often the first noticeable symptom, also known as Behavior Variant Frontotemporal Dementia (bvFTD). Major changes in personality and interpersonal relationships often occur in their 50s and 60s.

Mom's journey was far more than Bipolar tendencies and worsened between her 40's and 50's. From Vascular Dementia in her mid-40's to progressing towards FTD in her mid-50's and advancing by her 60's.

I shared the same information with Mom's 2nd neurologist, who also seemed to disagree with me at first simply because she did not seem to exhibit symptom #8 – speech difficulties or any language problems. Thankfully, she understood my concerns and agreed that this could be true based on Mom's history with TIAs (Transient Ischemic Attack or mini-strokes) and behaviors even without speech difficulties.

The doctor scheduled an appointment for Mom to be seen by a forensic psychiatrist who performed a list of tests over 5 hours. Soon after, Mom had another series of tests done which involved blood work, CT, and PET Scan. Roughly six weeks later, we had a diagnosis for Mom. This diagnosis was my private football touchdown spike in my sisters' face. The medical referees vindicated me. I know that was not the humble response because it still confirmed a rougher road ahead of us.

The diagnosis validated our sibling rivalry, but there are no winners in this blame game.

As a side note, one thing that stood out to me and made me feel it was a sign was Mom's hairline. I know that women also struggle with hair loss for many other factors. However, Mom's hair had receded evenly just above her forehead, pushing her hairline back about an inch or more as if she wore a headband too tight for too long.

My first thought was poor circulation from inactivity or Vascular Dementia. Then as I read more medical journals, it connected a dot for me. Clinically, this form of Dementia is also misdiagnosed as a psychiatric disorder. It is a neurological impairment and is associated with Parkinson's Disease. The hairline to some may pass as a coincidence, but to me, it was an indication of her deterioration timeline. So, while we were dismissing her behavior or mood swings over the years, Mom's hairline had receded more than just normal hair loss. As her hairline receded, she too declined faster than in previous years.

My sisters and I came to accept what we witnessed was indeed different from Bipolar Disorder. No more excuses, no more denial, no more laughing at crazy Mom. Her behavior was becoming quite serious and more destructive. Driving on the wrong side of the road and not having any memory of time loss or ability to find her way back home in the past was no longer silly. Ranging from insomnia to driving in the middle of the night was certainly no laughing matter. It was finally making sense.

The negative tone society places on mental health became our reality and one we hid from neighbors, friends, co-workers, and relatives. It was frustrating coping with Mom day to day and embarrassing to cope with her out in public.

The very little that society understands about Dementia is 1) it is genetic and 2) it is memory loss. The variations leave so many, like my family, not only dismissing the signs and symptoms but harshly judging their mental health. It was easier to say Mom had Alzheimer's so people could understand or even sympathize with her lack of judgment and memory loss rather than look at me as if I was next. The look showed sympathy because I carry her genes as her daughter; therefore, I must be 'crazy' too.

Of course, this fear was running rampant in my mind already, so projecting that onto others was not a stretch. As soon as Mom's neurologist asked if I would get tested, it was hard to say 'No' without sounding defensive. I was not going to let Mom's story become my story. Knowing what was happening to Mom lifted the fog of frustration.

Knowing was half the battle. Now finding the strength to do what needed to be done for Mom, including encouraging her to live what life she had left to the fullest, would take more than the medical referees going forward.

FTD is uncurable or reversible with no approved therapeutic pharmaceuticals. It is also far more aggressive than Alzheimer's. Doctors can only treat the behaviors and manage the medical body symptoms, depression, diabetes, heart, and gut functionality common with FTD.

Key differences between FTD and Alzheimer's, as described on Alz.org, point out age at diagnosis as being the most important clue. Most people are diagnosed in their 40s and early 60s. Alzheimer's grows more common with increasing age. However, these symptoms may be more commonly linked with Early Onset Alzheimer's.

FTD is frequently misdiagnosed as Alzheimer's, depression, Parkinson's disease, or a psychiatric condition like Schizophrenia or Bipolar manic depression. Eventually, people with FTD die because of the physical changes that can cause skin, urinary tract, or lung infections like pneumonia.

Trusting God to guide me through the remainder of Mom's journey did little to calm my panic at first. The more I focused on what was best for Mom, the less I was concerned with keeping the peace with my sisters. I had to trust God with what our relationships became in the long run.

The medical referees can only do so much for Mom when it is related to her appointments. I still had to find a way to manage her days without losing myself in the routines. I also had to accept I was continuing this journey with Mom without my sisters. No matter how much information I can gain from the doctors, nurses, specialists, or medical journals, there is still a varying view of what quality of life looks like for Mom with the delicate boundaries she needs.

I have finally reached a point in my journey to accepting prayer over researching. Yes, knowledge is power and peace of mind to an extent. Knowing more has helped me understand our journey and lean into it without fear. At the beginning of every day, I must remind myself I AM enough. At the end of every day, I give thanks and praise for the strength and guidance given to me.

There is still so much more to learn at this point in our journey. Self-reliance is not the only answer. Learning when to ask for help is allowing pride to step aside. As time continues to pass, my community of caregivers and supporters has grown. I see and feel the grace of God. I pick my battles carefully. When I cannot figure it out, then I give it to God.

Chapter 12
Proactive Measures

During my adolescent years, Mom would ironically tell me, *"It's not what you're eating; it's what's eating at you."* And yet, we never understood what was eating at her until it was too late. Had we known her food cravings mixed with her depression masked the early signs of Dementia, then we could have acted sooner. Unfortunately, by the time I stepped into Mom's daily living full time, it quickly became a matter of taking a long hard look into my own life to stop the generational, cultural loop. How do I stop the boomerang effect to keep this from becoming my way of living?

Mom built a life through perseverance and self-reliance. Yet, this self-reliance created a set of ideals as she learned a different survival cycle. A cycle I desperately intend on breaking. Another reason I no longer believe Dementia to be genetic is that our poor dietary habits can create an imbalance in the gut, leading to dysbiosis.

Rosanna Lee is a practicing registered dietitian with the College of Dietitians of Ontario specializing in senior nutrition in the greater Toronto area. She explains how long-term, chronic dysbiosis can cause gastrointestinal conditions (diarrhea, constipation, upset stomach), allergies, weight concerns, and psychiatric and behavioral problems. Common conditions affected by dysbiosis include inflammatory bowel disease, irritable bowel syndrome, diabetes, rheumatoid arthritis, obesity, cardiovascular disease, and even Alzheimer's.

Part of my desperation to stop the boomerang led me to many different ideals of my own. One very important approach is changing my mindset to protect my heart and gut. Gut health cannot be overlooked. Everything matters.

Our gut's microbiome contains trillions of microorganisms. These work together to regulate digestion, immune function, metabolism, detoxification, vitamin synthesis, and weight control. All of this suggests a strong link between the gut's microbial state and emotional functioning, particularly with stress, anxiety, and depression.

My daily regimen had to change if I not only prevented Dementia but also maintained sustainable energy. My care routine built around Mom meant I needed a flexible regimen. Her regimens had not changed much since I was a kid. They had worsened. I also did not need to add more stress to my day by preparing special meals and then something simple or unhealthy for Mom and my family. The changes had to be gradual and fulfilling.

Over the next two years, I began weaning myself off coffee and switching to real green tea—none of those sugary drinks with yellow #5 for coloring and fructose corn syrup for sweetening. Then I decided I could trade the beverage for a green tea supplement. It was great because I could drink more water in place of the tea. Until I ran out of the supplement and opted to replace it with a green tea fat-burning supplement, I could benefit from weight loss and mental focus. Right?

About 4 to 5 weeks passed when I started to feel palpitations and dizziness as I stopped for the day to sit down on the couch after dinner to watch tv. I kept thinking I just needed to drink more water, so I did. Then over the following week, my right arm started to have pain, and my chest would feel a little tight like it was hard to catch my breath.

I was beginning to panic because my mind immediately went to Mom's heart and age when her symptoms of Dementia began to present more regularly. I tried to justify it based on other things happening in my life that would cause enough stress and anxiety to mimic my symptoms. When the dizzy spells got a bit stronger, I finally made a call to see a cardiologist.

After answering the doctor's questions about when the symptoms had started and what may have been different, I realized the symptoms started shortly after taking the new green tea supplement. I did not connect the correlation at first because it was just a supplement. I arrived at the doctor's office a week later to take a stress test on a treadmill. I was hooked up to the machines with leads stuck to my upper torso as I nervously watched the monitor displaying the vitals, which did not make much sense.

Even if I wanted to see a good result, I wasn't sure what it would look like so I could mentally focus on something more positive. The anxiety was a bit too much because I struggled to breathe and had to stop as the speed increased.

I was wearing a required COVID mask, so breathing my own exhale was not helping, but I immediately thought again, *"Oh no, it IS my heart."* For a moment, the thoughts occurred - *"Could Mom have been right to assume she had a bad heart just because Grandpa did? Could I have inherited her broken heart at some cellular level?"*

I was scheduled to return for a nuclear stress test in a few days because I could not pass the first one, and the doctor did see an issue with the vitals. A few days before the next stress test, my husband and I talked through what had changed over the last month and a half. I brought up the green tea supplement because it was the only thing that had changed. He was not having any issues taking the supplement, but I was.

We read through the ingredients again to find the active ingredient for weight loss was caffeine. After weaning myself off coffee over the previous two years, I realized that I was reacting badly to a daily supplement that had the equivalent of two cups of coffee. My husband was drinking at least one cup a day. I stopped taking this supplement immediately. I had three days before my stress test to allow the supplement to get out of my system.

I arrived at the doctor's office in my workout gear, ready for a hike. I was prepped with the leads again, plus an IV this time. I was able to complete my test with all good marks. My heart was healthy. The doctor explained the results while urging me not to take those supplements anymore, so I finally took a deep breath of relief.

My heart is fine. No more fear that Mom's bad heart is automatically my genetic time bomb. This experience did reinforce my sense of responsibility to protect my heart to prevent Vascular issues as much as possible.

I committed to a whole new lifestyle. In Let Food Be Your Medicine, Dr. Don Colbert lists a modified Mediterranean Diet to follow, which can prevent Dementia in those not yet experiencing symptoms. It can also aid those in early stages to slow or postpone advanced stages in our loved ones living with Dementia already.

Our body systems are similar, yet each response is different to sugar, sodium, and protein. It is a lifestyle, not a diet, because diets signify temporary where lifestyle is life-changing. I have found a nice balance between Mediterranean, vegetarian, and partially vegan lifestyle helped me lose weight and maintain stamina. The nutrients provided me with energy to exercise, experience more restorative sleep, and help me to be more focused.

The more I learned I could take 'some' control of my destiny through lifestyle, the more nutrition became a central focus. This nutritional focus became the bulk of my 20% focus of the 80/20 Pareto Principle. Exercise is great for muscles, circulation, and heart health but what we provide our bodies in the first place is far more important.

Knowing something is good for you but not why does not help. Labels can claim great taste, but the taste does not equal healthy. Knowing the nutrients, you get from various foods and beverages will make it more likely for you to commit to a lifestyle change permanently. The variations of lifestyle I have come across to produce positive changes are Ketogenic, Paleo, and the Mediterranean.

Lifestyles are not one-size-fits-all, no matter what you choose. Whether you choose to change to one nutritional lifestyle or another based on necessity driven by medical history or proactive choice for prevention purposes, accept this is a lifelong committed way of being, not a trendy diet.

You could commit to guilty pleasures as easily as you can commit to life-sustaining practices. If you are not committed to a lifestyle, then any diet you choose will be temporary. Therefore, falling prey to the familiar term *'Yo-Yo diet.'* This commitment is like any other relationship. You will get out of it what you put into it.

It is helpful to drop the word *'diet'* to avoid the garbage in garbage out approach. Try to see this lifestyle change as an opportunity for mental reprogramming. Approach this commitment with more than a mindset as a quick test to see if it works because many diets are temporary but not sustainable.

Ketogenic

Ketogenic is the most aggressive lifestyle to change, so be aware of some good pros and a few cons to maintaining this lifestyle. The focus on food is mainly a low-carb approach to help the body produce ketones in the liver as energy instead of glucose and excess insulin.

Maintaining a Westernized diet causes our bodies to produce more glucose for energy, so we store fat rather than burn it. Glucose production then causes our bodies to produce more insulin, leading to insulin resistance and, subsequently, type two diabetes over time. There has been a dramatic rise in type 2 diabetes and Dementia in the United States. Type 2 diabetes shares genetic, environmental risk factors and underlying pathology that contribute to Vascular and Alzheimer's Dementias.

This lifestyle works by lowering the intake of carbs so that the body may be induced into a state known as Ketosis. This state is a natural process where the body produces ketones, produced from the breakdown of fats in the liver. This process can happen when the body is starved of carbohydrates and not by starving the body. If followed properly based on your height and current weight needs, weight loss, increased energy levels, lower blood sugar, and better mental focus can be achieved.

Pros of Ketogenic Lifestyle:

1. Reduce insulin levels
2. Decrease insulin resistance
3. Reduce Appetite (cravings)
4. Reduce fat storage/increases fat burning
5. Increase thermogenesis (the number of calories you burn daily)
6. Spare muscle for better body composition (we lose 3% to 5% muscle mass after age 30 if inactive)

---

7. Improve cognition
8. Lowers cancer risk
9. Decreases neurological disease (Dementia)
10. Greater endurance performance
11. Easier time losing fat for weight class/aesthetic sports

The brain needs roughly 50 grams of glucose a day for energy, but those grams do not have to come from carbohydrates. Our bodies can produce glucose from amino acids, protein, glycerol from dietary fat or fat tissue in our body, and lactate and pyruvate, which are produced from glycolysis. These substrates go to the liver, turning them into glucose via the process known as gluconeogenesis.

The rest of the energy the brain requires is derived from Ketones. When the brain obtains most of its energy from Ketones, it can improve functionality which is why Ketogenic lifestyles are used to treat brain disorders.

Speaking with your doctor or a nutritionist who knows your specific situation would be beneficial because your brain has an adaptation period before noticeable positive results. I have heard many refer to this as the Keto-flu response. Brain function may slow, and fatigue may increase while adapting to the Ketogenic diet. Work with a nutritionist, so you learn the right way to eat and help avoid Keto-flu.

Cons of Ketogenic Lifestyles:

1. Requires an adaptation period of 1 to 2 weeks. May experience brain fog initially.
2. It is a restrictive way of eating which requires eating without higher carbohydrates foods.
3. It requires restraint, self-control, and forethought in planning before social gatherings or impromptu restaurant stops.
4. More than a general understanding of your metabolic rate, blood glucose level, and ATP resynthesis levels are needed since this is not your typical diet to follow.

What type of foods should you focus on then? Limiting carbohydrates means focusing on eating mostly vegetables, nuts, and dairy. Avoid refined carbohydrates such as wheat (bread, pasta, cereal), starch (potatoes, beans, legumes), or fruit—small exceptions for fruit being avocado, star fruit, and berries consumed in moderation. A typical goal is 70% fats, 25% protein, and 5% carbohydrate.

General Ketogenic – Do Not Eat:

Grains – Wheat, corn, rice, cereal, etc
Sugar – honey, agave, maple syrup, etc
Fruit – apples, bananas, oranges, etc
Tubers – potato, yams, etc

General Ketogenic – Do Eat:

Meats – fish, beef, lamb, poultry, eggs, etc
Leafy Greens – Spinach, kale, chard, etc
Above ground vegetables – broccoli, cauliflower, etc
High-fat dairy – hard cheeses, high fat cream, butter, etc
Nuts and Seeds – macadamias, walnuts, sunflower seeds, etc
Avocado and berries – raspberries, blackberries, and other low glycemic impact berries like blueberries
Other fats – coconut oil, high-fat salad dressing, saturated fats

Paleo

Paleo, better known as the *'Caveman Diet,'* is more adaptive and nutrient-dense. This lifestyle is focused on eating a variety of quality meat, seafood, eggs, and whole foods (raw) such as vegetables, fruits, nuts, and seeds.

The Paleo diet aims to improve health by providing balanced and complete nutrition while avoiding most processed and refined foods with empty calories or no value-added. This lifestyle incorporates two concepts being 1) adaptability to eat particular kinds of foods and 2) eating like our ancestors to stay healthy and strong.

Adaptability back then also translated to eating whatever and whenever you could to ensure survival, but in today's world eating whatever and whenever would liken human beings to pigs. We were not designed to consume processed or refined foods over our daily needs.

Once we learned how to make tools and fire, our daily consumption changed from raw to cooked foods. Our natural state of omnivorous hunter-gatherers has always been to feed on the food of both plant and animal origin. Still, the preparation and preservation of food are what made such drastic changes.

Rationing at home and K-rations abroad changed the eating habits of Americans and the business of farming, hunting, and gathering, as noted by Wessels Living History Farm in York, Nebraska author Claudia Reinhardt and Bill Granzel from the Granzel Group. *"Government rationing began in 1942 of sugar, coffee, canned goods, meat, fish, butter, and cheese. Ground beef took fewer ration stamps to buy than steak or roasts, so homemakers "stretched" the meat supply by fixing meatloaf, spaghetti, stuffed peppers, and meat rolls. During the war, there was a boom in frozen foods for soldiers."*

Products like Spam, which began back in 1937, are still in wide distribution today. Frozen and dried foods products also began to be more popular after the war. During the 1940s frozen orange juice produced as concentrate made by Minute Maid had people jumping on the convenience bandwagon. By 1960, powdered Orange Juice, better known as *"Tang,"* came around too.

Sales came from the convenience these products provided and not enough emphasis placed on safety or long-term effects. This convenience would eventually cost us health. The change in consumption brought about the change in appliances, which introduced us to refrigeration and microwaves. We continued to adapt but lost sight of health and strength.

We may adopt a Paleo Lifestyle to modern-day times to get back to our ancestral roots for healthier living. The logic is better to match the human body to today's modern world when farming and agriculture led us to more processed and refined foods. Back then, once gathered, the food was cleaned and consumed. And yet today, we gather and process it well beyond the original state, which causes us to lose value and even cause harm to our human genetics through mutated genes and cancer.

Pros of Paleo "Caveman" Lifestyle:

1. Consume more fiber through fruits and vegetables, protein from meat, omega-3 fatty acids from fish and nuts, and unsaturated fat.
2. Consume less saturated fat and sodium by avoiding all sugar (processed cookies or cakes), grains, dairy, legumes, or beans.
3. No consumption of foods with added hormones or artificial ingredients.
4. Consume more vitamins and minerals.
5. It is a plain and simple plan without calorie counting because some foods are allowed while others are not.
6. If done correctly, it may help manage type 2 diabetes regarding high blood sugar (hyperglycemia) or low blood sugar

(hypoglycemia) and lipid profiles. You must consult a doctor beforehand to know what your actual levels are before making significant changes.

Cons of Paleo "Caveman" Lifestyle:

1. Produce and meat have evolved to be very different from Paleolithic times in that livestock today tends to be higher in saturated fat due to the way it is fed and raised.
2. Prone to consume too much meat and not enough vegetables, adding saturated fats and cholesterol to a diet. If not taken seriously, then excess consumption of meat can lead to cardiovascular diseases or cause problems with kidneys. Red meats, in particular, are high in saturated fats.
3. Requires diligent food prep rather than calculating and journaling by cutting out food groups like Dairy; must find a sufficient calcium and vitamin D source to avoid developing osteoporosis.

General Paleo – Do Not Eat:

Grains or sugar cane
Legumes such as lentils, beans, peanuts, and peas
Tubers such as potatoes
Dairy Products
Processed foods

General Paleo – Do Eat:

Fruits
Vegetables
Limited salt
Meats, eggs, fish
Nuts and seeds

Mediterranean Lifestyle

This lifestyle is higher in vegetables, beans, fruits, and nuts and lower in meats and dairy products. This lifestyle has been associated with slower cognitive decline and a lower risk of Alzheimer's, mainly due to the high vegetable content and a lower ratio of saturated to unsaturated fats. It is also the best anti-inflammatory diet in the world to allow your brain to heal.

"A Harvard Women's Health study concluded higher saturated fat intake (sourced predominantly from dairy, meat, and processed foods) was associated with a significantly worse trajectory of cognition and memory. Women with the highest saturated fat intake had a 60-70 percent greater chance of cognitive deterioration over time. Women with the lowest saturated fat intake had the brain function, on average, of women six years younger."

Dr. Michael Greger explains even though *"your brain is only about 2 percent of your body weight but may consume up to 50 percent of the oxygen you breathe, potentially releasing a firestorm of free radicals. Special antioxidant pigments in berries and dark-green leafy may make them the brain foods of the fruit and vegetable kingdom."*

"Then, in 2012, Harvard University researchers quantified these findings by using data from the Nurses' Health Study, in which the diets and health of sixteen thousand women were followed starting in 1980. They found that women who consumed at least one serving of blueberries and two servings of strawberries each week had slower rates of cognitive decline – by as much as two and a half years – compared with those who didn't eat berries."

Whole foods truly are our medicine.

Pros of Mediterranean lifestyle:

1. The best thing is it is easy to stick with since it covers all major food groups with diversity.
2. It has robust flavors
3. It's low in saturated fats and higher in monounsaturated fats or "good fats."
4. It's heart healthy.
5. Some studies have shown this lifestyle to prevent colon and prostate cancer.
6. Lowers risk of developing Alzheimer's or Parkinson's disease and improves brain function for those living with mild Dementia.
7. People following a Mediterranean lifestyle lost more weight than any other low-fat diet.

Cons of Mediterranean lifestyle:

1. Must pay attention to calcium intake since this diet is low on dairy. One can replace milk with Greek yogurt or hard cheese but must be

mindful of processed sugary types or oily hydrogenated processed cheeses. Too much cheese can contribute to constipation.
2. Must be disciplined not to drink wine more than one to two glasses a day. Overconsumption of wine can increase the risk of other cancers such as esophageal, oral, laryngeal, and liver cancers.
3. The American Heart Association points out that while the Mediterranean diet meets heart-healthy diet limits for saturated fat, your total fat consumption could be greater than the daily recommended amount if you are not careful.
4. This lifestyle relies heavily on your ability to cook aside from eating whole raw foods, which is more time-consuming and even a bit costlier.

General Mediterranean – Do Not Eat:

Candied, honey-roasted, or heavily salted nuts
Sausage, Bacon, and other high-fat meats like beef
Butter or Margarine
Hydrogenated peanut butter

General Mediterranean – Do Eat:

Primarily plant-based foods, such as fruits and vegetables, whole grains, legumes, and nuts
Replacing butter with healthy fats such as olive oil (primarily Extra Virgin) and coconut oil
Using herbs and spices instead of salt to flavor foods
Whole-grain rice and pasta (Quinoa, Couscous, and plant-based pasta)
Limiting red meat to no more than a few times a month
Fish (Mackerel, lake trout, herring, sardines, albacore tuna, and salmon) and poultry at least twice a week
Limited whole-grain bread dipped in Olive oil instead of spreading with butter or margarine
Limited dairy such as fat-free yogurt, skim milk, and low-fat cheese (consider oat, almond, or rice, or coconut milk instead but be aware of sweeteners added)
Purple grape juice can be an alternative to red wine if you prefer not to drink or have a family history of alcoholism

After researching these diets, we quickly knew what to eat, when to eat, and where to improvise. The mental perception of a dinner plate should help gauge portion control when it is filled with more fruits and vegetables. As I adapted to this way of eating, I gradually became more vegetarian. Still, research has not proven enough benefits to becoming a full vegetarian or vegan for me just yet.

There have been scary stories released about how our livestock is raised and processed from slaughter to packaging, which has become a good reason to research more. I hope it encourages you to do the same. As we continue to learn to eat better, we all need to consider the source of our food regardless, which applies to meats and produce. Farm-raised animals do not always mean what you might expect.

The goal of any business owner is to control costs to make a profit. This goal includes mass-produced livestock. The only way to consume meat responsibly is in moderation, if at all. Plus, selecting whom to purchase from may eliminate most concerns, but you still have to consider the processing and packaging process. I know families with large deep freezers that split the cost of one healthy farm-raised cow to be butchered, which lasts them months to consume.

I understand some choose to become vegetarian or vegan for personal or religious reasons, so there is no right or wrong choice. The main choice should come from a healthy viewpoint to mitigate risk. Research these lifestyles to decide what is best for you and your loved ones. Knowledge is power, so take control of your health with gusto.

Chapter 13
Brain & Gut Food for Thought

Ecclesiastes 7:12 (ESV)
For the protection of wisdom is like the protection of money, and the advantage of knowledge is that wisdom preserves the life of him who has it.

No diet is better than the other because we are all different shapes and sizes with different nutritional needs and metabolic rates. Finding the right balance to the number of inputs (food) versus outputs (exercise) will be similar for most. The biggest challenge is our own free will to commit with honest and consistent effort or self-discipline. Taking control of our gut health will be the fastest approach to balance that will benefit us in the long run. Could it be a simple balancing act?

Dad's doctors did their job to warn him of a potential heart attack, stroke, or eventually, become diabetic. If he could not stop eating to reduce his waistline drastically, he faced more health challenges. Once Dad focused on what he could no longer have, the more he seemed to crave it or buy more of the bad stuff. I felt this feeling of lack made it easier to give into Mom's sugar cravings too.

Taking sweets away from Mom made her grumpy and mean, so portion control with substitutions was the only other way to go for her. She was already living with Dementia, so I did not want to see her also need insulin shots daily. Telling her no would only set her off and added more stress for both of us. When I added more fiber to her meals, she was often too full for dessert. Showing her a bigger picture now was not going to work.

You see, Dad did not understand the bigger picture. Having to cut back on coffee, bacon, and cow milk made him focus on losing pleasure rather than discovering new ones. The bigger picture was gaining a wider variety of flavorful food, losing weight, improving health, sleeping better, no longer injecting himself with insulin, and perhaps a longer life with better quality. Change is hard without incentive and understanding of how.

Once I understood the different lifestyles between Ketogenic, Paleo, and Mediterranean, I could mix up the details to find my flexible regiment. My next step in planning our new lifestyle was figuring out the medicinal fuel provided through produce.

I was finding the 'Why' made the 'How' simple and grocery shopping more deliberate. The following is a list of foods I have learned to eat and why. The more I learned their significance related to healing the heart, which heals the mind, the easier it was to adapt to healthier eating. I continued to improvise as provided by Dr. Don Colbert's and Dr. Michael Greger's research.

Water

First, let's revisit the essentials of life through a big picture, little picture perspective. The Earth's surface is 71% water, while the adult body has up to 60% water. Our brains consume at least 50% of the water we drink. The planet's drinkable water is depleting faster than you realize because of the population and how we use it.

Rather than drink clean water to aid our body in its natural functions, we use more water to produce harmful drinks heavily sweetened, caffeinated, or both. The amount of water used to cleanse the factories and machinery post-production is not considered either. Convenience has a cost much higher than any trending aluminum can or recyclable bottle.

Coffee and Alcohol are dehydrating, mood-altering, and appetite suppressing. If you are struggling to get your loved one living with Dementia to eat, reconsider the amount of coffee throughout the day. Caffeine by itself is not bad. Our willpower and lack of self-control are what make coffee and alcohol dangerous.

Sodas and most fruit juices contribute to weight gain and tooth decay. These beverages also affect the body in other ways aside from harming the brain, gut, and heart with mood swings.

If you say, *"I don't like the way water tastes"* or *"I get tired of water,"* then consider why you do not like the taste. We have become accustomed to highly addictive sweet drinks or trendy coffee beverages, so the water our brain needs seems boring in comparison. Consider the power of water with the following alternatives to drinking plain water.

1. Water lubricates your joints to help with the joints' shock-absorbing ability.
2. Water helps us form saliva and mucus to help digest food and keep our mouth, nose, and eyes moist.
3. Water helps our blood carry oxygen effortlessly through the parts of our body.
4. Water can be an antiaging agent to boost our skin health and beauty by avoiding premature skin wrinkling and other skin disorders.
5. Water cushions the brain, spinal cord, and other sensitive tissues. Dehydration can affect brain structure and function. It is involved in the production of hormones and neurotransmitters. Prolonged dehydration can lead to problems with thinking and reasoning.
6. Water helps us to regulate our body temperature. We sweat when the body heats up to cool it down.
7. Water aids our bowels to work properly. Constipation and overly acidic stomach or ulcers can cause more than irritability.
8. Water flushes the waste from our bodies through sweat, urine, and feces.

9. Water helps our bodies maintain blood pressure. A lack of water causes the blood to become thicker, strains the heart while increasing blood pressure and possibly causing headaches.
10. Water helps our airways to minimize water loss which can make asthma and allergies worse.
11. Water makes minerals and nutrients accessible as they dissolve in water, making it possible for them to reach the different parts of our body.
12. Water helps us to prevent kidney damage by avoiding kidney stones and regulating fluids in our bodies.
13. Water, when consumed during a workout, can boost your performance.
14. Water helps us with weight loss when consumed instead of sweet juices and sodas. Drinking it before and during meals can help prevent overeating.
15. Water reduces the hangover effect—alternate water with your alcoholic drinks to prevent overconsumption and dilution.

Many liquids we drink have so many sugars and artificial sweeteners or processed ingredients that our bodies are not getting what they need. They leave us feeling thirsty and bloated. We are creating molasses to flow through our veins which overworks the heart without even knowing.

Urinary Tract Infections (UTIs) are the second most common type of infection in the body and can be deadly to your loved one living with Dementia. Flushing our system naturally is aided with water after the kidneys clean our blood overnight. If the UTI spreads to the upper urinary tract, including the kidneys, permanent damage can happen, leading to septicemia (blood poisoning, caused by bacteria or toxins).

UTIs can cause sudden confusion or delirium in older people living with Dementia. They may experience confusion, agitation, or withdrawal. If they cannot communicate how they feel, it is helpful to know the symptoms to help them get the right treatment ASAP. The fastest way is monitoring how much water they drink throughout the day with how much they are losing by relieving their body of waste.

Any infection, especially UTIs left untreated, can speed up the progression of Dementia. As the bacteria in the urine spread to the bloodstream and cross the blood-brain barrier, other cognitive difficulties can occur. You may also experience what is known as brain fog and fatigue when you do not consume enough water.

Tips: When You Think Water is too Plain to Drink – Find Healthy Alternatives

Water with a lemon - Adds vitamin C, improves skin quality, aids in digestion, detoxes the body, freshens breath, and helps to prevent kidney stones.

Hot Lemon water - [first thing in the morning] boosts your immune system with the added Vitamin C, B-complex vitamins, calcium, iron, magnesium, potassium, and fiber. Potassium is beneficial to heart health as well as brain and nerve function.

Water with Cucumber- Aside from keeping you hydrated and helping with weight loss, you get antioxidants that help prevent and delay cell damage from oxidative stress caused by free radicals from junk food and sugary sodas. Oxidative stress leads to cancer, diabetes, heart disease, Alzheimer's, and eye degeneration.

Strawberry ice cubes- Get an ice tray and fill each empty cube with a slice of strawberry. Fill the cubes with water or lemon water. Then freeze. Each cube strawberry cube will add color to your beverage and much-needed nutrients as well as they dissolve into your water.

Coconut water is high in ascorbic acid, B vitamins, and proteins. Coconut milk and water help protect against kidney disease and bladder infection.

Fiber

The next essential, water in concert with fiber, is very beneficial. Mom and I needed to introduce into daily habits an abundance of fiber, phytochemicals, and probiotics. Fiber neither requires insulin to be disposed of nor raises blood sugar. Fiber also increases the sense of fullness while slowing the absorption of food, which helps curb overeating and bad craving habits.

As we get older, we need to have more fiber in our daily nutrition to help our guts. The average adult eats only 15 grams a day. According to the American Journal of Lifestyle Medicine, women need roughly 25-30 grams of fiber daily, and men need 38 grams per day.

Nancy Ferrari, Managing Director and Executive Editor for Harvard Health Publishing, explains, *"getting to a healthy weight and staying there is an important way to prevent heart disease, diabetes, some cancers, and other serious conditions. Something as simple as aiming to eat 30 grams of fiber each day can help you lose weight, lower your blood pressure, and improve your body's response to insulin just as effectively as a more complicated diet."*

Before you think, *"Great, now I have to eat bark to get skinny,"* think about all sources of fiber like enriching the soil for plants to grow and thrive. Our guts need this fiber by consuming more fruit, vegetables, fish, and high-fiber foods such as whole grain (i.e., barley, brown rice, or legumes). We can also help our guts by cutting back on salt, sugar, fat, and alcohol. We can make health differences by encouraging our loved ones to have healthy behaviors rather than enabling unhealthy ones.

Healthy gut soil refers to balancing the healthy bacteria in our gut. There was a time when Mom continued to have more UTIs every 4 to 6 months when she lived alone, which meant she had to take more antibiotics to kill the infection. Antibiotics kill all bad and good bacteria, so she needed probiotics to replace the good bacteria. Eating non-sugary Greek yogurt could have helped her, but her craving for cheap and sugary junk foods kept her from eating healthy yogurt.

We had to find a happy medium for her between sweets and healthy foods to increase the balance of her gut's microbiome. This new approach became quite the creative project in the kitchen, so I could get her to look past the sweets and enjoy the healthy foods that would help promote better gut health. With all her sweets and medications, constipation was an issue before and after taking antibiotics.

In addition to fiber, Phytochemicals are found mainly in the skin or peel of fruits and vegetables such as apples, broccoli, and carrots. The Polyphenols found in plants help to stop pathogenic bacteria growth and stimulate good bacteria while reducing gut inflammation.

Dietary fiber is material from plant cells that enzymes cannot break down in the human digestive tract. Although the quick way would be to include more supplements, they should come from various food rather than pills. The American Heart Association Eating Plan suggests eating a variety of food fiber sources.

Plant-based foods like vegetables, fruits, whole grains, beans, lentils, peas, nuts, and seeds are good sources of fiber. Some fibers function as prebiotics to fuel the good bacteria in our gut so they can thrive and function. They also help to improve joint and cardiovascular inflammatory issues. Foods such as bananas, onions, garlic, and maple syrup are notable prebiotic fibers.

Probiotics provide beneficial bacteria to support gut health. Probiotics can be found in cultured foods (yogurt, kefir) and unpasteurized fermented foods (kimchi, sauerkraut, tempeh, kombucha). There are two important types of fiber: water-soluble and water-insoluble. Each has different properties and characteristics.

Soluble: Water-soluble fibers absorb water during digestion. They increase stool bulk and may decrease blood cholesterol levels. Soluble fiber can be found in fruits (apples, oranges, and grapefruit), vegetables, legumes (dry beans, lentils, and peas), barley, oats, and oat bran.

Insoluble: Water-insoluble fibers remain unchanged during digestion. They promote the normal movement of intestinal contents. Insoluble fiber can be found in fruits with edible peel or seeds, vegetables, whole grain products (such as whole-wheat bread, pasta, and crackers), bulgur wheat, stone-ground cornmeal, cereals (not sugary), bran, rolled oats, buckwheat, and brown rice.

When I understood the why, I made a point to eat them more often with breakfast, lunch, and dinner or snacks in between meals. The more fruit I ate, the less I craved processed sugar. The more vegetables I ate, the more energetic and content I felt after a meal. Even with less of a workout routine, my inputs were balanced with the outputs of energy.

Here are some specific foods to add to your weekly grocery list and why:

Almonds - Contain lots of healthy fats, fiber, protein, magnesium, and vitamin E. The health benefits of almonds include lower blood sugar levels, reduced blood pressure, and lower cholesterol levels. They can also reduce hunger and promote weight loss.

Walnuts - Packed with healthy fats and vitamin E, which reduces the risk of Alzheimer's and other types of dementia.

Cashews – Are Low in sugar and rich in fiber, contain heart-healthy fats and plant-based protein. Cashews contain a good source of copper, magnesium, and manganese, which is important for energy production, brain health, immunity, and bone health. It supports good cholesterol (HDL) and reduces bad cholesterol (LDL). Eating 3-4 cashew nuts will keep you satiated for a long time and aids in proper weight management.

Macadamia nuts - Although low in protein, they are rich in vitamin E, manganese, thiamin (B1), copper, fiber, antioxidants, and healthy fats (Omega 7- monounsaturated fat). One cup, or 132g, contains nearly 950 calories, so be mindful if you are calorie counting. Avoid the ones that have been roasted or contain extra oil, salt, or sugar.

Macadamia aids in weight loss, improved gut health, protection against diabetes, metabolic syndrome (lowers A1C), and heart disease by lowering bad cholesterol (LDL) and triglycerides. They prevent cancer with plant compounds called flavonoids which destroy damaging free radicals in the body and protect the brain from Alzheimer's and Parkinson's caused by oxidative stress. One cup, or 132g, contains nearly 950 calories, so be mindful if you are calorie counting. Avoid the ones that have been roasted or contain extra oil, salt, or sugar.

Blueberries – These berries are full of antioxidants to fight cancer and vitamin C for an immune booster. Blueberries have also been found in various studies to act as a concentration and memory enhancer. They will also help protect your brain against stress and premature aging.

Raspberries – Contain strong antioxidants such as Vitamin C, Quercetin, and Gallic acid that fight against cancer, heart, and circulatory disease and age-related decline. They are high in elegiac acid, a known chemo preventative, and have been shown to have anti-inflammatory properties.

Cranberries - are packed with polyphenol antioxidants and anti-inflammatory benefits, vitamins C E & K, dietary fiber, manganese, copper, and pantothenic acid (a vitamin of the B Complex essential for the oxidation of fats and carbohydrates.

Strawberries - The super berry of berries! It is rich in Vitamin C and minerals such as potassium and manganese, which our nervous system needs to help drive the electrical signals they carry.

Strawberries are a natural diuretic with both soluble and insoluble fiber and can help suppress your appetite. Trying to avoid stress eating, then drink uncarbonated strawberry-infused water throughout the day. This berry absorbs water and slows down digestive processes while expanding the stomach. Strawberries also help to stimulate the immune system and have anti-inflammatory properties.

Super strawberries promote the growth of good intestinal bacteria, which plays a role in physical and mental health. Strawberries help fight cholesterol (bad or unhealthy LDL cholesterol) by preventing plaque buildup in our arteries. Without the buildup, it keeps your blood vessels healthy and flexible. They even help us increase the nutrients we get from other berries and good foods we eat. And with all those benefits, they also prevent constipation and help lower blood pressure naturally while increasing urination.

Lemons - In addition to providing vitamin C, lemons reduce inflammation and clean the system. It helps to keep your skin blemish-free. The vitamin C in lemons can help alleviate stress and fight viral infections and sore throats. The fiber contains pectin, which helps fight hunger cravings.

Concord Grapes – 1 cup of concord grapes has 13.4 micrograms of vitamin K and flavonoids, powerful antioxidants. Stronger than found in oranges that may decrease your risk of heart disease by reducing the effect of bad cholesterol (LDL). They also have been found to decrease platelet function, which may lower the risk of a stroke or heart attack. Drinking Concord grape juice is not as healthy because of the sugar content and loss of fiber.

Broccoli - This vegetable is packed with choline, vitamin C and K. It's a powerful combination that can enhance focus, provide backup to your immune system, and sharpen your memory.

Cucumbers - High in vitamin K. Our bodies need vitamin K to help form proteins needed for making healthy bones and tissues and help your blood clot properly.

Spinach – This rich green leaf contains vitamin A, E, K, iron, zinc, thiamin, calcium, protein, and dietary fiber. When sautéed, the nutrients are denser since heating removes the water from it. Aim for at least ½ cup per day.

Kale – Another rich green leaf contains vitamins A, K, B6, C, E, folate, potassium, copper, and manganese. Although bitter, it can reduce the risk of various types of cancer. The only people who may need to avoid or limit kale intake are those that form oxalate containing kidney stones or take blood thinners such as Coumadin or Warfarin. Kale types are Curly, Dinosaur, Redbor, and Russian depending on your geographical availability.

Chard - is an excellent source of vitamins A, E, K, & C and a good source of calcium, magnesium, copper, zinc, sodium, and dietary fiber. Swiss Chard contains antioxidants beta carotene, lutein, and zeaxanthin to support our vision to help prevent macular degeneration.

All nutrients in Chard help maintain our heart, lungs, and kidneys while supporting our immune functions. You get more benefits for proper blood clotting for wound healing and bone-building. Amazing that this rich leafy green can also help regulate muscle and nerve function, plus balance blood sugar and blood pressure levels.

Celery – Excellent source of antioxidants, enzymes, and phytonutrients. One stalk of Celery contains fiber, vitamins A, B6, C, K, potassium, folate, iron, magnesium, and sodium.

This vegetable helps to reduce inflammation known as arthritis and osteoporosis thanks to an alkalizing effect from the minerals. The antioxidants and anti-inflammatory nutrients protect the digestive tract, improving the stomach lining to decrease stomach ulcers. Eating the leaves from the stalk instead of discarding them will provide you with calcium, potassium, and vitamin C.

Cucumber – Provides Vitamins A, B, and C while hydrating you. Aids in weight loss, revives eyes, cuts cancer risk, stabilizes blood pressure for both high and low, soothes muscle and joint pain, keeps kidneys in shape, helps to reduce bad cholesterol.

In addition to all those benefits, patients with diabetes can enjoy cucumber while also reaping its health benefits since the cucumber contains a hormone needed by the cells of the pancreas for producing insulin.

Garlic – The main ingredient in garlic is allicin, which has antibacterial, antivirus, antifungal, and antioxidant properties. It helps blood flow, lowers cholesterol, and stops heart disease.

Lentils - high in fiber for better digestion and packed with folate and Vitamin B-1 for a brain boost. Vitamin B-1 helps brain cells produce energy from sugar. When levels fall too low, brain cells cannot generate enough energy to function properly.

<u>Whole Grains</u> - decrease the risk for cognitive disorders, such as Alzheimer's disease. They lower inflammation levels and decrease chances of stroke; be highly selective of the type of brands you purchase. Brown rice, buckwheat, barley, oatmeal, or whole-wheat bread are good examples of whole grains that provide B vitamins, iron, folate, selenium, potassium, and magnesium.

Keep in mind that refined grains have the germ and bran removed, which gives them a finer texture and longer shelf life. White flour, white rice, white bread, many kinds of cereal, crackers, desserts, and pastries are refined grains. The refining process removes fiber along with many of the nutrients.

Enriched grains have lost the nutrients during processing, so they are fortified by adding nutrients back like B vitamins or additional nutrients that do not occur naturally. Most sugar "kiddie" cereals have been fortified or enriched with vitamins and minerals to seem "healthy." Even if they can be fortified, the amount of sugar in one serving size is still too much to be consumed when you add in other sources of sugar from juice, sodas, and pastries consumed the remainder of the day.

For our loved ones living with Dementia, agitation from sugar spikes or drops needs to be considered. With added sugar to the diet and lack of movement, constipation also adds to their agitation.

Food can be the first line of defense to help you stay healthy and your loved one from declining faster.

Chapter 14
Superfoods, Protein, and Vitamins

Proverbs 3:13 (NIV)
Blessed are those who find wisdom, those who gain understanding, for she is more profitable than silver and yields better returns than gold.

The bigger picture of health and longevity was finally formed in my mind. Learning the difference between existing paycheck to paycheck and now desiring health over convenience was a whole new perspective. Each new meal prepared outside of my comfort zone gave me more hope with added energy. Many things did not come to mind as I tried to think outside of the tv marketing box, but my curiosity in the kitchen was growing.

Herbs and spices, pairing veggies with carbs, and portion control became a new way of thinking. I started to be excited about grocery shopping because it was no longer a respite hour when I looked forward to new recipes.

Shopping turned into treasure hunting in the produce isles, knowing I could maintain my weight with food without feeling like a failure because I could not run 3 to 5 miles a day. Before my back surgery, my way of maintaining weight and energy was solely through food. I found a huge stress reliever.

I was not so crazy about celery or beets until I understood how great they were for Mom and me. Learning to adapt by finding recipes to cook with them, making smoothies, or even raw for snacking is easier than you might have thought before. Deciphering between what my body needs versus what it was craving made an incredible difference in my overall day-to-day energy and mental focus.

I dusted off the blender and started making shakes out of fruits and veggies with Greek yogurt, Rice, Oat, or Coconut milk. Your inner child might be thinking, *"yuck,"* but it is very important to at least try. I usually watched Mom's face scrunch up when I handed her a visibly green shake. Then she tasted it and liked it but turned down the shake only because it was green which made her think of salad. She is not a salad eater.

If I handed her a pink or purple shake loaded with strawberries or blueberries, she was more willing to drink it. Little did she know the pretty pink or purple shake also had spinach and Kale in it too. She sipped it, smiled, and drank it all. So now I had a way to get better nutrients into her gut with a lower glycemic effect.

I use local honey rather than Stevia to sweeten because natural, local honey has also helped me over the years with allergy prevention. You can improvise while remaining on the low sugar side by adding vanilla, ground cinnamon, and maple syrup. Eating foods that are high in the glycemic index can stimulate hunger and contribute to obesity. Mom no longer cared about weight gain or diabetes, but I did, so knowing where to cut sugar became easier.

Having an Avocado, Kale, and Green Apple smoothie with either

Greek yogurt (which is more filling) or Coconut Milk was tastier than I would have ever imagined. I sweetened with roughly a teaspoon of local honey. If you are used to sweet juice drinks or sodas, then aim to slowly wean from the sugary drinks by substituting at least one sugary beverage each day with a glass of water or healthy smoothy.

One Easter season, my husband gave up sodas for Lent - 40 days. The first week was rough, especially when it came time to go to the movies. Buying a tub of popcorn without the added butter and no soda was a sacrifice for sure; this was his Kryptonite.

As the days passed, we all drank more water and tea. By the time Lent was over, I did not care for soda, so I did not buy them anymore. Going to a movie was still the one-off treat, but the sodas started to taste differently. Even my favorite Barq's root beer soda no longer tasted as sweet as I remembered. My pallet was refined because cutting back on processed sugar with more shakes and natural sweeteners helped me taste the difference.

Since I did not want an all-liquid diet, I also had to figure out how to add protein into my daily meals as I also weaned off eating pork and beef. Substitution for smell, taste, and texture can be a bit tricky, so finding the replacement in a mushroom may not be your first thought.

I already began stocking the fridge with a variety of green leafy produce, fruits, and vegetables. Next came learning how to find plant-based protein to replace animal-based protein gradually. Keep in mind these substitutions were not so I could transition to veganism. I started to substitute animal protein earlier in the week and then increased the amount of fish for the remainder of the week. We eat far more animal protein than we should which affects our gut, heart, and brain more than most organizations will admit to for the sake of protecting profits.

Here are some suggested substitutions for plant-based protein:

Mushrooms - Even with a variety to choose from, mushrooms are a rich, low-calorie source of fiber, protein, antioxidants, and immune-boosting zinc. They mitigate the risk of developing serious health conditions like Alzheimer's, heart disease, cancer, and diabetes. Great source of vitamin D, selenium, copper, thiamin, magnesium, and phosphorus. They are also an important component in bone and immune health. They can replace the texture and flavor of a steak when seasoned and cooked well.

Avocado - This fruit holds an incredibly high nutrient value. The meaty flesh of this fruit contains vitamins A, B1(thiamine), B2 (riboflavin), B3 (niacin), B5, B6, C, E, K, potassium, and folate. The avocado contains small amounts of magnesium, manganese, copper, iron, zinc, phosphorus, protein and is loaded with fiber. Our bodies use folic acid to make DNA and other genetic material while aiding in cell division. Without it, we are susceptible to anemia, depression, and cancer.

With the healthy fats and being a fruit, it is still a low-carb friendly plant food. Avocados contain more potassium than bananas, making them healthy for our heart and brain. They can also help to lower bad cholesterol and triglycerides.
The raw avocado provides these nutrients but making guacamole for salty tortilla chips isn't healthy. Now it's a happy hour since guacamole usually means margaritas might follow. At least in my caregiving neck of the woods occasionally. 😊

Pomegranate – Dates back to Egyptians when they used the juice as a cardio tonic for improved health. Pomegranates are packed full of polyphenols, tannins, anthocyanins, and punicalagin, containing more antioxidants than cranberry juice or green tea. You will experience improved blood flow which helps aid our hearts again coronary heart disease by stopping plaque from building up in blood vessels which also helps keep cholesterol from being so damaging.

Other pomegranate benefits include the prevention of cancer (prostate & breast cancer in particular) by helping repair DNA. Impressive anti-inflammatory effects to help with arthritis and joint pain. Aside from helping with bacterial or fungal infections, the juice can also help with erectile dysfunction. Improves memory and performance with exercise. Because of the high levels of vitamin C, the fruit also helps uplift mood and maintain flawless skin. The seeds contain fiber, protein, vitamin C, K, Folate, and potassium.

Pomegranates also aid in weight loss by boosting your metabolism because of the high fiber content and are great for people with diabetes. The low sugar content and antioxidants help to keep a check on elevated blood-glucose levels.

Coconut – Coconut flesh helps restore oxidative tissue damage and contains healthy fats, proteins with vitamins C, B6, iron, magnesium, and calcium. In addition to the antiviral, antibacterial, anti-fungal, and anti-parasite properties, adding coconut to snacks or meals improves digestion and absorption of nutrients. The crunchy flesh also helps protect the body from cancers due to insulin reduction and free radicals that cause premature aging and degenerative disease.

Sunflower seeds - Contain immune-boosting zinc and selenium, vitamin E, thiamin (B1), helps convert food into energy, high levels of protein, improve heart health, and lowers cardiovascular disease caused by high cholesterol and high blood pressure with flavonoids and other plant compounds that reduce inflammation. Be mindful of the salted sunflower seeds because added sodium can be counter-productive for your heart.

Pumpkin seeds – A 1 oz. Serving, or 28 grams, contains Vitamin K, Phosphorous, Manganese, Magnesium, Iron, Zinc, Copper, polyunsaturated fatty acids, potassium, Vitamin B2 (riboflavin), folate, and fiber. This seed is high in antioxidants, reducing certain cancers, improving prostate, bladder, and heart health, and lowering blood sugar.

Hemp seeds - technically a nut, yet also referred to as hemp hearts. These seeds are rich in two essential fatty acids, Omega 3 (alpha-linolenic acid) & 6 (linoleic acid). Great source of high-quality protein more than chia and flax seeds, vitamin E, phosphorus, potassium, sodium, magnesium, sulfur, calcium, iron, and zinc.

Nutrients from hemp seeds are more known to help reduce heart disease and boost our immune system. The benefits of hemp oil are also known to improve skin disorders such as eczema and relieve dry skin without medication.

Chia seeds - known to the Aztecs and Mayans for sustainable energy as the word Chia means strength. These seeds are related to the mint plant as a whole-grain food, non-GMO, and gluten-free. One ounce (28 grams) or two tablespoons of chia seeds contains 11 grams fiber, 4 grams protein, 9 grams fat, and roughly 18% calcium, 30 % manganese, 30% magnesium on the recommended daily intake, and 27 % phosphorus.

I love to add these morning yogurt mixes, salads, or even bottled water with a pack of emergen-C when I am on the go. Chia is the best source of fiber in the world, with very high-quality protein. Both of which aids in healthy weight loss.

Quinoa - Gluten-free, high in protein, and contains all nine essential amino acids. Quinoa is also high in fiber, magnesium, B vitamins, iron, potassium, calcium, phosphorus, vitamin E, and antioxidants (quercetin). As a grain crop, Quinoa was a very important crop to the Inca Empire. They referred to it as the *'mother of all grains'* and believed it to be sacred. These grains hold powerful aids by being anti-inflammatory, anti-viral, anti-cancer, and anti-depressant qualities.

One cup of cooked quinoa (white, red, or black quinoa) will provide you with 8 grams of protein, 5 grams of fiber, vitamins B1, B2, B3, B6, and E, in addition to 58% manganese, 30% magnesium, 28% phosphorus, 19% folate, 18% copper, 15% iron, 13% zinc, 9% potassium of the recommended daily amount.

Spices For Consideration:

Saffron – A powerful spice high in antioxidants that have been linked to improved mood, libido, sexual function, and reduction of PMS symptoms. This spice is also known to enhance weight loss and not just a strong fragrance or distinctive color.

Saffron spice is derived from the flower Crocus Sativus. A double-blind twenty-two-week study was proven to be just as effective as the well-marketed prescription drug Donepezil (better known as Aricept), without the side effects of nausea, vomiting, and diarrhea. Donepezil is prescribed to patients with Alzheimer's and other forms of Dementia with lower levels of acetylcholine. It is used to slow the progression of memory loss, problems with thinking and reasoning.

Spirulina – better known as a superfood and a great replacement for meats from livestock, even though it is classified as blue-green algae. This superfood is being investigated for regions suffering from malnutrition and long-term space missions to Mars. A food source to the Aztecs until the 16th century is once again an abundant resource because a serving of 3.5oz of dried Spirulina contains 24% Carbohydrates, 8% fat, and about 60% protein. Great in shakes or sprinkled into yogurt mixes.

Spirulina also has plenty of vitamin A, beta-carotene, Thiamine (B1), Riboflavin (B2), Niacin (B3), Pantothenic Acid (B5), Folate, Choline, C, E, and K. It also contains the minerals calcium, iron, magnesium,

---

phosphorus, potassium, sodium, zinc, and 3.6 grams of fiber. There may be adverse effects for those with weakened immune systems and problems with blood clotting. The source needs to be highly scrutinized because some have been found contaminated with Microcystis.

Moringa - Another superfood is a plant native to the sub-Himalayan areas of India, Pakistan, Bangladesh, and Afghanistan. It is also grown in the tropics. The leaves, bark, flowers, fruit, seeds, and root are used to make medicine. Also, great in shakes, added to tea, or sprinkled into yogurt mixes. It contains vitamins A, thiamine, riboflavin, niacin, folate, calcium, potassium, iron, magnesium, phosphorus, and zinc.

Moringa is used for "tired blood" (anemia); arthritis and other joint pain (rheumatism); asthma; cancer; constipation; diabetes; diarrhea; epilepsy; stomach pain; stomach and intestinal ulcers; intestinal spasms; headache; heart problems; high blood pressure; kidney stones; fluid retention; thyroid disorders; and bacterial, fungal, viral, and parasitic infections.

It is also used to reduce swelling, increase sex drive (as an aphrodisiac), and boost the immune system.

Turmeric – Contains curcuminoids which can help the immune system reduce the amino acids in the brain associated with Alzheimer's disease. It fights inflammation at the molecular level with powerful anti-inflammatory effects, making it a very strong antioxidant.

Unfortunately, Tumeric is poorly absorbed into the bloodstream without black pepper. You may benefit from a Turmeric supplement and adding black pepper to season your food. Once absorbed, turmeric will help your body fight foreign invaders and repair damage.

The curcumin in turmeric can increase hormonal brain levels of brain-derived neurotrophic factor (BDNF), which have been linked to depression and Alzheimer's when these levels decrease. An improvement in memory and reversing of age-related decline as the levels of this hormone are raised. This spice can also reduce heart disease by improving the lining of your blood vessels and has been deemed just as effective when compared to the drug Atorvastatin.

Sage - can increase recall abilities, memory retention, and anti-inflammatory of the cardiovascular system, resulting from heart diseases and high blood pressure. This herb helps with other health issues such as arthritis, gout, and menopause. It can assist in lowering blood sugar levels, bad cholesterol (LDL) and supports brain health. It also contains a superior level of Vitamin A, C, E, & K in addition to magnesium, zinc, copper, protein, and fiber. Sage is also loaded with antioxidants.

Rosemary- a cognitive stimulant and an increase in memory retention. The aroma of rosemary alone has been linked to improving mood, clearing the mind, and relieving stress in those with chronic anxiety or stress hormone imbalances.

When consumed, Rosemary becomes an antioxidant, anti-inflammatory, and anti-carcinogenic in nature to fight against many other diseases. Rosemary acts as a stimulant for the body and boosts the production of red blood cells and blood flow. Consuming regularly can help the immune system fight any infections that do occur.

Olive Oil - Cholesterol is an important part of anyone's diet. Studies have suggested that a larger intake of saturated fats and cholesterol can clog the arteries, making foods high in cholesterol an Alzheimer's trigger food; however, good cholesterol can help to protect your brain cells. If possible, eat more polyunsaturated and mono fats, such as olive oil, and stick to grilling, baking, or dehydrating over frying and smoking. It contains Omega 3 & 6 fatty acids. Olive oil has been proven in studies of over 841,000 people with the only source of monounsaturated fat associated with the ability to reduce the risk of stroke and heart disease.

Avocado Oil - adding this to salad or salsa can increase antioxidant absorption. Some nutrients are fat-soluble, meaning that they need to be combined with fat for the body to utilize their nutrients. Vitamins A, D, E, And K are fat-soluble, so using avocado oil when you eat veggies will help insure the nutrients do not go to waste. Additional nutrients in this oil include carotenoids lutein and zeaxanthin, which are incredibly important for the health of our eyes.

Dark Chocolate – The chocolate I love is made from the cacao tree's seed and is loaded with nutrients. Real chocolate with 70% cocoa or higher has shown positive results in focus tests. Good quality dark chocolate contains antioxidants, fiber, iron, magnesium, copper, manganese, potassium, phosphorus, zinc, and selenium. It also promotes the natural release of endorphins while improving the blood flow as it lowers blood pressure.

Dark Chocolate can be bitter, so that it may be an acquired taste. Pairs well as dark chocolate blueberries, almonds, or raisins. Must monitor portion control to become aware of how many pieces complete one serving. You can still have too much of a good thing!

Green Tea - Indian and Chinese medicine use green tea traditionally because it helps promote focus and clear brain fog. L-theanine, an amino acid in green tea, also promotes a healthy brain by increasing dopamine production and shutting down sensations of anxiety.

It is easy to find imposter green teas, but quality green tea will also help burn fat, reduce bad breath, and prevent type 2 diabetes and cardiovascular disease. Not crazy about the taste at first? Then add half a cinnamon stick, a nickel size of local honey, or a touch of lemon juice.

Chai Tea - This spicy Indian tea is also referred to as masala chai. Chai tea helps boost heart health by lowering cholesterol, reducing blood sugar levels, aiding digestion, and helping with weight loss. This spicy, fragrant tea combines black tea, ginger, and other spices like cardamom, cinnamon, fennel, black pepper, and cloves.

Some Chai Tea versions may include star anise, coriander seeds, and peppercorns. Chai is brewed with warm water and milk (I use oat milk or unsweetened coconut milk).

Mint Tea - peppermint is an aromatic herb that is a cross between watermint and spearmint. Peppermint leaves contain several essential oils, including menthol, menthone, and limonene. Menthol gives peppermint the cooling properties and minty scent. This mint tea aids in digestive issues such as gas, bloating, indigestion, and irritable bowel syndrome (IBS).

The mint also reduces the severity of nausea and vomiting, relieves tension headaches and migraines, menstrual cramps, and relieves clogged sinuses. We benefit from mint because peppermint has been proven to kill the growth of common food-borne bacteria, including E. coli, Listeria and Salmonella.

Peppermint oils also kill other bacteria, including staphylococcus and pneumonia-linked bacteria. For these reasons, I would like to add a mint tea bag to my green tea with a drop of local honey to combine the benefits.

Red wine - one single 4-5 oz serving of red wine 3 to 4 times a week can reduce the risk of Alzheimer's disease by improving cholesterol and fighting free radical damage. We also get the added benefits to help manage diabetes by regulating blood sugar, fighting obesity, and preventing cognitive decline.

When drinking red wines, you provide rich antioxidants such as polyphenols, preventing unwanted clotting by keeping the blood vessels flexible. Resveratrol in red wine inhibits the formation of beta-amyloid protein in the brain, which aids in keeping memory sharp. The same resveratrol converts into a chemical compound, piceatannol, which helps to reduce fat cells in our body. Piceatannol fastens the insulin receptors of fat cells, which blocks the pathways required for immature fat cells to grow.

The anti-bacterial nature of red wines has enabled them to treat stomach irritation and other digestive disorders like Helicobacter pylori (H-pylori), usually found in the stomach. H-pylori infection can be passed from person to person through direct contact with saliva, vomit or fecal matter, or contaminated food or water. Mom was on antibiotics of 12 pills a day for three weeks to clear H-pylori. A difficult moment in time for us.

Disclaimer: Drinking red wine has the potential to become habitual, so do not rush out to the grocery store to start stocking the pantry as your new weight loss regimen. As with everything else, consume responsibly and in moderation.

Why Are Vitamins So Important?

We here so much around flu season to get plenty of rest and Vitamin C that we know C helps fight colds. Not many of us know that if we do not get enough Vitamin D, our body cannot efficiently absorb other vitamins and minerals. After reading the previous chapter, you know salads are good for you, but you probably did not consider what each vitamin provides you.

I know I listed what seems like basic fruits and vegetables, but there are far more to be considered for gut, heart, and brain health to prevent Dementia and other serious conditions. If you understand what the vitamins provide us, you can begin to venture into more supermarket areas to know what to look for once you get sick of Kale. I did after a few months! I had to switch up our home menu to stop reverting to convenient unhealthy fast food and continue learning what my body needed.

The following are only intended to get you started. I encourage you to continue researching and changing your mindset to maintain a healthy body on your caregiver journey and beyond.

Vitamin D – Aside from helping us maintain healthy bones and teeth, this vitamin helps support the health of our immune system, brain, and nervous system. It also helps to regulate insulin levels and aid diabetes management, lung function, and cardiovascular health.

Vitamin D is considered more prohormone than a vitamin because our bodies produce it as a response to the sun in as little as 10 minutes, 2-3 times a week. Bodily storage can run low in the winter or if kept indoors, leading to depression, among other ailments.

Vitamin C – as a supplement, found in Citrus fruits, broccoli, Brussel sprouts, raw bell peppers, and strawberries. This vitamin is needed every day and not just in the flu season. This nutrient helps our body to form blood vessels, cartilage, muscle, and collagen in bones. It helps our body heal because it is an antioxidant that protects our cells against free radicals from bad food, stress, tobacco smoke, and radiation from the sun or x-rays.

Vitamin K - the human body requires the complete synthesis of certain proteins prerequisites for blood clotting. The body also needs K to control the binding of calcium in bones and other tissues. Without K, the body cannot produce prothrombin. Vitamin K also increases cognitive health and heart health by improving memory and lowering the risk for stroke.

Vitamin A - is a group of unsaturated nutritional organic compounds that includes retinol, retinal, retinoic acid, and several pro-vitamin A carotenoids (most notably beta-carotene). Vitamin A has multiple functions: it is important for growth and development, the immune system's maintenance, and good vision. The eye's retina needs vitamin A in the form of retinal, which combines with protein opsin to form rhodopsin, the light-absorbing molecule necessary for both low-light (scotopic vision) and color vision.

Vitamin B12 – Is also called cobalamin. B12 is a water-soluble vitamin that has a key role in the normal functioning of the brain and nervous system via the synthesis of myelin (melanogenesis) and the formation of red blood cells. It is one of eight B vitamins. B12 is involved in the metabolism of every cell of the human body, especially affecting DNA synthesis, fatty acid, and amino acid metabolism.

Vitamin E - known to protect the cell membrane tissue in the brain and acts as a peroxyl radical scavenger, disabling the production of damaging free radicals in tissues; plays a role in eye and neurological functions and inhibition of platelet coagulation; protects lipids, and prevents the oxidation of polyunsaturated fatty acids.

Folate - known as folic acid and vitamin B9; Folic acid is the form of folate used to treat anemia caused by folic acid deficiency; Long term supplementation is also associated with small reductions in the risk of stroke and cardiovascular disease.

Choline - Found in almonds, soybeans, broccoli, cauliflower, sunflower seeds, and cooked kidney beans, to list a few. Choline is the precursor molecule for the neurotransmitter acetylcholine, which is involved in many functions, including memory and muscle control. Our bodies make it in our liver but can benefit from more by adding to your daily nutrition if your liver does not make enough.

Omega 3 - promote cell regeneration, reduce inflammation, and lower your risk of arterial buildup, which could cause a stroke. Inflammation is the root cause of memory loss, dementia, and Alzheimer's.

Foods to avoid that may contribute to memory loss:

Wheat Products and the not so skinny facts according to the author of "Wheat Belly" by Dr. Davis:

- o   It is high in FODMAPs, a type of carbohydrate that can cause digestive distress in many people, which leads to inflammation.
- o   Regardless of the type of wheat you purchase, it is full of sugar, leading to blood sugar and insulin spikes, which leads to visceral fats or belly fat that harms the heart.
- o   Sugar keeps your cells from regenerating, so it loses elasticity and causes wrinkles (found in pastries like cakes, pies, and sodas). Stay away from NutraSweet and products like this that contain aspartic

acid, which can be found in many processed foods claiming to be sugar-free.

o   Linked to hair loss such as alopecia areata, which is caused by celiac–like inflammation

Wheat products (gluten) are not only in the bread aisle or bakery. You may also find gluten in frozen dinners, salad dressings, couscous products, different gums, canned soups, soup mixes, Artificial food dyes, and fast-food fries (since they are often fried in the same oil breaded patties). It can be hard to avoid wheat products overall, so minimizing or rotating every four days between wheat and corn is better if you can.

Corn Products – It is so hard to believe one single grain can create a multibillion multifaceted industry yet wreak havoc on our health at the same time. The production of corn dominates American agriculture due to its use primarily for ethanol, animal feed, and high-fructose corn syrup. Due to the increase in pesticides usage, the GM corn crop has created "superbugs" or rootworms that are no longer vulnerable to GMO (genetically modified organism) corn.

o   Corn is mainly a GMO used in cereals, snack foods, salad dressings, soft drink sweeteners, chewing gum, peanut butter, hominy grits, taco shells, and other flour products, specialty corn including white corn, blue corn, and popcorn.

o   Animal feeds — Distiller has dried grain, gluten feed, and meal, high-oil feed corn for cattle, swine, poultry, and fish. If you have gluten allergies, eating meats with a diet from gluten feed could inhibit the effort to avoid the grain.

o   GMO corn was found to be more filler than a nutrient by only containing trace amounts of many key nutrients necessary for life. De Dell Seed Company of London, Ontario, shows that GMO Corn is nutritionally deficient and wholly unfit for human consumption. One study had the World Health Organization (W.H.O.) recently recognized as *"probably carcinogenic to humans."*

o   Labeling and marking phrases of products makes it harder for the average consumer to determine whether they are purchasing a GMO Corn-based product or non-GMO corn that does not contain glyphosate.

o   High Fructose Corn Syrup is one of the most toxic substances that your body can consume. It turns into fat and cholesterol. It causes insulin resistance, which is detrimental for people with diabetes.

Some words on labels that tell you corn may be in food are dextrose, glucose, dextrin, maltodextrin, lecithin, fructose, high fructose, vegetable starch, "thickeners," sweeteners, syrup, vegetable oil, maize, and sorbitol. Corn may also be used in bakery products (bread, rolls, biscuits, doughnuts, pies, cakes, cookies, pretzels, etc.)

Many of the foods we crave and have come to expect at certain events or nostalgic outings, so we not only become addicted to these types of foods, we even have fond memories from eating them, making it harder to give them up.

The line between the brain and the gut is very thin, confirmed when Dr. Michael Greger writes in his book *How Not to Die*. *"The brain possesses a miraculous ability to heal itself, to forge new synaptic connections around old ones, to learn and relearn. That is, however, if you don't keep damaging it three times a day."*

Finding a better balance to living a healthy lifestyle that includes a healthy gut to prevent Dementia is a personal choice. Whether it is for you or your loved one, it is worth taking the time to make some adjustments now rather than when it is too late.

We do not wake up one day, and we are suddenly demented or suffer severe memory loss. Unless, of course, an accident of some kind like a car wreck that caused amnesia (sport-related collision or fall) or severe brain damage from a stroke.

Our heart and brain will not receive the benefits of all the types of foods as listed if our gut is sick with overly processed foods, high sugar content, trans-fat, and bad bacteria. We are programmed with marketing campaigns designed with subliminal messages to boost your interest in purchasing the product.

The ingredients in highly processed foods cause addictions that can lead to a leaky gut while breaking down your immune system, increasing bi-polar-like cycles, and accelerating aging. According to the Web MD article published by Matt McMillen, we recognize leaky guts through bloating, gas, cramps, aches, and pains.

Choosing a healthy lifestyle is a total shift in thought process and commitment to our overall well-being. Go beyond a weight loss program for a head-to-toe, physical and mental change overall.

I have met several young adults and even mature seniors who grip tight to the concept that we only live once, so we should enjoy life while we can. Their idea of enjoying life is what causes poor quality of life in the long run.

With this YOLO mentality (you only live once), you are shortening what life you have been blessed with and creating a burden for your loved ones with pending care needs.

I have also met others saying that if they knew they would live to 70 or 80, they would have taken better care of themselves. Reactive mindsets are useless because they bring about nothing but regret.

Each of us is unique in God's plan and purpose, yet still similar in so many ways. Having self-awareness of what we eat and how we think coupled with our free will can help us avoid living in a state of regret.

Chapter 15
How to Effectively Switch Roles

Philippians 4:13 (NIV)
I can do all this through him who gives me strength.

Most of my caregiving journey began trying to understand what Dementia is and how to proactively prevent this kind of demise. There is also an amazing transformational component when roles are switched. I did not recognize the roles switching between Mom and me in the beginning. I was still compartmentalizing life with the many emotions I was willing to deal with or those I was still avoiding.

For one, I did not want to acknowledge that Mom was not only getting older but was not the survivor persona she had been desperately trying to uphold since the divorce. Mom's anger was an amazing fuel for the kind of determination required to prove to others that she didn't need them when deep down she did. I was not ready to step into her world in the capacity she needed me. Plus, I still had not begun my transformation towards healing, so my anger and resentment dominated my thoughts most of the time.

Secondly, what I had perceived as one of my many strengths to multi-task, only added Mom to part of my lengthy To-Do list. Taking her to a doctor's appointment during my work lunch hour was my way of squeezing her needs into my busy day. Cooking meals for her during the weekdays, doing her laundry, or helping her shower were necessities I knew had to be done just as I cooked for my family, did our laundry throughout the week, and cleaned our house on the weekends.

I was checking off the boxes on a list and not stopping long enough to feel my way through the challenges. I was convinced that if I allowed myself time to feel, my clever ways of doing instead of being present would make me crumble.

Each caregiver will face a variety of areas that will demand emotional, mental, and physical challenges. The items listed below are areas you can expect to face and helped me as I faced them.

1) Let the Calendar be the "bad guy" or tool for reasoning.

I learned the proactive response to Mom's protests to shower days or doctor appointments needed to be *"Yes, and…"* responses to not only agree but redirect to allow the calendar to be the "bad guy." For example, *"Yes, you did take a shower yesterday, and now you need to shower before we go to the doctor's office. The calendar shows we're going to Dr. Smith today."*

I hung calendars throughout the house in her bedroom, bathrooms, and kitchen. Her bedroom calendar kept "shower" marked days after she showered to see visibly. She liked it since it was like receiving a gold star. A breakthrough was thinking like a teacher now to incentivize her on shower days without giving her extra sweets.

I eventually started using her bedroom calendar to keep all her doctor's appointments for her to see them. I added her weight on the days we checked it, days she had a BM, blood sugar count, and anything else I needed to track. The next time she started to bicker about taking a shower or drinking fluids, I would point out the day we were on and the last day she showered or the last day she had a BM. She had nothing more to say after seeing the calendar other than *"Okay, okay, okay!"* Small victory when she realized I was not tricking her all the time because the calendar did not lie.

I could not believe this was what our lives had become together. No matter how much I could organize onto the calendar for Mom to see, I needed to be released from being the bad guy or truth-teller. I had become the teacher, and she had become my student.

2) Create a consistent yet flexible daily routine.

Just as kids need structured environments to learn and grow in, our loved ones living with Dementia need a structured environment to retain the skills they have. Keep the daily routines consistent to help your loved one remain accustomed to what comes next. Having Mom shower before lunch helped with some nausea. It also helped avoid arguing after lunch since she usually wanted to nap on the couch once her belly was full. Showers eventually came after lunch, and before she could snuggle in the recliner, she became a bit more of a messy eater.

Announcing the day when you wake them and repeating the day's name throughout the morning helps establish the plans for the day and reinforce their muscle memory. For example, the morning greeting *"Good Wednesday Morning to you!"* Later during breakfast, reiterate the day and daily routine for this day. *"Well, since today is Wednesday, you will get to shower after breakfast. In the meantime, here are your Wednesday morning medications."*

3) Schedule regular monthly appointments with a therapist for yourself.

The benefits of therapy are endless and priceless during your time of switching roles into a caregiver. You are not only starting a new role but stepping into a new relationship. Your loved one has changed from the person you loved in the past or hated growing up for whatever reason. There are differences in each of you that must be acknowledged and understood as the roles switch.

My soul became more at rest as I continued therapy to address my resentment and anger with the family drama. Understanding who and what I was angry at helped reduce resentment. I also was able to communicate more effectively with Mom without letting my emotions cloud our time together. Deciding what was more important and what I needed to let go of or fight for was still a daily struggle. Still, having a therapist helped make more sense of this caregiving journey co-mingled with life in general, past, and present.

4) Set healthy boundaries and communicate them when possible.

I gradually understood I was enough for her to work on my self-doubt by replacing the doubts with more self-care. This kind of self-care starts by setting healthy boundaries and learning to communicate with Mom, who was my next challenge. In this way, self-care is about an expression of feelings in a healthy, positive way. Bottling up feelings, trying to correct your loved one, or losing your temper with them will only add more tension to a hectic situation.

One area of communication that created an uncomfortable elephant in the room was Mom's choice of chatter on a sexual level. These odd conversations about needing a man and what she wanted to do usually came upon shower days as I ran out of reasoning or bargaining options to get her into the shower. Learning how to redirect her train of thought was one side of the conversation. The rest was all in trying to understand where her mind was and then letting her know how I felt when she talked in such a vulgar way, especially in front of my husband and sons.

I had similar conversations when Mom chose to use name-calling as either a defensive response or an attempt to be funny. Since she lacked empathy and the ability to reason, she could not see calling me or any other caregiver a bitch, the 'N' word, or 'pain in the ass' in any language as rude and hurtful.

Mom called our youngest son what she thought were cute pet names, but they only pointed out physical characteristics he was already insecure about, which hurt too. All I could do for our son was explain Grandma's mental status and explain to Mom why it was unacceptable. Setting boundaries is not selfish. Unfortunately, the boundaries may need to be reset daily as short-term memory continues to fade.

5) Purchase a Dementia digital clock for their main room.

Aside from using a monthly calendar to be the bad guy, you can also purchase this clock from Amazon called SVINZ-Dementia-Auto-Dim-Calendar for roughly $47 US dollars. Even if your loved one has issues with short-term memory, the clock can still help them know what day of the week.

Mom's general doctor would ask her what day it was and then the date. Many times, Mom had no idea what day it was before we started using the calendar daily. Other times she would recall some date in February even though we were in late summer or fall.

Watching the news may help anchor them to a day and time of day, but the news also has the potential to upset or anger them. This reaction is especially difficult if they are dealing with a later stage, including separation from reality.

Meaning they may watch the news and create a new narrative in their life with it or tell a story about their past that sounds a lot like what they watched on tv. It is more helpful to have this clock in their living room or bedroom to see it early enough in the day or throughout the day as a gentle reminder.

6) Learn about who they were before their changes began, as far back as possible.

As your loved one continues to go through their changes, who they were before Dementia began intensifies as the progression continues. If they were joyful, they most likely would remain that way but become a bit more withdrawn, quiet, not as happy, or full of smiles.

If they were mean or temperamental before their changes, they might become more so. Check-in with their siblings or family members to share stories to help provide insight into who they were back in their glory days. That is if it does not cause any family drama or bring about more stress.

If this is not possible, chat with them about their favorite moments growing up or the toughest challenges as an adult. These kinds of conversations should unlock many memories with or without a photo album. Their story may not be the real story, but it is real to them.

As I began to ask Mom about her childhood through to the early years of her career, I not only began to see a new person but also could understand to whom she was reverting. This understanding helped me to decipher the type of care tailored to her preferences in food, clothes, music, games, and, more importantly, the types and gender of doctors treating her along with any outside caregivers.

7) Learn to be comfortable during times of silence.

Mom raised us with the rule that you did not have anything nice to say, then do not say anything at all. I knew this was to teach us to bicker less or nicer towards each other growing up. Unfortunately, as adults, it is sometimes difficult to determine whether Mom was silent because she did not have anything nice to say to me or struggled with maintaining a conversation.

I continued to keep the small talk going beyond the typical yes or no questions and answers. If Mom became frustrated with my inquiries to begin the small talk, it indicated something else needed closer observation. I eventually asked her if she would prefer not to have any small talk which she replied with a nod – yes.

Mom has also become a quiet passenger in the car. Each trip to the doctor's or grocery store was no longer considered hanging out or catching up. The car rides were more of her staring out of the car window while I focused on the road. Any attempts to get a conversation going ended with her head nods or shoulder shrugs. If I were lucky, a familiar song would play on the radio, which triggered a memory or pleasant response for her to sing along. I remained silent to enjoy hearing her voice and watch her have a pleasant moment.

I realized I might multitask by driving, talking, navigating, and changing radio stations. Still, Mom was privately reminiscing or silently panicking because she could not remember where we were going and why. If your loved one is not in danger or pain, then attempt to be in the moment silently with them.

8) Find your balance (center) before you spend time with them.

Whether they live with you or not, always try to check your workday stresses at the door. You do not need to be easily shaken by abnormal aging behavior. Whether you work outside the home or are a home engineer, you will still have to take a couple of deep breaths while reminding yourself who you are about to interact with, especially if you are picking them up to rush off to an appointment.

If they live with you, then find recess time during the day where you can take a breather or be able to walk away if emotions get too high. Never underestimate the power of breathing techniques. There is a reason it is part of Lamaze classes! Men need to breathe through emotional pain just as much as women do. Find privacy in your home, car, or backyard so you can have those cleansing breaths before stepping back into the room with your loved one.

9) Don't always expect the truth or honest answers.

It can be very frustrating when you have a teenager stretching the truth or flat out lying to you to avoid consequences. When your grown adult parent lies, it is even more frustrating. However, it is more like a white lie because they often believe what they tell you, even if you know the difference. Mom eventually could not make sense of a lie to get what she wanted, which usually was dessert for breakfast or lunch and not brushing her teeth.

For example, Mom would often feed her dog table scraps even though I repeatedly asked her not to because it would give him diarrhea or make him vomit, aside from teaching him bad begging habits. I watched her do it, and she would still adamantly state she did not do it.

It was annoying trying to explain how I knew she fed the dog scraps because I watched her put the food down or found the food on the floor next to her chair. It becomes a stalemate argument of *"Yes you did"* then *"No, I didn't."* The dog was no longer allowed in the kitchen while she ate. She eventually would admit she was full and did not want anymore. Rather than tell me she was full, she was giving her leftovers to the dog because, as a child, she was not allowed to waste food.

I keep pictures of her near my workspace at home to remind me of the woman I knew and loved as a mother rather than allowing myself to get excessively flustered with childish tantrums and the strange child she is becoming.

10) Always remember to be kind with your words, touch, and intentions.

When my first son was a baby, I was advised to place the baby in his crib or playpen whenever I felt my jaw clench from frustrations. I naively said I would never hurt him and believed this was advice I would never use. Until the moment occurred when I was exhausted and needed him to sleep. When I felt my jaw clench, this advice repeated in my mind. I placed him in his crib and stepped away for a moment to take a few deep breaths.

I often experience moments with Mom that left me frustrated because of her bipolar tendencies and anosognosia. During the week, I tried to convince her why she needed a shower, explain the seriousness of diabetes, attempted to work with her on a computer to enhance cognitive skills or keep existing skills sharp. I began to speak through a clenched jaw which revealed my annoyance, lack of compassion, and loss of respect.

A simple touch can make anyone feel uncomfortable but can specifically make a loved one with PTSD and Dementia feel threatened or place them in a fight or flight response. A pat on the arm may be intended to be comforting but may not be welcomed in their mind.

We may have to resort to bribery to encourage them to do things independently, creating delicate boundaries or new bad habits. For example, I intend to encourage Mom to exercise more by providing an incentive like a small scoop of ice cream as a reward for reaching a daily goal. Sometimes it worked, and other times she declined to avoid having to get up from the couch.

11) Don't take it personally.

Try to put yourself in their shoes. When I was frustrated or angry with Mom, I kept asking - *"Why couldn't she take better care of herself?"*

Dementia presents all sorts of reasons why, yet the feelings vary. I struggled to care about Mom's needs in my angry mindset, but later, when I considered what it must feel like to lose abilities, I could imagine the lack of independence and isolation. I realized I could not take her frustrated responses personally. Whether she understood what she was saying or not, her words had to roll off my back in an impersonal manner so I wouldn't get rattled.

Yet another adage I learned from Mom growing up - *"Say what you mean and mean what you say."* At the beginning of our journey, I took that to heart because often, the truth comes out in moments of anger. As Mom transitioned through the stages, this old saying no longer fit her moods and behaviors. I figured out what emotions she meant to express when her actions and words were lost in translation.

12) Make time to meditate.

What you choose to focus on is your choice. Being able to continue to do so without getting sick or finding yourself in a downward depressive spiral makes finding time to meditate a necessity.

I started meditating outdoors to clear my mind from the daily distractions. This time was difficult at first to calm my mind because I focused actively on situations with Mom. Eventually, I learned to read scripture as part of my meditation time. I was letting the Holy Spirit in to help me refocus on letting go. I asked for guidance. I asked the Holy Spirit to melt me, mold me, fill me, use me and work through me.

For Example, Psalm 23 (NLT)

^{1The} *Lord is my Shepherd; I have all that I need.*

^{2He} *lets me rest in green meadows; he leads me beside peaceful streams,*

^{3}*He renews my strength. He guides me along right paths, bringing honor to his name.*

^{4}*Even when I walk through the darkest valley, I will not be afraid, for you are close beside me; your rod and your staff protect and comfort me.*

^{5}*You prepare a feast for me in the presence of my enemies. You honor me by anointing my head with oil; my cup overflows with blessings.*

^{6}*Surely your goodness and unfailing love will pursue me all the days of my life, And I will live in the house of the Lord forever.*

13) Make a list of pros and cons regarding your current mental and physical state.

Be proactive instead of reactive. Taking better care of ourselves to avoid becoming a burden to our loved ones is the first step in being honest. I refuse to get tested to see if I carry any genes for any form of Dementia. I know better now. No test will change the fact that I need to take care of the body and mind I have been blessed with. Having my own base line could be helpful in years to come.

14) Pray.

Even after we do as much as we possibly can, it still falls into God's hands in the end. When my questions run out of answers and I struggle to find a way, I pray for guidance and strength. I repeatedly learned to pray before moments of helplessness brought me to my knees. Giving thanks or gratitude prayers for the good days became a daily practice as I prepared for bed. The bad days usually brought about an important lesson, so I learned to give thanks for those days as well.

15) For siblings, keep in mind, not all roles will switch.

As my resentment grew with Mom, it also grew between my siblings. Neither of us wanted to do what needed to be done. Either way, we did what we could and criticized the others in the process. I started to recognize what Mom could do or when she was manipulating us to get what she wanted.

For example, Mom wanted ChocoVine wine, and I told her she could not have it because of her medication. Instead of taking no for an answer, Mom asked Little Sis to take her to the grocery store another day so that she could buy it herself. When I found the wine in the refrigerator days later, I poured it down the drain and got rid of the bottle without asking where it came from or why she disregarded my reasoning about her meds not mixing with alcohol.

So, you can imagine the flare-ups between us, both Mom and I, then later between Little Sis and me once they figured out the wine was gone.

I started to feel like a parent to both of them. The more little things like the wine happened, the angrier I became as it became a battle of our egos.

16) Pets need care and attention too!

Many people have live pets and not just imaginary or life-like robotic stuffed dogs or cats. They are great companions, but if your loved one is dealing with memory loss, you cannot assume they can remember basic care for their pets.

Mom's Schnauzer was her mighty protector in the house, but she began to neglect him as much as she neglected her own needs. I lost sight of his needs because Mom would say she was doing it all in between my brief check-ins. I foolishly believed her.

I guess deep down, I wanted it to be true, so it was not only proof she was still capable of living on her own, but it would be one less chore on the mental daily task list. Sadly, if I did not see her with my own eyes, I could not trust her words.

This gut reaction was validated one winter holiday break. Big Sis stopped in to groom her pup and save Mom some money. By the time she was done grooming the dog, she had called me to explain. Mom had not been feeding him as we thought. A couple of months before this grooming, the dog was roughly 15 pounds but dropped to 9 pounds on his last checkup. His little body was proof to see he was starving and eating whatever scraps he could get from her. The reality of it did not seem to faze her other than saying, *"Oh poor baby!"*

His dog food in the pantry was gone, and the water in his bowl was dirty or slimy. He then sat on the top of the couch like a cat waiting for scraps. Mom's mighty protector was hangry and tried to bite your face if you attempted to lean in to hug or kiss her. Pets can get hangry too!

17) Remember, you're not intended to go on this journey alone!

As I began to come to my wit's end before Mom moved in with us, I read an email from a woman in our neighborhood offering her services as a caregiver. My prayers were answered! But first, I had to convince Mom this could work for her to keep her in her own home longer. When I casually mentioned it to Mom, she shut me down right away – *"No, I don't want any strangers in my house!"*

For the sake of conversation, I will call our neighborhood friend Hope. I called Hope and invited her over to our house first for an interview. She answered my prayers alright and arrived with a plan to proceed with Mom's care. I was so nervous this would not go over well with Mom, so I decided on telling Mom a bit of a compassionate deception out of desperation.

I arranged a time for Mom to meet my new friend, Hope, who happened to be her age. Hope, also divorced, wanted to find a friend to hang out with that lived in our area. All true, of course, except for the fact that I was going to be paying Hope. Mom needed a new companion to help around the house part-time. I needed the respite time.

Mom met Hope and was a bit put off by her at first. She rolled her eyes each time Hope kept trying to talk with her, asking so many questions while opening the window blinds and tidying around the house. Hope was great! Well, to me.

Then Hope started to talk about her ex-husband, and Mom fell right into step with the ex-husband gossip. *"He said this or that, He did or didn't do this or that, He always did this, and he never did that"* It was like girlfriends catching up again. Before too long, Mom began to enjoy Hope's company and invited her to family holiday dinners.

Thanks to Hope, Mom exercised regularly with fresh air from the outdoors and helped Hope clean in the house on other days. This exercise over the next year became so beneficial for Mom; her A1C lowered to the point of stopping a diabetic medication. Mom's spirits were lifted. I was relieved.

18) Learn the power of "Yes, and..." statements to keep from getting discouraged.

Learning how to make suggestions rather than telling Mom what to do was how I started to ease into parenting her. This kind of parenting was very similar to raising my sons when they were little yet complex enough because I had to identify her boundaries.

Respecting her needs over what she wanted was a definite learning curve when it came to figuring out the gentle *"not right now"* response instead of a firm *"No."* Of course, throwing in a couple of *"Yes, and..."* responses as well to her resistance helped too.

I did not want to fight with her throughout the day for every little thing. I hated my parent's response of *"because I said so"* when I was growing up. It was so dismissive and hurtful. Even if I became frustrated enough to dismiss Mom, it did not go well. I was quickly reminded that SHE was the matriarch of the family, even if it was time to help her highness into her mickey mouse pajamas for the night.

Mom asked me one day, *"Haven't I earned the right just to sit here if I wanted to?"* Very true, she worked very hard and is now in retirement as she understood it. Instead of traveling the world during her retirement or engaging in activities socially, she wanted to remain put on the couch. So, in response, I said, *"Yes, you have earned the right, and I know you would feel so much better on the couch after a warm shower with clean pajamas."*

Sometimes it worked with a surprising *" You're right, okay"* response Other times she would give me the middle finger as she said in Spanish, *"¡Chingada Madre!"* or *"Shit!"* and *"No seas maricón"* or *"Don't be an asshole!"*

The more my communication improved with her, the more I connected the dot to a very important lesson – **This is not about ME**. It is not about the easiest or fastest way to deal with or avoid her for my convenience. I was learning the skills of compassion. God used our journey to free me from my past in a gentle, compassionate, grace-filled way.

What worked one month, week, or day may no longer work the next day. Like so many other breakthroughs with her, suggestions eventually left too much open for interpretation. I kept telling myself it was her choice and her right to choose. At some point, things change enough that you must make the decisions for them yet present them nicely or creatively.

19) Be aware - God uses everything to teach and help us grow.

Rather than becoming frustrated with Mom's present behavior, I had to mentally step aside to ask myself, *"what am I supposed to be learning from this moment?"* I had to create a safe environment for her health and wellbeing. I needed her cooperation which did not come easy most of the time, as her daughter was telling her what to do.

Even if she was still trying to be the survivor she once was, her body was beginning to fail her. Understanding this helped me find a different mindset to approach the day with a plan and a *"can do"* attitude. Many days, I would say, *"I can't do this."* The panic would fill my chest immediately for not only the moment I was reluctant to move forward but for the future of what was yet to come.

From the outside, looking into Mom's world, all I could see was disorder and darkness. Most of my frustrations, later, came from the instinct to fight for life. Only this was me trying to convince her demented mind to fight for her own life. Knowing she had a DNR on file with all her doctors for end-of-life wishes did not change living in the moment for me. Not every day included a major medical procedure or potential for an end-of-life situation, but there was an element of letting go of her each day.

Being at peace with her wishes yet continuing to live for her made me see God was not done teaching me through her just yet.

20) Forgive yourself.

I have already stated this, but this requires a repeat: caring for someone other than yourself is emotionally and physically exhausting. No one expects you to be perfect because there are no perfect situations when caring for your loved one. It is a messy, frustrating, thankless opportunity. You are a normal human being to feel upset, angry, impatient, resentful, ungrateful, unappreciated, annoyed, unkind, or anything else, which falls into this pity party.

However, it is not normal to act on those emotions by taking anything out on your loved one verbally or otherwise. So, if you have not started yet, begin meditation daily to forgive yourself for being normal (review step #6 again).

As I learned more about Mom's health and the pending journey, I beat myself up for not doing more or being there sooner. We do better when we know better. Where there is a will, there is a way. When their will has broken, a caregiver is born. Forgive the past and have faith in yourself. You were chosen for a reason.

Chapter 16
Caregiver Compliance: Legal Documents, Trusts, Probate, & Estates

Acts 19:39 (NIV)
If there is anything further you want to bring up, it must be settled in a legal assembly.

Five Legal Documents Caregivers Must Have Created

I assumed I had plenty of time to pursue topics of Estate Planning. I naively thought I could forego the advice and pick that back up years later when Mom would need it. The problem with waiting is the progression of the stages may rob your loved one of cognitive skills. The proactive approach is to begin having conversations with your loved one as soon as possible. You never know what could happen, from basic medical procedures to short-term progression to random accidents.

FTD and early-onset Alzheimer's tend to be more aggressive, so time is extremely important to consider. You will want to get their affairs in order while still mindful of their information with passwords to accounts. For example, bank accounts, investment accounts, bills paid online, and even social media accounts, to name a few. You will need to understand what they want for the future of their estate and of their death. You will even need to know who they would want to care for them.

Suppose you need to consider sibling rivalry, divorce, and blended families. In that case, these documents will eliminate most of the potential drama created with the difference of opinions or connections to birthrights. Designees for these forms do not always fall to firstborn.

Below are the five main documents of estate planning you must have to establish your legal rights to be their caregiver to manage their estate and well-being.

1. Statutory Durable Power of Attorney (DPOA) – Written document in which one person, known as the principal (your loved one), designates another person, known as the agent or attorney-in-fact (you as the caregiver), the authority to act on their behalf.

The difference between a POA and Statutory Durable POA means the Durable POA remains valid and in effect even if your loved one becomes incapacitated and unable to make decisions for themselves. If the document is not a Durable POA, then the power to manage their Estate ends if they become incapacitated. A POA may be of use for a specific event instead of being all-inclusive like the SDPOA.

Some people misunderstand the difference between a DPOA and a living will, which does not provide the same caregiver right. A living will delineate your loved ones' wishes specifically in terms of property. In contrast, a DPOA allows you the right as the caregiver to make decisions for them regarding their property or business transactions during their lifetime as needed.

---

2. Declaration of Guardian - In the Event of Later Incapacity – Estate code Title 3, Subtitle D, Chapter 1104, Subchapter A explains only one person may be appointed as guardian of the person or estate.

One person may be appointed guardian of the person, and another person may be appointed the guardian of the estate if it is in the best interest of the incapacitated person or ward. It does not prohibit the joint appointment if the court finds it in the best interest of the incapacitated person or ward (i.e., Husband and wife or both parents of an adult who is incapacitated).

Your loved one may designate you as the caregiver to be their legal guardian in the event of later incapacity to avoid having to go through a court-appointed process later down the road.

3. HIPAA Authorization – According to HHS.gov, the HIPAA (Health Insurance Portability and Accountability Act) privacy rule and sharing information related to Mental Health provides consumers with important privacy rights and protections concerning their health information. Including important controls over how health information is used and disclosed by health plans and health care providers.

This document will allow you to make appointments, inquire, and receive health information regarding your loved ones' care with physicians to ensure they receive the best treatment. You will be able to provide the doctors with as much information as possible to aid them in decisions regarding their care plan, but they will not be able to share test results or care plans with you without this form on record.

Many doctor's offices have their release form you can sign, but it is specific to their office and cares only. To have overall access, it is more beneficial to have this form signed, enabling you to provide it to each doctor's office (i.e., General M.D., Cardiologist, Neurologist, ENT, any other specialists) and hospital as needed.

4. Advance Directive to Physicians – This is a document by which a person makes provisions for health care decisions if they become unable to make those decisions themselves. This directive would alert the physician when your loved one can no longer verbalize their decision to fight for life or do not resuscitate (DNR).

Your loved one may have a predisposed position to do everything medically necessary to keep them alive, including resuscitation with subsequent life support measures or not to proceed with the hospital protocol to save a life and allow them to pass. If your loved one signs this while still coherent enough to do so, it removes the burden from you to make this choice later down the road.

Emergency responders will follow through with protocol to save a life in a tragic episode where you are not present. Assuming they were saved, the doctors will ask if they have an advance directive signed upon arriving at the hospital. It will be your moral and legal duty to provide the sworn statement for them to maintain life support or begin comfort care should they continue to decline.

5. Medical Power of Attorney (MPOA) – This is another form of the POA to designate you as the caregiver to speak for your loved one on health care matters and enables you to make financial decisions related specifically to health care services.

These documents not only provide you with legal rights as a caregiver, in my experience, they have also aided me in solving family disputes on who can make decisions based on my mother's best interest and who cannot. These documents carry a high level of fiduciary responsibility and require the utmost level of integrity to protect your loved one's physical, mental, and financial means.

Caring for your loved ones is physically exhausting, but the emotional stress from unresolved disputes will worsen matters. When the family begins to engage in disputes over who will care, when they care, how they care, or who has financial responsibility for the care, it quickly becomes legal matters for an attorney or even the courts to decide.

Deciding between Revocable Trusts (also known as a Living Trust) or Irrevocable Trust

As care for your loved one becomes more expensive, then qualifying for Medicaid is yet another frustrating process to go through for legal and tax implications. Medicaid planning often includes the selection of a trust.

Revocable Trust

A revocable living trust, also known as a revocable trust or inter-vivo trust, is simply a type of trust that can be changed at any time. In other words, if the Principal (your loved one) has second thoughts about a provision in the trust or changes their mind about who should be a beneficiary or trustee of the trust, you can modify the terms of the trust through what is called a trust amendment fairly easily.

Likewise, if you decide that you do not like something about the trust, you can either revoke the entire agreement or change the entire contents through a trust amendment and restatement.

A revocable trust is still considered your assets for a creditor and estate tax purposes. Therefore, a revocable trust offers no creditor protection if you are sued. All the trust assets will be considered yours for Medicaid planning purposes.

All assets held in the name of the trust at their death will be subject to state estate, federal estate taxes, and state inheritance taxes. Either way, assets held in the name of a Revocable Living Trust when a person becomes mentally incapacitated can be managed by their disability trustee instead of a court-supervised guardian or conservator.

Assets held in the name of a Revocable Living Trust at the time of a person's death will pass directly to the beneficiaries named in the trust agreement and outside of the probate process. To protect the privacy of your property and beneficiaries after you die, this type of trust will aid you by avoiding probate, which keeps the trust agreement as a private document instead of becoming a public record for the entire world to see and read. To protect the details about your assets and who you have decided to leave your estate will remain a private family matter.

Irrevocable Trust

An irrevocable trust is simply a type of trust that cannot be changed after the agreement has been signed. It is also a revocable trust that becomes irrevocable after the Principal (your loved one) dies or after some other specific point in time. Irrevocable trusts may remain intact for up to 21 years after the principal's death but must be liquidated and closed after that time.

Irrevocable trusts, such as irrevocable life insurance trusts, are commonly used to remove property value from a person's estate so that the property cannot be taxed when the person dies. In other words, the person who transfers assets into an irrevocable trust is giving over those assets to the trustee and beneficiaries of the trust so that the person no longer owns the assets. Thus, if the person no longer owns the assets, they cannot be taxed when they later die.

Another common use for an irrevocable trust is to provide asset protection for the Principal and the Principal's family. In the same way that a revocable trust can be used to reduce estate taxes by placing assets into an irrevocable trust, the Principal is giving up complete control over and access to the trust assets.

Therefore, the trust assets cannot be reached by a creditor of the

Principal or be registered as an available resource for Medicaid planning. The Principal's family can still be the beneficiaries of the irrevocable trust which still provides the family with financial support but outside of the reach of creditors.

There are also irrevocable trusts called self-settled trusts or domestic asset protection trusts. Some states, including Alaska, Delaware, Nevada, and Tennessee, offer creditor protection and allow the Principal to be a trust beneficiary.

Depending on your situation and type of assets, it would be best to discuss the options with an Elder Law attorney proficient in these types of trusts to aid you in your decision.

In the event of an untimely demise of a designated DPOA, the power would pass to the first alternate DPOA designated. By having only one DPOA, decisions can be made timelier and help alleviate issues caused by sibling rivalry, which can accelerate beyond reconciliation. At the same time, your loved one waits for care, or their business matters are not attended to while you wait for reconciliation appropriately.

You might expect this when families live scattered out of state and cannot often visit to see the condition of their loved ones. Or the family drama that existed long before your loved one's progression of Dementia began may require more empathy than all involved are willing to give.

If they can still stand to be in the same room or talk to each other online, then all siblings can still meet and discuss changes or details of care provided to your loved one. Should disagreements arise, then the single DPOA can make the necessary decisions for your loved one without them suffering from lack of care while the siblings struggle to find common ground or agree to disagree in the least.

We struggled in our family for a couple of years to make sure everyone was involved and doing their "fair" share of caring, but it came down to logistics and a considerate level of understanding. Once these documents were in place, I no longer had to choose to please everyone because I now had a legal obligation to be a fiduciary of her trust. It required me to act in the best interest of my mother's financial assets as well as her wellbeing.

The legal documents did not resolve disagreements or stop any name-calling or selfish behavior. Many of the decisions for your loved one may require a great deal of research to make logical or best-case scenario conclusions. These types of decisions made me feel guilty because the outcomes were based on more than opinion.

I eventually stopped trying to be an understanding sister and embraced the Caregiver Compliance documents' full rights. I was warned that our situations could become emotionally charged within the family, but I never expected it to happen. I thought we would be able to stay above that kind of fighting, but sometimes caregiving brings out the worst in us.

Sticks and stones, you know, the elementary school rhyme we're taught to stand up to bullies. *"Sticks and Stones may break my bones, but your words will never hurt me."* We had our moments of exchanging words that felt like stones against my heart. Ironically, keeping the peace and our family out of the courts meant I had to make a stand and throw stones too.

If decisions are made early on, then the burden is removed along with the fear. The documents are filed away in a safe place until the time they are needed. Now you can continue to live and be the best caregiver to honor your parent(s) or spouse till death do you part.

Additional documents to gather and set aside for your loved one's estate would be:

- Wills
- Bank and brokerage accounts
- Deeds, mortgage papers, or ownership statements
- Pension and other retirement benefit summaries
- Social Security payment information (establish online accounts)
- Stock and Bond Certificates
- Monthly or outstanding bills (Credit Card statements, reoccurring bills, collection, or lien status)
- Insurance policies (particularly any Long-term Insurance policies as covered in Chapter 5 Protect Your Future with the Caregiver's Trinity)
- Your loved one's birth certificate with their parent's birth and death certificates.
- Military discharge papers
- Any business ownership documentation (Registration with IRS, Tax records, Financial status, Asset listings) for the continuation of business or liquidation plans.
-

Probate Process

Probate is the court-supervised process of gathering a deceased person's assets and distributing them to creditors and inheritors. As an executor, your probate process will depend on whether your state has adopted the Uniform Probate Code (UPC), a set of probate laws written by a group of national experts.

The UPC's goal is to make the probate process simpler, especially for small estates, and to give executors more flexibility in how they proceed. Although the law is very similar in the states that have adopted the entire UPC for probate, it isn't identical. You'll need to learn your own state's (and sometimes your own county's) particular rules. Under the UPC, there are three kinds of probate: informal, unsupervised formal, and supervised formal.

States that have adopted the UPC (as of this print):
Alaska, Arizona, Colorado, Florida, Hawaii, Idaho, Maine, Massachusetts, Michigan, Minnesota, Montana, Nebraska, New Jersey, New Mexico, North Dakota, South Carolina, South Dakota, Utah

States that have not adopted the UPC:
Alabama, Arkansas, California, Connecticut, Delaware, District of Columbia, Georgia, Illinois, Indiana, Iowa, Kansas, Kentucky, Louisiana, Maryland, Mississippi, Missouri, Nevada, New Hampshire, New York, North Carolina, Ohio, Oklahoma, Oregon, Pennsylvania, Rhode Island, Tennessee, Texas*, Vermont, Virginia, Washington, West Virginia, Wisconsin*, Wyoming.

*Texas and Wisconsin have an informal probate proceeding similar to that used in UPC states.

Informal Probate – This relatively simple process is used when inheritors get along, and you don't expect problems with creditors. If anyone wants to contest the proceeding, you cannot use informal probate. The whole process is just paperwork -- there are no court hearings.

After distributing the property, you can close the estate informally by preparing and filing a "final accounting" with the court. Finally, you will file a "closing statement," stating that you have paid all debts and taxes, distributed the property, and submitted the final accounting.

Unsupervised Formal Probate- Unsupervised formal probate in UPC states is a traditional court proceeding. It is generally used when there is a good reason to involve the court. For example, suppose there's a disagreement over the distribution of the estate's assets. In that case, the heirs need to be determined (if there is no valid will), or minors inherit significant property.

You may need to get the court's permission before you sell the deceased person's real estate, distribute property to beneficiaries, or pay a lawyer or yourself for work done on behalf of the estate. To close the estate, file an accounting that shows how you handled the estate's assets.

Supervised Formal Probate - Supervised formal probate is the rarest form of probate. It's used only if the court finds it necessary to supervise the probate procedure. For example, a beneficiary can't adequately look after their interests and needs the court's protection. As you might expect, you must get court approval before distributing any property in this case.

Administering the Estate

As executor, you're in charge of keeping estate property safe during the probate process. You or an attorney will need to prepare a list of the deceased person's assets and, if necessary, get assets appraised. You'll need to:

- Get an employer identification number for the estate from the IRS.
- Notify the state health or welfare department of the death, if required by state law.
- Open an estate bank account.
- Arrange for the preparation of income tax returns.
- Prepare and file an inventory and appraisal of estate assets.
- Mail a notice to creditors and pay debts (state law may impose a deadline on you).
- If the court requires it, file a list of creditors' claims you have approved and denied.
- If required, file a *federal* estate tax return within nine months after death. (Most estates are not large enough to owe federal estate tax).
- If required, file a *state* estate tax return, usually within nine months after death. (Fewer than half the states impose their tax.)

Closing the Estate

When the creditor's claim period has passed, make sure you have paid debts and filed all necessary tax returns. After any disputes are settled, then you are ready to distribute all remaining property to the beneficiaries.

You'll need to:

- Mail a notice to heirs and beneficiaries that the final hearing is coming up. (This must be done in a certain period before the hearing; the court will have a rule.)
- File proof that you mailed the notice as required.
- Get the court's permission to distribute property.
- Transfer assets to the new owners and get receipts.
- After distributing assets and concluding all matters, file receipts and ask the court to release you from your duties.

From beginning to the end of becoming a caregiver to finalizing your loved one's estate, you may sometimes feel stuck on a Ferris wheel with limited views. Your work may go unrecognized and often scrutinized, but it is valuable nonetheless. Your support group of caregivers knows what you have endured and what you have survived.

Chapter 17
Chasing Validation

1 Corinthians 12:6 (NIV)
There are different kinds of working, but in all of them and in everyone it is the same God at work.

Finding Support Along the Way

Along my caregiving journey, I continued to utilize the benefits of support groups and started my own. The distance created by all the fighting with my sisters left me desperately seeking validation. Having medical referees, in the beginning, was helpful. However, many other areas created doubt, which created the constant need to know if I made the right choices and feared consequences.

Unresolved childhood trauma clouded my ability to become an objective caregiver until therapists helped me see I had a repetitive script in my mind that needed to be broken or replaced with a more positive one. Convincing myself, I was doing what needed to be done for Mom to meet her needs and protect her from others made me search for a new family or surrogate sisters in the support groups.

I was raised with both concepts that family comes first no matter what, and blood is always thicker than water. The problem with these concepts is they created a very toxic relationship to provide care within. The irony is that we did not always live by these concepts, which is why Mom's Dementia went unacknowledged for so long.

If I had a conversation with a total stranger and we came to a difference of opinions, I could graciously agree to disagree out of respect for their opinion. Within the family, this approach was impossible. My caregiving journey has turned into an internal emotional cleansing I would not have considered before. Why? Because of the tough decisions, I wanted to make them as a family and not on my own. For various reasons, I grew to be someone who unknowingly fell prey to needing validation.

Growing up with Mom and Dad, I wanted their love and appreciation that was not tied to getting chores done or making straight A's. They did not accomplish as much as they wanted growing up themselves, yet somehow their expectations of us were extremely high. This need for validation that I am a good employee, wife, mother, friend, sister, and daughter manifested unhealthy and toxic relationships personally and professionally.

No matter the situation or the fact that I am the Power of Attorney and Medical Power of Attorney for Mom's care and well-being, I continually needed validation and appreciation from my sisters. I needed them to know that I was doing what was best for Mom, even when it came time to make the hard decision to transition her to a memory care community.

Instead, our difference of opinion became a source of heartbreak time and time again. If my sisters would not agree with me, then somehow, I felt I was in the wrong or made a mistake even though I knew from countless others it was the right or best choice to make at the moment.

Attending more support groups helped me find this coveted validation. I found a new tribe in support groups which included surrogate brothers and sisters with mutual appreciation and understanding. They were able to see me, and I could see them as well. Seeing into a person's soul creates a bond just as strong as any family.

This journey is filled with many ups and downs, left and right turns, but the emotional roller coaster mixed with continual mourning without a supportive family makes it even more difficult. The isolation and situational depression grew as I felt more disconnected from family, knowing I would never be given their validation.

Once again, learning to let go of who/what no longer served me added to my transformational process. Allowing those into my life to bring about joy and harmony took practice living by faith and trust.

The items listed below helped me stop searching for validation and actively live by faith and trust in God's plans.

1) Journaling

It is a therapeutic form of expression to vent, create goals, document transitions, or be honest with yourself when it is too hard to be openly honest with others. If, at the moment, you feel like life sucks, then write it down! *"Life sucks! - this too shall pass."*

I gradually challenged myself to write more and find a bright side or alternative thought to reprogram my mind through this exercise. When there was no bright alternative side, then I chose the gratitude prayer. When my inner wounded child needed a pity party, I wrote about that too. Just as I started to see new and different sides to Mom, through writing, I began to see new and different sides within me as well.

You are now a student in the school of hard knocks. Rather than write on the board - *"I will not..."* whatever you feel called on the carpet for, then write the Serenity prayer. Write this every day until it sinks into the depths of your being.

God grant me the Serenity to accept the things I cannot change; Courage to change the things I can, and the wisdom to know the difference.

2) Art Therapy

Find time to rescue your inner child and create with an innocent mind once again. This journey can become too serious for me at times as I watched Mom transition towards the next stage, getting closer to her end of the journey. Indulging in art therapy helps to relieve stress and anxiety by tapping into our creative side. Give the logical left brain side a break to allow the creative right brain to flow more freely.

Taking time to get messy with paints on a canvas, porcelain or wood, or walls in the house helped the emotional pain transition onto the canvas or item and out of me. The smells of the paint, texture, and colors created quite a mood changer, especially if I could get Mom to join me in making a mess. When I felt stuck in my ability to help Mom or lost my confidence after family drama, finding another creative outlet was as beneficial as a nature walk.

3) Comedic Tension Relief

It is important to watch more comedy or attend a comedy club to laugh aloud now and then. Not only is it good for your lungs, but it can also be food for your soul as well! You are the hero on a very unpredictable journey. The more you can smile and laugh your way along the journey, the better your heart, mind, and soul will be. You may even hear a funny story that resembles your serious situation and gain a funny way to look at or appreciate your situation in the least.

4) Volunteer for a relatable cause

Many caregivers might think they don't have the time to volunteer because of their responsibilities to their loved ones. Some of you may even think I already do this at home for my parents or spouse; why in the world would I do it some more for others?!

Well, this kind of volunteering not only provides a distraction from your world of caregiving, but it also provides a network of new friends, connections to services, and a new perspective overall. This perspective made my journey seem less traumatic or shed light on the purpose-driven life I was learning to lead.

Several programs or workshops need extra hands. I was able to meet so many wonderful individuals who had already gone through to the end of their loved one's journey. Others were in different stages than I was with Mom. Volunteering became a wonderful sanity check knowing so many others had experienced very similar moments. Hearing their hero's journey validated my own and even prepared me for steps ahead on my caregiving journey.

We are stronger together.

5) Find a local support group

Having a network of family and friends who support you and show they are with you no matter what is vital because they will quickly become your rock of salvation. You are given an opportunity to meet the ones who know exactly how it feels as they lend their shoulder to cry on. The ones that understand when you say through tears, *"I just want this to be over with already."* And they get it 100%. A sentiment that comes from a place of emotional and physical exhaustion, not selfishness or cruelty, is truly understood by those who attend support groups. Sometimes understood more so than family.

Each person comes from a different background story but experiences similar responses. Those moments that gave rise to your frustration or the event that left you with feelings of helplessness or hopelessness are all part of the journey. The reactions to those moments are normal, and yet it is common for caregivers to experience guilt.

Family can be supportive to an extent, but sometimes family might be too busy trying to be strong for others or buried in their mind of obligation, which keeps them from being as supportive. Having a soundboard with the group to express many feelings gave me a safe and confidential outlet. It also gave me sound advice to take back home and put into practice with Mom.

6) Big picture - Little picture - Change in perspective

One afternoon I sat outside to meditate under my meditation tree. As I watched the clouds passing overhead, I could see the shape of a man lying down, looking up at the stars with his arms crossed over his chest. At that moment, I realized as I stared up looking for peace, the Lord also looked around the universe for peace as well. It's the difference in perspective.

As caregivers get through the day-to-day routines, our perspective can narrow. We begin to lose sight of the bigger picture and let small moments of frustration or hopelessness become our focus. Thankfully, my new programming reminds me that my perspective can be small compared to the broad perspective God attempts to show. We are presented with the big picture and the little picture. The difference is between the moment when our minds and hearts shift focus and we slip into survival mode day to day.

Life lessons are to teach us to expand and grow while broadening our perspectives. Sometimes those lessons are painful to endure, so it may be hard to extract the actual lesson at the moment. Real-life experiences with Mom were real trial and error lessons. Most led to knowing better ways, and some led to moments of forgiveness.

7) Each day is a new day.

Each day is a new day. Each day is a new opportunity to learn and grow together. Each day is a blessing, even when some days feel like a curse. The frustrations of yesterday are done and over. Try your best not to bring the recent past into your present. When I felt I had made a mistake initially, I dwelled on it far too much, which only discouraged me from going forward. Later, I let myself off the hook of perfection and acknowledged the moments as lessons learned rather than mistakes.

Each new day brings about new opportunities to try something different, like experimenting as a cook in the kitchen. Ingredients, in this case, are compassion, kindness, understanding, retreat or respite, reflection, or allowance, to name a few. Even when the repetitive routines are set in motion for the good of your loved one's safety and the environment - you are still on a new day with another opportunity to see life in a new way.

8) Pick your battles.

It is difficult to reason with chaos, so picking the battle you are willing to stand firm on is as important to the moment as it is to your sanity. Many parents know the types of behavioral battles that occur with each age group, so applying the same concept to our loved one aging with Dementia is not always the rational approach. We eventually come to the point of comparison with the mental age of our loved one and that of a young child or teenager. As long as you can remember, they may look like an adult but not entirely think like a rational adult, so some battles can and should be avoided.

Deciding to keep Mom's dog out of the kitchen while she ate was easier than arguing with her about having to pick up doggy diarrhea since she DID give him table scraps. It sounds like something so trivial to understand, but it is not always easy deciphering when one moment to the next is truly a "senior" moment in the heat of an argument. One good day does not erase many bad days or should give rise to a denial of their condition. Lack of sleep or unresolved issues may prompt you to fight or bicker before you stop to think why you're bickering in the first place.

9) **Know your limits.**

Knowing my limits is what helps stop me from the recurring *'Should's attack.'* I should have done, said, or planned this or that. Knowledge is power! There are forms of care that can be learned like checking blood pressure, blood sugar, administering insulin, or even CPR for emergency purposes. Although there are many classes for these types of care, it does not mean you have to learn them.

My limit was when I had to wipe Mom or be more of a nurse than I felt comfortable. When the day came for the first time I had to wipe Mom in the bathroom, I found myself feeling resentment and guilt when I thought I had come to terms with caring for her. This moment was a new level of care, an intimate level of care I was unwilling to do. Assisting with the shower, rubbing lotion on her legs and back, and dressing her were activities of daily living that brought me concerns. Sure, it was a challenge to get through shower day with as little cursing as possible, but wiping her crossed a line for me.

The caregiver compliance documentation must be done well in advance with a plan for when you reach your limits. You cannot and should not try to please everyone. Some may be able to handle all levels of care, including end stages in their homes, regardless of financial status. Others may have more of a hard and clear stop line to their limits. Either way, your limits are your limits for whatever reason.

10) **Become a better listener.**

Listening is a learned skill. It may not seem like much of a skill, but when you are caring for your loved one living with Dementia, you are listening for more than just the words coming out of their mouths. Reading between the lines sharpens skills as a listener or observer. Just as a parent learns the difference between their baby's cries for hunger, wetness, or need for comfort, we must learn to listen to the sound of our loved one's breathing, grunts, gestures, and yes, words spoken or mumbled.

I am quite the talker, so sitting in silence can be awkward when I am not meditating. Learning to be silent to hear the words helped me understand if Mom was speaking about a past moment as if it was her present or sharing a memory with me. I validated her when she shared stories, whether true or false, which meant showing her respect regardless. Sometimes the story she recalled was her way of telling me how she felt without expressing the exact words.

Listening to how she cleared her throat or how long after a meal she became fidgety in her chair let me know to refresh her water and encourage a bathroom break. Listening became less about filling the awkward silence with sound and more about analyzing her behavior with her actions. I became accustomed to anticipatory listening.

11) Seek Respite Care

If I compared my efforts to others in my family, I did not feel that I deserved respite time. If I allowed my self-doubts to linger too long, I felt as if I did not have time to allow for respite time. You have to make time for yourself. It starts by patting your own back for a job well done. It is NOT selfish to want time to refresh because your loved one will benefit from your recharge once you return.

Schedule an afternoon for a massage, a day at the salon, or a dinner with friends to catch up guilt-free for men and women alike. Getting away alone is good for you, but being around others without Dementia will remind you how precious life is and what a great service you are providing to your loved one with Dementia. Having something to look forward to that is special to you will recharge your batteries and reset the level of tension or tolerance until your next break.

We can learn to identify and cope with Dementia symptoms in our loved ones. Still, the symptoms of burnout in a caregiver can be easily missed by ourselves and even our family members. It is important to establish boundaries as a caregiver to avoid depression and burnout.

Caregiver Burnout

Caregiver burnout is a sign that the caregiver has gone above and beyond their physical, emotional, and mental limitations. We give out of love but forget to include ourselves in the same frame of mind towards safety, environment, and well-being.

Wondering if I was doing something right or wrong made me search for others for validation. Taking Mom to multiple doctors and learning what questions to ask was one way to find validation. Sometimes I had no clue what to expect next, so I did not know what questions to ask.

Not knowing what direction to go in on this journey only added to my depression. I wanted to throw up my surrender flag. That is until someone explained to me to do the same thing I had already done and why. I felt vindicated and validated, yet still exhausted emotionally.

The more I learned about reprogramming my old mindset and the fact that I was not alone in this journey, gave me the emotional strength to keep going. The problem was, even though I found someone to validate my actions regarding Mom's care, I did not feel any added energy. I had experienced the beginning of extreme exhaustion from caregiver burnout.

The following are ways to avoid caregiver burnout:

1) **Prepare a list of all the tasks - Share the load.**

Hopefully, as the family becomes aware of all the tasks needed for your loved one to live independently or with you, it might become easier to understand the present demands. Regardless of your loved one's condition, there are still plenty of chores to be done that are overwhelming for anyone to handle. Aging with or without Dementia, your loved one would still need help with indoor chores such as vacuuming, dishes, cleaning floors, laundry, dusting, cleaning bathrooms and showers, changing bed linens, and even caring for a pet by grooming and feeding.

There are also outdoor chores with mowing and edging, maintaining flower beds or pulling weeds, pest control issues in and around the home, and other home repairs like fences, gutters, windows, and doors. These chores can be easily solved by finding a neighborhood teenager to help or pay to assist since some services can be quite expensive for a senior on a fixed income. If neither of those solutions is available, you might be left with more chores to maintain, which quickly leads to burnout or depression from the overwhelming To-Do list.

2) **Bring in an expert**

Sometimes the need is keeping up with chores which is where the list comes in handy. Sometimes the need requires an expert for areas such as dealing with hoarding. Explaining the need without fear of judgment might keep some caregivers from bringing in more help. You may be able to start by checking with neighbors who might be willing and able to help on a part-time or regular basis. Then investigate your local services available for caregivers or respite care. Some help can be provided by government agencies such as DADS or the Department of Aging and Disability Services.

Other local agencies or home health services such as Visiting Angels, Home Instead, Hospice, or Senior Helpers are also helpful. When professionals take over the grooming and hands-on care, it frees the family to spend time together doing what they enjoy. Outside help also provides an extra measure of dignity for the elder who still needs some help with personal care. Some services are private pay, and others may be paid by Medicare or Veterans benefits.

The *"ask"* is the hardest part. You may get directed to another service, but help is out there if you are willing to ask for it.

3) Trust your gut and listen to your body!

I had several moments when I decided on Mom's care and felt confident about it, only later to second guess myself when the family did not agree. Disagreements were sometimes more than a difference of opinions and included a hidden agenda or reason for self-preservation..I understood where their motivation was coming from, but this self-doubt kept me from listening to my body intuitively.

Whether you need validation or genuine support, your body will tell you what it needs. Muscle aches and pains, upset stomach or GI tract, and headaches are all indications that your body is stressed for a variety of reasons and needs attention. Taking over-the-counter (OTC) medicine to treat a symptom so that you can push through the discomfort will not get down to the root cause.

I had severe muscle aches and pain caused by sciatic nerve damage for years. Before I was able to get cortisone injections, I was taking quite a bit of Advil, Tylenol, and Aleve. All provided temporary relief, but none fixed the root cause. Avoiding self-care and not going to my doctors out of fear that I would not be there for Mom when she needed me made matters worse. The truth is because she will continue to need me, I must listen to my body and keep myself as healthy as possible for both of us.

Chapter 18
In Hindsight

1 Corinthians 13:12 (NLT)
Now we see things imperfectly, like puzzling reflections in a mirror, but then we will see everything with perfect clarity. All that I know now is partial and incomplete, but then I will know everything completely, just as God now knows me completely.

Before our lives became consumed with Bipolar episodes and mixed Dementia, before Mom and Dad became my parents, they were individuals growing up in families just trying to get by. Some of the stories Mom shared with me made her life seem driven solely by survival rather than goals. No one asked either of them what they wanted to be when they grew up. Leaving to go to college or the military became an escape from their day-to-day lives. Dreams were a luxury.

Taking the time to reflect on who Mom was before my existence helped me see past my initial anger and resentment to appreciate who she truly had become aside from the title of Mom. The woman I knew throughout my life, who became my caregiver first, is more than a person living with mixed Dementia.

Let me properly introduce you to my mother, Lizel, born in Barceloneta, Puerto Rico, to loving parents Rafael and Leanora. Mom's twin sister is named Grizel. They were the 6th and 7th births among ten children. The name Lizel is English, meaning 'God's Promise.' The name Grizel is German, meaning 'Christian battle.' They shared a womb for some time but became quite the opposite outside of the womb.

According to Mom, she was a tomboy, while Grizel grew to be a prim and proper baby doll with perfect hair and make-up worn most of the time. They were not the type of twins to go everywhere or do everything together, nor did they confide in each other. As I learned from my aunt Vilma (5th born), Mom was grandpa's favorite. While the other siblings had regular chores to do, Mom could pal around with grandpa, leaving Vilma with extra chores.

Each time Mom had the chance to go roller skating or off independently, Grizel would try to tag along, but Mom would not have it. She would push Grizel away and tell her she could not go. Mom took advantage of the opportunity to ride by herself to visit her favorite aunt. She loved visiting with her because this aunt would give her a quarter each visit. Each quarter was saved until she was able to buy rice for the family.

Mom became quite the saver throughout her life. Thankfully, she taught me the same value of how to save for the rainy day. Mom used to say, *"When it pours, it pours, but your savings can soften the storm."*

I was only able to meet and visit with my maternal grandfather a few times as a child before he passed. I was fortunate enough to meet the silly, loving man with a fierce sweet tooth before I grew to know a more serious side to him.

Grandpa Rafael was a survivor of the Korean war who smoked cigars, drank heavily, and owned a candy store on the side of his house during his retirement. Grandpa had a *'bad heart,'* which I feel gave Mom the excuse not to take better care of herself. By her logic - Grandpa had a bad heart, so it was inevitable for her to have a bad heart.

Grandpa died at the age of 69. Mom held tightly to this idea of having to live until 69 herself. Until then, she would eat and sleep herself into a diabetic coma if you let her. As I write, she has made it well past 69 and into her 70s.

Grandma Leanora was a petite woman who stood at 4'11" yet birthed ten babies. I was not fortunate enough to get to know her. My only memories were of her cooking fried chicken in the kitchen and smiling in her rocking chair once she cleaned the house for the day. She did not understand much English, so everyone else translated for her.

Grandma died when she was 82 from pneumonia. She was very gentle and quietly observed everyone in the room with a smile when we did visit. Although she died of complications from pneumonia before she passed, the doctors diagnosed her with Parkinson's disease.

Even though Mom was quite the tomboy, she had an appetite for education and learning languages. She eventually left Puerto Rico to attend Brooklyn College in New York City to obtain a Liberal Arts bachelor's degree in Language. Later she continued with a master's degree in Bilingual Education at Hofstra University in Hempstead, New York, where she met Dad.

My father, Hector, returned from the Vietnam War to live in New

York. The Big Apple became their divine meeting place, back when Mom was reserved and weighed 96lbs.

The name Hector is an English, French, Scottish, and Spanish given name meaning restrain or protect. Dad was nicknamed Hector the protector and in Spanish "Tanque or Tanco" as in the tank. Yet Dad was just as gentle and romantic as he could be a fierce protector. He mustered up the courage to say *"Hello"* to a beautiful young woman reading the paper at a diner one afternoon. Even though this young woman was too distracted to catch his gaze or attempts to capture her attention, Dad pressed on.

I tried to imagine Mom playing hard to get, but in hindsight, she was already jaded. Dad's courage remained persistent long enough to grab her attention. Going forward with breaking down her protective barrier would take more than courage, but something worked because I am here in existence able to tell you about our family dynamics.

Mom entered this marriage with plenty of emotional baggage, as did Dad after returning from the Vietnam war. Therapy for both individually and as a newly married couple would have put them on a better marital path. I can't help but wonder if maybe they would have become more aware of the difference in moods by looking for a cause instead of defensively attacking each other. Would they have divorced?

Unfortunately, PTSD combined with Bipolar Disorder created one hot mess before they began to add little humans to this mix. Ironically, now as caregivers, we are told not to take those same emotional outbursts personally. We understand there are underlying physical and psychological reasons, but we had no way of knowing back then. We were taught to suck it all up and move forward rather than stop and reflect.

Before Mom began to withdraw and isolate herself in her living room, she was quite the ambitious go-getter. Learning these details was so important to see her through compassionate eyes. Hearing these stories from Mom, Dad, and my aunts put this journey into a new perspective for me.

The feelings of finally knowing and respecting Mom as an individual and parent were so uplifting and at the same time heartbreaking because now the sense of time is a painful reality. I felt the weight of losing a woman I finally began to understand and enjoy, yet was declining faster than in previous years.

In Hindsight, we all wasted valuable time with Mom unknowingly. Had we learned about the power of reflection that we are aware of now, so much of our childhood would have made more sense. I believe so much of it would have been different simply because we could have embraced Mom more and understood her physical struggle to balance life. Not just a work/life balance but an emotional, mental, physical, and spiritual life.

Why You Should Make Time to Reflect

Reflection is about careful thought. This type of careful thought does not mean meditation. We are not trying to quiet the mind to listen to the universe. On the contrary, this type of careful thought is a thoughtful, conscious consideration to analyze your beliefs and actions or those of your loved ones.

This time of reflection allows us the opportunity to become the detective in our life, an observer, to unravel our experiences to create meaning out of them. During this time, you might identify a timeline, pattern, or connection of events that have created the teachable moments in your life that made you who you are today. You might even identify a pattern of your loved one slowing down, approaching their end.

We can teach ourselves by taking time to reflect more often. The problem with the practice of reflection is the time it takes. Before I began to add this practice to my daily/weekly routines, I was not particularly eager to slow down, and when I started, I was not too fond of the inward-looking glass.

Learning from my actions or mistakes and then owning up to my actions was not easy to do at first. Understanding my actions over time made reflecting more enjoyable. I understood myself and others on a deeper level. I eventually was more confident and at peace, because this kind of reflection, sometimes guided, helped me fall in love with myself in the present. I no longer chase the ghost of my future self.

For years I was puzzled by the bizarre dreams I could remember. Now, as I take the time to reflect, I see messages that perhaps I would not have gleaned from my waking life, too busy to appreciate. For example, three years before I stepped away from the corporate world, I had a dream that puzzled me until I was further along this caregiving journey.

In this dream, I walked on a cement pathway through a forest under an invisibility cloak with a male friend behind rows of soldiers. Even though none of the soldiers could see us while they stepped in unison in front of us, we whispered to each other, *"Where do you think they are going?"*

My friend whispered back, *"I have no idea; let's follow and find out."* Just as he said that another woman that resembled an older cousin of mine, whom I had only seen in pictures, called over to me. Somehow, I was visible to Carmen but not the soldiers. She said, *"You need to go over there where they need you."*

Carmen motioned back over her right shoulder into the woods in the opposite direction of the soldiers to a structure in the distance. I had no idea where she came from or why she was there, but somehow, I felt absolute trust in her instruction. There was a sense of familiarity with her.

I stepped away from the cement path, setting the cloak aside. My friend followed me, ready to embark on this adventure with me. I took a few more steps past Carmen with my friend, then stopped and turned to him. *"There is something I need to do alone, but as soon as I am done, I promise I will come back to get to know you even better, Ryan."*

I had no idea who this friend was, but I also felt a deep familiarity with him. I placed my hands on his cheeks, pulled his face close to mine as I kissed him gently on the lips, and said, *"Goodbye for now. We will meet again soon."*

He looked a little sad but understood as I walked away from him towards what appeared to be a large cottage. Once I entered the structure, there was a woman on a table who was cut in half. A man was holding his hands above her body, infusing a red light into the center of the table, trying to reconnect her two halves. He looked up at me with sweat across his brow and said, *"Thank God you are here,"* with extreme fatigue. *"I keep trying to put her back together, but it is not working. We need your help."*

I could not believe what I was seeing because what I thought resembled a woman was somewhat of a different kind of being, possibly a fairy. I had the sense that her being cut in half was a battle wound.

Without any direction or understanding, I suddenly knew what had to be done. I turned to step towards the door of the cottage and said, *"keep doing what you can. I need something. I will be right back."* He nodded and continued to infuse this warm red light towards her separated body.

There was a giant 400-year-old tree outside of this cottage with energy that drew me to it. I walked over to the tree and placed my hands on it to draw in as much power as I could. My hands began to glow in a brilliant golden yellow light.

I ran back to the cottage and motioned for the man to step aside. The instant he pulled his hands from above the woman, she began to fade fast, turning pale. I held my hands over her just like he had done with thoughts of healing her. The brilliant golden light flowed from my hands and down into her separated body.

The light between her halves began to glow brightly as the two separate halves slowly grew back together, making her whole again. I was exhausted but knew this woman was important to our world and the challenges ahead of us. The man thanked me through tears. The woman smiled and thanked me as well. I started to step out of the cottage to find Ryan, but he was gone. The man stopped me and asked, *"Where are you going?"*

I looked around the space but had no clue other than to get some rest. *"I am drained and need to rest. You both need to rest as well to prepare for the war ahead."* I have no idea who this man or woman was because they did not feel familiar, but I did know they were important to save because the war was coming. What war or why, I have no idea, but I just knew it was coming.

When I woke from this dream years ago, I believed strongly in symbology, so I first looked up Ryan's name. The name Ryan is the English language of Irish origin used for both males and females. It comes from the Irish surname Ryan, or Rian. The name means *'descendant of the king,' 'little king,'* or *'illustrious.'*

I did not know anyone named Ryan in my waking life, which felt like a message to find him. Then I focused on what I said, *"There is something I have to do alone, but I promise to come back and get to know him better."* Life had become drastically different from the corporate world. Acknowledging my transformation was something I had to do alone, which made me wonder if the Spirit had been trying to prepare me years before.

I stepped off the cement path (away from the corporate world) and met a descendant of the king (Ryan). Not *a* king, but **the** king (Jesus). I was not needed in the corporate world because I intended to create change in a different way.

I found an ancient tree (the tree of knowledge) and knew it was a source of healing. The man with the warm red light (symbol of red chakra - grounding, security, courage, physical and emotional survival energy) could not bring her halves back together.

The yellow light (Solar Plexus chakra), which I could find and possess within, could heal her because her courage and security had been damaged, disconnected. The yellow energy is related to perceiving and understanding, connecting us to our mental self. She was disconnected from her mental self or true self. Like me, I felt so disconnected from all that I had identified within the corporate world, prohibiting me from connecting to my divine, true self.

How to Make Reflection Time More Effective

1) Start by selecting a reflection process that works for you.
As long as you are comfortable with it, you will most likely stick to it and look forward to it. You might want a separate journal specifically for this if you prefer to do it privately by writing your thoughts down. If you prefer having a companion to reflect with, perhaps as a sounding board, then invite a friend to join you.

2) Ask yourself a question.
I don't know about you, but my time of reflection ends up being when I am in the shower or driving alone. That seems to be when a question comes to me, which I accept now as being Spirit-led. My questions often end up being deep right off the bat.

What are you avoiding? Why are you putting {it/them} off?
What upset you? Why did that get under your skin?
How can you fix this? What do you want out of this relationship?
How did this happen? Where do we go from here?

The question triggers the memory of the moment, which then gives me the time to look at the moment, dissect it, and honestly answer myself. Based on my answer, I can be selfish or judgmental and still learn something or be led by yet another question.

3) Start Small - Don't overwhelm yourself.
Like any exercise regimen or lifestyle change, the key to success is starting small. With meditation, I started with five minutes and worked up to thirty minutes or more. With Yoga, I started as a beginner, barely reaching my shins, let alone my toes. Push-ups - I did a miserable three push-ups a day for a week until one day I did five, then seven. You get the idea. If you sit down and attempt to reflect for an hour, your mind will wander, you might get frustrated, or you'll find reasons why you don't have the time for it. Five to ten minutes can make quite an impact.

4) Challenge your thoughts.
Until I started reflecting, my thoughts lingered on the negative events or statements made to me. The negative thoughts opened the door to dwelling on my perceived weaknesses, which allowed more self-doubt.
I had to reach down and ask myself the tough questions, almost becoming my own therapist. Once I did, I took my thoughts to my

---

therapists to understand whatever I got hung up on. We can look in and learn, but sometimes we need an interpreter along the way. The more you are willing to challenge yourself, the more self-awareness you can achieve.

5) Be your own hero - Inspire self-acceptance and live intentionally.

We have already established that the caregiver's journey is long, stressful, and lonely, but it does not have to be. Some days may feel like a rinse and repeat, but the days are different. Our repetitive thoughts make the days feel the same. I focused on the negative present when I stepped into Mom's isolation which kept me focused on what I should or could have done differently.

When I began to reflect on her past, how she was raised, how she chose to live, I had to accept life as it was in the moment. There was nothing I could do to change her past or her intentions to live her remaining years. Through continual reflection, I learned how to live more intently, which meant quality of life, not simply quantity.

Chapter 19
Spousal Distress

Matthew 19:8 (NIV)
Jesus replied, "Moses permitted you to divorce your wives because your hearts were hard. But it was not this way from the beginning.

Any married person willing to share their experience once the honeymoon wears off will most likely tell you marriage is a work in progress. Even those who dated for many years or held lengthy engagements experience changes in connection after the marriage is consummated. There are very few perfect marriages because the majority of marriages have cracks. Once communication and intimacy begin to erode, stepping into a deeper role of caregiving may allow the cracks to fracture further.

Most of my adult life was consciously spent on not becoming my parents. Aside from wanting more in life, I did not want to be like either of them. Ironically, I have a better idea now of the wonderful people both of them tried to be. I did not want to experience what they represented, what seemed like a failed marriage. The sad thing is that until I began to research Dementia to avoid my demise, I assumed their failed marriage was inevitable for my marriage, like Mom and Grandpa's bad heart.

During my adolescent years, I felt sorry for Dad. All he wanted was the same thing I wanted from Mom, to be loved and appreciated. Nothing I did seemed to be enough back then. What I know now, as a parent, she only wanted me to have a better life than she had.

Whatever life she envisioned for me would take quite a bit more effort than I was able to put in during those adolescent years because of my overworking inner parts. On the other hand, Dad put in an incredible amount of effort to keep his family safe with a roof over all of our heads and fed. Except his efforts were expected by Mom and not reciprocated. Before Mom began to show obvious signs of something wrong, her passion was in her classrooms, not the home Dad tried so desperately to keep together.

Dad and I used to go to my high school track to walk and talk about life. As an adult, I can see how those long walks around the track became Dad's time of reflection and confession. Walking lap after lap around the track, Dad shared details that perplexed us both, which seemed to be the beginning of his heart hardening.

While he mentioned one moment after the next, I watched the football team run drills in the center of the track, cheerleaders off to the far left practicing their routine, and off to the right were track and field athletes practicing shot put or straddling hurdles. We were surrounded by all sorts of people exercising. Then Dad started to explain when he tried to talk to Mom, yet she seemed to go blank. She had a blank stare like the lights were on, but no one was home. He recalled how he waved his hand across her face saying, *"Yoo-hoo, where'd you go?"* He thought she was bored with him and tuned him out.

We finished our last lap and headed back to his Volkswagen van to go home. I remember him apologizing for sharing things like that about Mom because he did not want me to think he was talking bad about my mother. I loved Dad, but at that time, I was not prepared for the mature friendship and could not appreciate being placed in the middle. He was just so frustrated and confused with her actions or lack of affection. Besides, back then, he was not open to therapy of his own or sharing the family's 'dirty laundry' with anyone else.

I was placed in a delicate position. The pressure of right and wrong as I understood it morally as a 16-year-old raised in the Catholic Church grew heavier. I had to tell my Mom what I knew, in case she died. I had to do more than simply clear my conscience.

As far as I knew, her health was mainly challenged because she had an inoperable tumor near her pituitary gland. I did not grasp what this meant medically or what could be done at the time. I only understood that Mom's behaviors were due to the stress of being a junior high teacher, including the challenges of faculty politics.

One day after volleyball practice, Mom and I stopped at Henry E. Butts (H.E.B.), our local grocery store. Once we finished picking groceries off our list, we walked up to the closest checkout line. My heart was pounding fast, butterflies swirled through my stomach, and my mouth felt dry. We loaded the groceries into the back cargo area of our burgundy 1995 GMC Jimmy and then hopped in. The dark smokey grey interior with dark tinted windows seemed to envelop me with only the turquoise light of the stereo clock for my focal point as I sunk into my bucket seat.

With the smell of fresh French bread lingering in the vehicle, Mom reached to grip the black leather steering wheel with her left hand as her right hand began to place the key into the ignition. I blurted out, "Wait, there's something I need to tell you." I paused to take a deep breath.

"Remember the Saturday you had to go to school to work in the classroom?" I said while rubbing my hands, trying not to make eye contact with her.

"Yeah, what about it?" She squinted her judgmental eyes down at me as if I was going to confess something I had done.

"Well, Dad had a friend over, and he kissed her goodbye on the driveway before she left." I paused to catch my breath and braced for impact when her eyes widened, wishing I could sink further into the bucket seat.

"What kind of kiss? Who else was there? Where were you to see this? My God, He did this in front of you and the neighbors! I knew it. And what else? Then what did he do?" She took a breath when she saw me fidget more with the seatbelt and then calmly said, *"it's okay, I want to know. I need to know."*

As a teenager, I did not know much about monogamous relationships. It took being married for many years before I could understand how complex situations within relationships can be. This moment was one of the most uncomfortable situations I reflected on from my adolescence.

Caring for someone with Dementia does not eradicate the need for connection, which became clearer to me not only as a married adult but as an adult caregiver. Domestic married life impacts intimacy even before Dementia has the potential to rob the relationship of a beautiful connection.

Spouse Caring For A Spouse

According to AARP, Spousal caregivers are more prone to depression than adult children who are caregivers. These spouses often lose physical intimacy with their ill loved ones and deep friendship if those partners are no longer emotionally or cognitively capable of serving as their confidants. They frequently must mourn their past joys as a couple along with the dreams they had held for future happiness.

Spouses eventually face the dilemma of going or staying in their relationships. This type of decision to some may seem inconceivable. Those who honestly contemplate the pros and cons of leaving or staying are wracked with resentment because they give so much more than they are getting back. I know what this feels like firsthand as I became Mom's sole caregiver.

I still find myself experiencing Aha moments as I interact with Mom. Those are the moments I thought about wanting to step away from her care and then thought about how much Dad sacrificed to keep the marriage together but wanted to leave himself. He had his own dilemmas to keep the peace and please everyone. I was experiencing with my siblings as he had when we were vulnerable children and then later young adults.

If a spouse decides to leave, they are frequently wracked with guilt for abandoning the people they are supposed to love. The vow of *'in sickness or in health'* is broken for the sake of sanity. An estimate as high as 75% ending in divorce for couples with an ill spouse.

Each form of Dementia presents various issues for coping. There are no easy answers for these dilemmas because it is a personal choice to live with, along with real consequences. Keeping hope in the equation could lighten the burden by seeking as much education in the form(s) of Dementia your spouse is living with as early as possible. It will not change the situation, but it will help you make a better decision and find the brighter sides or what logically makes sense to you.

The proactive approach to avoiding this dilemma would be to manage your relationship more closely to ensure you are in a healthy balanced relationship. This balance comes from an equal give and take between the two of you before the relationship becomes spouse and caregiver. Life happens to every couple, which causes the imbalance at some point, which is normal. Many of the causes for an imbalance can also strengthen a couple as you learn about each other's needs. It is allowing yourself to be vulnerable that adds beauty to transformation.

When the imbalance is caused due to an illness, the imbalance places more strain on the couple's strength, which pushes the healthy spouse to give more than they were prepared. Meanwhile, the unhealthy spouse is forced to take more than they are often comfortable with. The unhealthy spouse's involvement can contribute to their mental well-being and help rebalance the give and take to an extent.

Being able to rebalance the relationship throughout time also helps both spouses to learn how to love differently and receive love. Over time, the word love may become 'care,' so the spouses learn to give and receive differently. Spouses will be able to switch roles like the parent and child from the spouse to a caregiver. You do not love your spouse any less because there is still a genuine fondness and level of respect for them. By caring in such a way, your actions continue to show and express the love you had before.

When the love you had before seems to be dissolving as you look at your spouse and begin to feel you no longer love them, it is usually the first sign of being overwhelmed. By this point, it is time to seek outside help with therapy. It is not uncommon for spouses to try to handle this all independently out of embarrassment or fear of judgment for any reason.

Sometimes it takes a therapist to help sort issues out to redirect your focus. It certainly will help knowing many of your fears or anxieties are quite normal. As soon as a spouse begins to withhold feelings from the other, communication breaks down, and feelings get hurt.

Worst case scenario may call for a separation of some kind. No longer wanting to be married but still wanting to care for your spouse is a normal feeling. With the various forms of Dementia impacting people at various stages in life, the concern for the quality of life is a decision for both the healthy spouse and the unhealthy spouse to consider.

Spouses may consider the following questions in advance before considering divorce:

1) **Boundaries** - How much are you willing to endure before you can no longer choose to remain married?

2) **Logistics** - Would it be feasible to agree to stay together as a legally married couple but have a more open relationship. Hence, is the healthy spouse free to pursue happiness elsewhere in a discreet manner?

3) **Private Space** - Would it be possible to live together under the same roof but in separate rooms rather than living apart altogether? A valid decision to make to help the healthy spouse remain a reliable caregiver.

4) **Sacrifice** - Are your own needs to honor vows leading to resentment and poor care of the unhealthy spouse? Without pointing fingers, is it possible to remain "in like" instead of "in love" and come to an amicable arrangement for both?

5) **Communication** - Are you able to share your feelings and concerns with your spouse?

I did not understand the end of my parent's marriage until I reflected on my past conversation with Dad and stepped in as Mom's caregiver. When communication broke, leading to an imbalance in their relationship, they continued to withdraw from each other instead of seeking outside help.

Dad loved Mom and was more than willing to care for her, but she stopped caring for herself while pushing him away. Her brokenness would not allow him to get emotionally close even though she expected him to care for her no matter what. The push-pull relationship was maddening.

I thankfully was aware of this push-pull potential when I had lower back surgery, making me the care recipient. Communicating my needs and asking about my husband's needs became very important to me. Creating space for our vulnerabilities helped us grow as a couple.

Of course, my needs were temporary compared to Mom's decline, but knowing these five points in advance has helped get even more conversation going for the potential of future illness. I needed him to understand that should I begin to show the signs of Dementia, then I understand there may come a time when his needs for intimacy may have to be met outside of our marriage, along with the guilt it might create. I accept that our vows will still be kept with a caveat to include another natural form of self-care.

Spouse Helping To Care For An In-Law

The other perspective is having a perfectly healthy spouse but learning to live with your in-law as the care recipient instead. If a marriage has cracks before being asked to assist, then those cracks may splinter to the point of separation or even divorce. This end can be avoided as well.

While caring for a parent, it is common to feel unappreciated or taken for granted. It is less common for one spouse to have similar responses and feel neglected or jealous when their spouse tends to their parents or other family members. Making time for both of you to receive the attention you need is important.

If you have children, you might recall the demands a newborn presents and how drastic your family dynamics have changed. It is such an exciting yet exhausting time, with each of you eagerly wanting to contribute to the newborn's care. The opposite is true when only one of you eagerly contributes care while the other begins to feel neglected because a newborn demands so much attention. *"You never have time for me anymore."*

The main caregiver may have an entirely different focal point of their days and nights, which leaves the other spouse blurred into the background. Traditional roles by design bring about an unbalance of giving and taking in a relationship. One parent works outside of the home while the other is the homemaker or *'home engineer.'*

As daily routines take over and we are pushed to exhaustion with work, school, and family, it is too easy to lose sight of the balance. We not only lose sight of the line to keep the balance, but we also lose a sense of gratitude for each other.

As I attended our marital therapy long before we ever became active daily caregivers for my mother, I learned the three most common reasons marriages break down, which, not in any specific order, are Sex, Children, and Money.

If communication breaks down because of these three areas, you can imagine how quickly a marriage would break down by adding an in-law under the same roof. With time for less sex, more money spent, both areas might create more arguments.

Although some cultures have learned to live with multi-generations under the same roof, it is not the norm. Having a village to raise the children and caring for the elderly within the same family can benefit. Still, it takes open communication and consideration to make it work for everyone.

If you are accustomed to multi-generational living, then having a feeling of loss of freedom and individuality is something you may *not* understand. I knew my mother's habits, Dementia related or not, would make my spouse uncomfortable.

A friend of mine knew this well, so he told his wife that she would never care for his parents early in their marriage. He explained how it initially made her feel confused and almost hurt because it felt like a trust issue. Later, as both of their parents aged, she could see why he declared this statement more in-depth.

There was no trust issue at all but an issue of consideration. My friend loves his wife so much and knew how his parents could be. He did not want her to experience them negatively. As time continued with both of their parents aging into their mid-80's, she was grateful he had the foresight to not only forewarn her but to be so considerate early on. They both tend to their own parents and lean on each other for support and advice, creating more understanding and consideration as caregivers. They remain optimistic and utilize the support to strengthen their marriage instead of allowing the caregiving to pull them apart.

Since I eventually cared for Mom in our home, it felt like my problem to solve no matter how willing my husband was to help me. For me, It was more than wanting to maintain a level of privacy or intimacy with my husband. No, this was me trying to keep Mom's care as tidy as possible.

I knew caring for her this way would affect more than my life or her life being disrupted; this was *our* way of life in our own home, having to be adjusted in ways none of us were prepared. For him, he simply wanted to help reduce stress on me.

I quickly found a care routine with Mom to keep life as simple as possible for all of us. The morning ritual routine of hygiene and breakfast was basic yet regular. The afternoon routine was a bit more flexible because we had to incorporate shower days, doctor appointments, errands to run, and time for her to walk for exercise. The evening routines also had to be flexible because preparing dinner between our schedules of support groups, bible studies, or even downtime was hectic.

Routines came together to make life simple for sure. I could not complain because I like structured routines, which provide a sense of stability and security. The one thing I did not expect from this simplicity was monotony. Life became too simple for me.

Conversation with Mom eroded down to the routine checkpoints. I wanted to be around people who could strike up conversations. Yet, conversations would take more attention from me, so I could not engage for long without having to run away to keep Mom from running off abruptly in public. My moments to connect started to disappear.

The evening routine was usually lively; staying on the go because preparing dinner and rushing off to meetings left little time to chat. I eventually kissed my husband goodbye in the mornings as he left for work and started my day. By the time he was returning from work and picking our son up from school, our dinners were a bit later. He needed to catch up on his To-Do list while I was trying to wind down emotionally from the 'simple' day.

I tried to discuss the day of frustrations with him, but I could tell I was bombarding him with so much emotion at the end of his busy day before I ever asked how his day went. Somewhere along the lines, I felt guilty for unloading my frustrations on him, so I started to default to the short answers.

As we advanced over the years, our day, between Mom and me, was just 'fine.' Surprisingly, his day at work was also just 'fine.' This went on for some time. No amount of wine, cookies, or game apps on my phone could fill the emptiness. We were both fine, and yet we weren't fine.

Being fine or showing the survivor's smile all the time allowed something unfamiliar to creep in before I knew what to call it. I was lonely, unhappy, and depressed. Life was so simple I did not feel alive anymore. I was going through the motions, checking the boxes of the daily routines, and daydreaming of a life somewhere else.

These changes in our lives were expected yet not truly understood. I was not only mourning the loss of who Mom was, but I was also beginning to mourn the loss of who I was. I was mourning a marriage that was quietly falling apart. I was losing connection with my purpose and no longer feeling passionate about life.

Withholding feelings from my husband did not help to make these changes any less bearable for him. Trying to stay strong or deny my feelings to remain the strong caregiver broke me down month by month. He also withheld feelings because he felt guilty about being able to leave for the day. He did not have to cope with what I was going through yet felt relief each day he left the house for work.

Some of my anger and resentment resurfaced, but it was not entirely towards Mom. I finally came to terms with caring for Mom, yet started to resent my husband for leaving for the day even though I knew it was for work. At the same time, I knew I could not keep the messy parts all to myself.

I felt the burden most and worried about what it would mean for him to feel the burden too. When I finally sat down to explain this through tears to my husband, he understood loud and clear we had to do this together, so we would all survive this caregiving journey.

The most important proactive step we learned to take was to schedule regular check-ins with each other. Here are a few tips on how you can create a healthy marital check-in.

1) Schedule regular monthly date nights to change up the scenery and conversation. Just as you might create a vision board, create vision topics, or visit new places for date nights.

2) Put regular weekly reminders on your phone or email to ask your spouse, *"How are you doing? No, How are you 'really' doing?"* Do not accept *'fine'* as the only answer. We know far more descriptive words to use – so use them!

3) In addition to attending couples counseling, continue individual counseling because if you cannot take care of yourself, you cannot take care of your loved ones. Therapy is a vital form of self-care that will save your vows and keep you in a healthy state of mind.

4) Create your own checklist – Sex, Children, & Money. Where do you stand on each of them today? Check-in each month or include them as part of your reflection time. When you feel your boundaries shifting, make time to talk to your spouse rather than brood over the changes or going silent.

5) Find ways to express the good, the bad, and the ugly. When we hold back to avoid an argument or hurt their feelings, we are not helping anyone. Those feelings you hold back will only drive you crazy and possibly make you sick. It's like having a bad case of gas – it's better out than in!

Chapter 20
Finding the New Home

Luke 14:28 (NIV)
"Suppose one of you wants to build a tower. Won't you first sit down and estimate the cost to see if you have enough money to complete it?"

When Mom and Dad mentioned life as retired seniors during my adolescent years, the context was usually dark sarcasm. They also had funny topics with the idea of being an old fart someday, but at the moment, they were going to enjoy a life of gluttony with no restraints—nothing was taken seriously at all.

Then in later years, as my sisters and I moved out to begin our own married lives with children, the concepts of getting old and not being able to go up and down the stairs as easily or keeping up with yard maintenance came about with much less sarcasm or humor.

While Mom and Dad were married, the talk about downsizing usually ended with a *"Let's agree to disagree"* kind of response. Dad could not imagine selling the house. He worked his entire career to pay it off. Mom was open to change just as long as it was not an old folk's community as they called it. Either way, my sisters and I did not want to let go of the home we grew up in or paint over the bathroom door frame where we logged our growth in height every year.

So as the years passed, we all did what we could to help Mom and Dad. After helping around the yard, we had several weekend barbeques and could not see letting go of this home full of memories. That is until Mom and Dad divorced, and then the idea of Mom living in the house alone with potential fall risks on the stairs or in the showers became a very big issue.

By the time she stopped checking the mail regularly, cancellation notices were delivered more often, and the house maintenance started to fall behind. Now it was clear the next phase of her journey to downsizing, or rightsizing as the market refers to it, was upon us. Knowing where to start included finding the courage to talk with her about getting this next phase in motion.

Every previous attempt had ended in protest because she was still too young to need this transition, or she did not want to part with a house full of extra furniture and stuff accumulated over 37 years. I could not argue with Mom successfully when it came to persuading her about safety and the environment.

I knew any change at this point was going to be difficult. We had to start somewhere because even if Mom felt too young in her mind or physically attached to our childhood home, the time would come soon enough when this kind of change had to happen regardless of age.

Clearing the stuff had to happen regardless, which eventually needed an organized plan to discard, donate, or pack for the new home.

The first right size moved Mom from a two-story house to a one-story with a smaller yard to maintain. Within three years of this transition, Mom moved in with us. Within three more years of living with us, I transitioned Mom into a memory care community. Each transition was painful, emotionally stressful, and challenging to get through without adding more family drama.

Here are some areas to consider as you think about preparing for this transitional stage of living arrangements:

1) **Consider your loved ones' current needs** with the length of time their abilities seem to be slowing. How long was it from their last step down? How healthy are they currently? Where are they cognitively? How quickly do they appear to be declining?

2) **Based on their current needs, assess their current living status** to see if their needs are easily met or require assistance more often than not. Are they a fall risk? Are you seeing bruises on their hands, knees, or face but get silly excuses? Can they navigate the kitchen or bathroom and showers easily? Are they avoiding meal prep, chores, or hygiene because of an issue in the home as-is?

3) **If they are still driving, are they getting lost more often?** Does their current home have access to public transportation nearby? You might be able to schedule transportation for appointments, but independence and sanity are hard to manage if you are not consistently tracking movements outside of their home.

4) **Could they stay independent longer** with in-home assistance? Once you can determine their level of competency, coherency, and cognitive status, you can figure out if staying in their current home with some assistance from an agency would help or if they need 24/7 assistance. Price comparison of hourly care in-home versus community cost with services provided helps get an idea of a budget needed.

5) **Start researching your area for the new home.** Whether your loved one can remain independent longer or not, you need to start researching your area for either a smaller, more ADA-compliant home or begin exploring assisted memory care facilities.

By the time I started to consider these factors for Mom, I had my accountant hat on tight and family dynamics set aside. Mom's medical needs were covered, and now her environment with safety and our peace of mind had to be addressed.

Since independent living was no longer an option for Mom, I began researching her alternative options aside from living with us. Moving Mom in with us helped us all adapt to her change in abilities but also helped save more money. The frustrating and sad point is that our society is driven by greed, and huge ROIs have also commoditized our seniors.

There is no way to avoid the investment that this new home will become, so if you look solely through the eyes of dollar signs $$, then you might experience buyer's remorse. Debating whether or not to invest in remodeling the current home to make it ADA compliant or put those funds towards a new community is a tough choice to make. Doing your homework will save you in the long run.

Research what regulations in your state may be regarding assisted living. What may seem extremely expensive to you for monthly rent is the cost of living to ensure those regulations are met. Of course, some communities are more expensive than others because they sell exclusivity or Cadillac versions yet may be poorly managed. Other group home styles may be better managed and less expensive but hard to find.

In this case, you DO need to judge the book by the cover. Paying for extra bells and whistles may not equate to better care when it comes down to the facts.

First homework note: Understand the difference between Independent living, Assisted living, Memory Care, and Nursing homes. Get the lingo down, so you know what you are seeking! The industry does not like an educated consumer. Your loved one is another sale of real estate space in large communities. I personally prefer the smaller group home style where less is more.

Independent Living: This is for those who can still live independently (not dependent on assistance for activities of daily living) but enjoy having access to dining, medical care, entertainment, and more as needed. Housekeeping, meals, and laundry may not be included with rent, but the benefit is no longer being responsible for heavy-duty household chores like costly repairs and lawn maintenance.

Many independent living communities offer seniors a calendar full of events in addition to weekly happy hours. The average cost of independent living ranges from $1,500 to $6,000, depending on your area and preferences. Medicare does not cover any portion.

Assisted Living: Better option for those having difficulties with activities of daily living and need regular support in a range of ways but can still live independently for the most part. Housekeeping, laundry, transportation, meals, and maintenance services are typically included with rent.

Additional care services such as medication management are also typically included. Your loved one will still benefit from activities, outings or trips, and other social engagements. The average cost of Assisted living starts at around $4,300/mth. Medicare does not cover any portion.

Memory Care: Better option for those who need to age in place with a continuum of care. If your loved one is at risk of wandering or getting lost if left alone, this is a more secure environment. Memory care communities are Dementia specific with activities or interactions tailored to unique cognitive abilities or challenging behaviors.

On average, Memory care costs 20-30% more than assisted living. Fortunately, Medicare and Medicaid will cover some specific expenses, but you must contact your local agencies to determine how much they will cover. Without long-term care insurance, you will be at the mercy of private insurance or Medicaid to cover physician visits, home health care, adult daycare, or skilled nursing care.

Nursing Homes: This option is what many assume assisted, and memory care communities are, which they are not. Nursing homes provide limited recreational activities with medical and personal care in a clinical setting rather than a home-like setting. Medical services that cannot be met in assisted living or memory care communities must be met in a nursing home provided your loved one is not utilizing Hospice care in their residence.

If your loved one has underlying conditions and would likely need nursing home services, then it may be more helpful to find a community with a nursing home branch for a smoother transition when the time comes. Medicaid covers most costs, so schedule time with a Medicaid Planner sooner than later. Average costs begin at $7500/mth.

When you are unsure what to consider or ask, you will only see a small portion of this larger picture. Finding the right place for your loved ones to live is about their well-being in a safe environment and quality of life for the remainder of their days/years. This process can be an emotional stressor for you because none of us look forward to this kind of change.

I used the services of our local Senior Living Advisors of Austin, co-owned by Sarah Hyde-Williams, to help me find as close as possible to the next *'forever home'* for Mom. Having their expert guidance to make an informed decision gave me peace of mind and confidence, knowing I could make this decision for Mom and not feel haunted for making it.

I originally avoided this service because my misinformed information was that it would be costly, but I was wrong. We spent roughly two afternoons initially discussing living plans, care options, and the kind of support Mom needed now and would eventually need. Still planning ahead but not stressing over the what-if scenarios.

We then scheduled two days to tour the communities, which fell into my criteria. The cost was not a factor in this respect because the community I finally chose for Mom paid what they call the finder's fee. I did not spend anything but gained a wealth of knowledge and perspective.

Through their expert guidance, I made an informed decision based on Mom's needs, not my preferences. Some places I looked at before using this service made me consider whether I wanted to live there. I was not researching hotels for a vacation stay. Yet, I looked at their layouts, staffing, or amenities and how it made me feel to determine how Mom might feel knowing what she already thought about *'old folk's homes.'*

The problem with this mentality was I was looking for my needs rather than Mom's continually declining needs. For example, I had already turned down one community I toured in my mind before the tour was half over. The layout reminded me of my son's daycares, and the starting cost was too high.

I was aware of the annual cost of living increases, but starting too high would have put quite a dent in Mom's savings from my initial perspective. Later, when I returned to the same community with an expert to explain why the layout was designed that way, it made perfect sense for Mom and others living with Dementia. The cost of the community even made sense once they broke down everything included in the monthly cost. There was still a difference in property values, so not all the cost was justified—all more, the reason to compare as many locations as possible.

My expert tour guide knew my top main concerns - location, care needs, and cost. I had other expectations, which I explained as well, but like a realtor helping to find you a home, the expert reminded me to make a list of wants/needs then weigh them by importance.

The added benefit of having the expert with me was their knowledge of several different forms of Dementia. Some communities will not accept your loved one with Lewy Bodies, for example, while others will.

Some places will wave deposits while others will not. Some places have ridiculous waiting lists because of the populated area and not their coveted care practices—some places I would never have considered because of my limited knowledge.

Understanding the form of Dementia your loved one is living with, and physical limitations will help decide between a group home style versus a large community home.

Making this decision was so much easier and far less stressful with an expert by my side who understood my emotional hesitations and even why I closed my mind in some cases. Each time I hear how well Mom is doing at her new forever home, I am given more blessings because she engages socially again and no longer isolates herself. Changes are still occurring, but her environment is well prepared for her pending decline.

Finding the right new home for Mom was a reality I fought because it was a promise, I tried to make years before that I had to break. Accepting my limitations with her growing needs was another bump in the road of our journey. Trusting my expert and seeing the outcome in Mom's smile, health, and improved daily interactions became food for my soul. We both have what we need now.

What To Expect Once You Find the New Home

The hard part was done once I finally chose Mom's "forever" home - or so I thought. Finding the new home was half of the challenge. The rest of the challenge came in filling out the paperwork before moving her in. You must have caregiver compliance documentation done far in advance to allow you to sign all the necessary forms.

Every community will have its own set of required forms by state, but you can certainly count on having to complete the following:

-Medical Release
-Patient Intake
-Discovery-Resident Information
-Pharmacy LTC Information (typically unique to the community)
-Out of Hospital DNR Physician (Mandatory and is different from Advance Directive)
-Physician Transfer Form (typically signed by Neurologist confirming mental health and medication)
-Essential Caregiver Designation (you and one other that is allowed

unlimited access)
-Dietary History
-Activities Assessment (ADLs and current status)
-Assisted Living Disclosure (with signed Acknowledgment)
-Resident Handbook (with signed Acknowledgment)
-Emergency, Disaster, and Evac Plan (signed Acknowledgment)
-Authorization of Electronic Monitoring
-Residence and Care Agreement
-Dental Care Designation and Acknowledgment (typically unique to the community)
-Medical Care Designation and Acknowledgment (typically unique to the community)
-Provide Medical Power of Attorney
-Provide Durable Statutory Power of Attorney
-Provide Advance Directive
-Provide HIPAA Form
-Provide Declaration of Legal Guardianship
-Provide Bank Draft information (with voided check) for automatic monthly drafts
-Provide copies of Driver's License or official ID of resident and SS Card
-Provide copies of Medical and Dental insurance with Medicare along with any other supplemental insurance
-Provide COVID vaccination card (new post-Covid pandemic)

Additional State Agencies Resources

   While you decide where the new home will be or if it is time to find a new home yet, consider state agencies for additional resources to keep your loved one home longer. If they wish to remain in their home or feel like there are no other options financially, try to exhaust all options before you throw in the towel or experience caregiver burnout.

Department on Aging and Disability Services (DADS) Now managed under the Health and Human Services in Texas.
Contact your local HHS department for help in Caregiver services such as:

- Aging and Disability Resource Centers (ADRC) – for help in long-term care services
- Area Agencies on Aging (AAA) - provides local services to anyone 60 and older and their caregivers for:
  -Information, referral, and assistance

-Benefits counseling and legal assistance
-Care coordination
-Caregiver support services
-In-home support services
-Legal awareness
-Nutrition services
-Ombudsman Program

- Community Services Regional Offices - provide administrative support to community services contractors and enroll people in community services programs.

- Department of State Health Services – Includes contact information for the health services region, community mental health centers, public health organizations, and state hospitals. Search by your state to know your area and what type of services are available.

- Local Intellectual and Developmental Disability Authorities (LIDDAs) – contract with Health and Human Services to provide services as the point of entry for publicly funded intellectual and developmental disabilities (IDD) programs, whether provided by a public or private entity.
-Includes state-supported living centers
-Home and Community-based Services (HCS) - persons living with their family, own home, or in small group home settings
-Texas Home Living (TxHmL)
- Service and Benefits Offices – provides a searchable list of benefit offices around the state of Texas for older people, have a disability, or care for a person with a disability.

  https://yourtexasbenefits.hhsc.texas.gov/programs/other/suppo rt-services
  -Help with daily living needs
  -Help for caregivers who need respite services
  -Treatment for mental health issues
  -Treatment for drug or alcohol abuse issues

Hospice Care Services

When I heard about Hospice Care by word of mouth, I assumed it was not a service that could help Mom because she was not actively dying of a terminal illness the way you might envision a cancer patient or elder. The truth I have learned to accept is that we are all actively dying, but some of us are dying faster than others. Our loved ones living with Dementia can benefit from Hospice care as their body enters the final stage, whether they remain in their residence or transition to an assisted living, memory care community, or nursing home.

Hospice care is suitable for patients facing life-limiting illnesses or health conditions. Your loved one may be able to use the service for 30 days to a couple of years. They may improve and no longer qualify for the care and then need it again later. It is holistic care and addresses the patient's physical, emotional, social, and spiritual needs. However, since this level of care is mainly medical support, you will need to make sure the caregiver compliance documents are completed.

For most patients, Hospice care is covered through a Medical Hospice Benefit or other health insurance plan. Medicare defines four distinct levels of hospice care as described below. A hospice patient may experience all four or only one, depending on their needs and wishes.

Routine Home Care: This kind of care includes pain management, symptom management, emotional and spiritual counseling for the patient and their family, assistance with daily tasks, nutritional services, and therapeutic services. These services can be provided to the patient wherever they call home, so residential or community based.

Continuous Home Care: Also referred to as Crisis Care, is for the patient who experiences a medical crisis or whose symptoms require more intensive management. This round-the-clock nursing care allows you to spend time with your loved one rather than continue to be their worried caregiver. If your loved one improves, then they may return or begin routine home care.

General Inpatient Care: This care is focused on controlling severe pain and stabilizing symptoms that may not be manageable at home. Some patients and their families know their end is near and choose to pass in a neutral, yet calm and safe place surrounded by their loved ones.

Respite care: This is beneficial because a caregiver can utilize a general inpatient care center as an occasional, short-term stay for their loved one. At the same time, they get some much-needed rest. Not many caregivers are aware this kind of service is available. You can ask your loved one's doctor to prescribe a stay.

Once you contact a Hospice Care service in your area, either through your loved one's doctor or private inquiry, then you can expect the following:

Advantages:

- Comprehensive, interdisciplinary care from a team of professionals such as physicians, case manager nurses, home health aids, certified medical social workers, chaplains, and trained volunteers.
- Care is available 24/7, even on weekends and holidays.
- Reduction in out-of-pocket expenses towards medications, durable medical equipment, and medical supplies.
- Choosing comfort care may also limit unwanted hospitalizations or treatments in support of the patient's wishes.

Disadvantages:

- Denial of some diagnostic tests, such as blood work and X-rays, even if the physician requests them.
- Hospitalization is discouraged once a patient enters hospice care because the provisions of short-term hospital stays are not very clear.
- Participation in experimental treatments or clinical trials is not allowed because they are considered life-prolonging.

Only you and hopefully your loved one will be able to decide to begin Hospice Care Services or not. Have conversations with your loved one's doctors, but if you feel the need and they disagree, do not hesitate to get a second opinion.

I ask you to please find the courage to have these conversations in advance with everyone that is of direct importance. You do not want to end up with caregiver burnout in attempts to provide care for your loved one beyond your limits. The time given to the very end should be as meaningful as possible, regardless of where they call home.

Chapter 21
Surviving the Holidays

Romans 12:15 (NIV)
Rejoice with those who rejoice; mourn with those who mourn.

When I was much younger, I loved the fall holidays from Halloween to Christmas, especially Thanksgiving break, to eat and sleep a ton between gatherings with family and friends. As I got older, the same holidays brought about more anxiety regarding planning to the shifting change in family dynamics based on the hostess versus the guest.

Now, as Mom declines more each year, the holidays are more emotionally challenging differently. There is more pressure around whether this might be her last. Mom still loves Halloween and attempts to dress up to hand out candy. It saddens me to see the difference between her usual excitement to engage with kids versus just sitting back to watch them pass by.

As Mom has continued to decline, I realized she shouldn't engage with kids and candy. Rising issues with diabetes, aggression and lack of filter for her comments make her favorite holiday she has to enjoy from her room.

Each year we need to stop and think about what the holidays mean to us and consider what they may no longer be to our loved ones. We go through new and different stages of our life, which brings about more and more change, welcomed or not. In addition to the changes your loved one is experiencing, you might feel sadder around the holidays.

The following are questions to consider as you head into the holiday season to avoid emotional landmines:

1)   What feelings are stirred up in you as the holiday's approach?

The holidays are often a time for our family to reminisce about previous holidays filled with gatherings in various types of weather, favorite meals, movies, or activities. It may be helpful to consider your feelings first but include considerations for your loved ones' feelings as well. They may not want, care about, or remember what makes you feel good about the holidays.

As our parents or spouses continue to live with Dementia, each holiday is different from the last. Consider whether or not this will be a positive experience for your loved one. Memories of your loved one in the past holiday celebrations might still be fresh in your mind. Those same happy memories you reminisce over may have become upsetting memories to them, knowing what once was, is no longer, or the memories may be incomplete, confusing.

What their abilities were years ago may now be diminished to less than basic. Decorations on the house may have been very important to them in past years, but physical abilities keep them from enjoying or participating in the decorations indoors and out. Asking for help to decorate may be difficult for them because it reaffirms the loss of abilities and independence. Planning to help them decorate before and after the holidays might increase your holiday blues or anxiety. It is also a form of mourning.

2) Are you planning something because it would make you feel better?

It might be time to rethink old traditions or adapt them to be more accommodating. Embrace the changes in their abilities by showing your enthusiasm to pick up the torch. Sometimes expressing your gratitude in lessons learned from their years of cooking and service to you is enough for them to sit back and allow the torch to pass graciously.

Dad would wake early Thanksgiving morning to put the turkey in the oven around 7 AM in our family. As it baked in the oven throughout the rest of the morning, he would work on other side dishes and homemade pumpkin pies. We had to clean dishes as Dad cooked and maybe sampled some food or grabbed a dinner roll when he was not looking. We would get 'the look' that said it all - to get out of the food dishes or else!

During Christmas Eve dinner, the same would happen as he prepared a pork roast with Spanish-style rice and beans that his mother, my grandmother, taught him to make. This tradition has since been passed to my husband.

3) Will you be traveling for the holidays with your loved one?

Consider the meal time since it may need to be earlier or later than originally planned to allow nap time. Road trips are exhausting for everybody in the car, both young and old, but certainly more difficult for a person living with Dementia.

Trips by car should be as short as possible or between 45 minutes to an hour at most between stops. Traveling to another city can be very agitating or cause distress, leading to unnecessary bickering or emotional outbursts.

Traveling by plane needs to be avoided if at all possible. In a car, you can make as many stops as necessary for bathroom breaks or even opportunities to stand and allow for circulation. An airplane can be more restricted for longer periods in pressurized cabins, which would lead to more potential blood clots and fatigue.

This is possible for both young and old. Still, for your loved ones living with Dementia-related ailments, this is exaggerated by extreme fatigue and the inability to bounce back as quickly. Swollen ankles are an indication of poor circulation which is blood not making it back to the heart.

Connecting flights include more stress and exhaustion of making it to another gate in time and exposure to more extreme fatigue. You might be energized by the excitement of being able to see family again that you have not seen in quite some time. Still, this energy is quickly drained from your loved one simply by walking to the plane, boarding, and sitting for long periods in pressurized cabins.

This extreme fatigue is caused by plane cabins which are pressurized to simulate a 6,000 to 8,000-foot elevation on land, which causes our bodies to absorb less oxygen at those altitudes. Suppose you are not a trained athlete or physically fit in general. In that case, you will most likely experience dizziness, sleepiness, and a general lack of mental awareness while on a flight. Your loved one living with Dementia is already battling those symptoms on the ground daily in their own homes or communities without the added pressure.

Cabin pressure may also cause gas fluctuations in your intestines and affect your ears. Difficult side effects for those that wear hearing aids or already experience problems with bowel movements.

Your loved one's skin may lose even more natural moisture from the dry, re-circulated air as well. Many of you may have learned how difficult it becomes to encourage your loved one to drink water and apply lotion to aging skin already. The dehydration alone in normal circumstances creates serious conditions aggravated by what seems to be one simple airplane flight. The lack of drinking water and exhaling moist air results in further dehydration.

On top of everything else, you also need to consider that your loved one most likely has a delicate immune system. Traveling by airplane and going through airports will provide more opportunities to be exposed to germs or viruses that the average traveler can handle but could become a potential hospital stay for your loved one.

The cons outweigh the pros by far, so if you can visit your loved one instead, then, by all means, avoid placing your loved one on a flight.

4) **Have you discussed in advance whose house should host the festivities?**

If your mom or dad still own their home but reside in an assisted living or memory care community and you choose to take them out for a holiday, it is better to take them to the home of a sibling or aunt/uncle, for example. Taking them back to their home can be somewhat traumatizing, especially if a surviving spouse still lives in their home.

Think about the end of the gathering as you plan because when the time comes to return to their assisted living or memory care community, their level of exhaustion could add to their confusion as to why they have to leave their own home again. Depression from longing to be in familiar surroundings instead of their new living quarters may hurt if they have not adjusted.

Avoiding their home may seem like a mean gesture and harder for you to accept. Keep in mind that change is rarely easy for any of us. Clinging to old holiday memories and longing for normalcy by having them home again, even if they are not the ones to be in the kitchen, might open up more old wounds.

Their memory may be fading as the weeks and months go by, but they will not forget the emotion of loss or anger, even when they cannot remember why they experienced the loss. They could potentially associate you with the loss at a point in time when their minds can no longer rationalize or comprehend the situation surrounding the loss.

Plan on extra travel time to arrive before the day of Thanksgiving or Christmas so that once you reach your destination, your loved one has plenty of time to settle in and rest. Having a quiet room for them to rest away from family is very important.

For those of us that have children, it's easier to be compassionate with other children in the family, yet it may no longer be the case for our loved ones. As painful as it may feel, accept that as they progress in aging with Dementia, their senses are changing, and their memory may no longer include the grandchildren.

No matter how precious the babies are or how badly you want them to love on your children, crying babies or children playing could cause avoidable stress. You may think they are kids who don't know any better or miss their grandparents, but you have to consider what is going on with sounds or sudden movements that could become triggers. Talk with young children before the visit and help them understand why it is important to be gentle with grandma or grandpa.

5) Do they still recognize family?

Consider name tags for everybody with easily readable large fonts. For our loved ones living with Dementia, it is like being in a new classroom trying to remember names. Grandchildren are the least likely to be remembered since they are mostly in their short-term memory. Don't be offended if you're called by the wrong name, either. Even if you're wearing a name tag, you may just look like someone from their memories instead. Improvise until their memory flickers back to you and be kind if it does not.

Good or bad, these memories may help them to have more fluent conversations, if at all. Some interactions may be avoided because they can no longer remember your name and fear a moment of embarrassment or offending you.

6) Avoid asking, *"Do you remember?"*

This question is the big one. Holiday gatherings bring together more people. It makes us feel good to see each other again. Before we realize it, our conversations go from catching up from the last visit to the reminiscent "do you remember when..." conversations.

Chat with your children or siblings beforehand to avoid asking, "Do you remember when...." And not correcting them when their memory is shared and it's not what you knew it to be. If you find the conversations leading down memory lane, try to be the one that states, "I remember when...."

They can join in if they feel comfortable or inclined to continue with their version of the memory instead of being put on the spot in front of everyone, making them feel pressured or embarrassed when they cannot remember.

7) *Does your parent or loved one live in a Community instead?*

If you're loved one cannot travel to be with you outside of their community for the holidays, that most likely speaks volumes to their physical health more so than their mental health. Be considerate of your loved one's condition or attention span.

Have extra consideration for the community and plan ahead of time to visit in smaller visits instead of the massive crowds with the entire extended family. Yes, they will most likely be happy to see you, but everyone together for the holidays can be overwhelming to your loved one and the community staff.

Speak with your siblings or family members in advance to coordinate dates and times. If this creates family drama, take a couple of deep breaths, try not to stress, and remember this is not about you.

Your loved one will pick up on the underlying drama, which can cause them to be indirectly upset as well. Visiting more often during the year is more important for your loved one than waiting until the holidays. This annual visit is more about soothing our stress and anxiety than bringing our loved ones joy.

Communities are designed for the care of your loved one and are typically not prepared for large crowds. If they do not have a room that would accommodate the whole family be prepared to take turns in your loved ones' living quarters. Remember that your loved one is most likely on a daily schedule in the community, so a call in advance to your visit will ensure availability to visit during appropriate times (i.e., not during bath time or nap time).

Be willing to let go of what used to be so you can embrace what is now. Holidays can be filled with less stress, feelings of loss, or mourning your loved one when we can accept what is and not force a happy moment.

Chapter 22
Mourning the Living

Proverbs 14:13 (NIV)
Even in laughter the heart may ache, and rejoicing may end in grief.

Five Stages of Grieving

I did not like the person Mom was becoming as her mixed Dementia progressed. I had resented her before for a big portion of my past for various reasons. Each time I adapted to the stage she was living in, it seemed as if I started to mourn all over again. Life was manageable until we stepped down again. Then life felt like living in quicksand as the decline happened faster.

I went from stepping into this journey as a broken and angry daughter. Further down the road, I began to resent her for the overwhelming burden her care had become. Then the family squabbling she seemed to be creating unknowingly between my sisters and me created even more feelings of loss.

Until I could separate the woman and mother from the behaviors that caused her deterioration, I felt emotionally stuck. I could not recognize this emotional stagnation on my own as mourning without therapy. Throughout my sessions, I gradually understood the difference between situational depression and mourning.

The loss of our loved ones begins way sooner than their actual passing. This mixture of emotions fluctuates with each stage of Dementia. Rather than allowing an emotional wall to protect me, as Mom did throughout her life, I began to appreciate the time I was given to dig deeper into the bumps along this emotional journey.

I needed to learn how to allow myself to be vulnerable, focus on gratitude, and accept help from others, so this kind of loss would not feel so final, long before her last breath.

I had finally begun to get to know Mom, aside from the parent that drove me nuts, and began to appreciate the parent she tried to be despite her struggles with Bipolar tendencies. When I could see past her survivor facade, I could see into her spirit, which also helped me see myself in her. I was not only mourning the loss of who Mom used to be, but I was also mourning the loss of my own identity along with the relationships I once held so dearly with my sisters.

So once again, I repeat the wisdom from Maya Angelou - When we know better, we do better. I hope this resonates more deeply by now as you read over the five stages of grieving next.

When you can reach a point of self-awareness and connect with your inner child, you may be able to process grief healthily as well. The pain of losing a loved one is still a pain because life as you know it without them or who they used to be leaves our minds in limbo trying to reconcile the difference. Your pain may finally be able to transform into joy and gratitude.

The demands of caregiving brought my siblings and me together for Mom's best interest initially, but as time passed, it tore us apart with irreconcilable differences. I was in a stage of mourning for years on top of experiencing situational depression from Mom's shifting care needs. As I gradually understood that my emotional fluctuations were normal stages, that awareness lifted the weight off my heart.

We experience grief from many different events in life aside from the death of a loved one. Grief is mental suffering or distress that is caused by experiencing the feeling of loss, sharp sorrow, or painful regret.

Below are the five stages of grieving according to Elisabeth Kubler-Ross with co-author, grief expert David Kessler of "On Grief & Grieving, Finding the Meaning of Grief through the Five Stages of Loss."

1) **Denial (or shock) and isolation -** are when grief is the most profound.

   The source of my denial was from not wanting to deal with the seriousness of our situations at hand on someone else's timetable. After downsizing her home, it took three years of denial for me to realize that Mom could no longer live alone. What we thought would be better for her in terms of safety (no stairs), less maintenance (yard and cleaning), and lower utility expenses with property taxes became more of a challenge for us all.

   Through reflection, I was using the corporate cubicle for my isolation. I could see stepping away from my career to spend valuable time with Mom as one of the best gifts I could have received. And yet, I still reached a point of wanting to run away or catch a flight somewhere, anywhere that did not include the drama.

   Only as I gave thought to the getaway plan did I know that running from it would only be temporary. Once I returned, I would still have to face that Mom is on an accelerated abnormal aging journey with the need for a tour guide along the way. I was willing to accept a shift in my day job, but I also knew that I could not be the only tour guide.

2) **Anger (retaliation) -** channeling grief towards someone else to hold blame or responsibility for your loss.

   My anger often flared because I was emotionally stuck in the moment of the good day, wishing we had more of them or thinking we could have more good days if she tried harder instead of simply existing in such a defeated way.

I could not get a hand on my inner child, stomping in a tantrum mentally shouting, *"This is not fair!"* I was angry because so much of this could have been prevented through simple lifestyle changes. Her refusal to change lifestyle habits left us stuck in reactive mode instead of proactively planning together. Each time the family drama flared, my anger would turn to rage, creating an internal 'Momma Bear' with a plan of legal action. This reaction not only got me nowhere, but it also added to my anger.

I was angry at the world! In reality, I was angry that I was running out of time with Mom and losing an opportunity to have the relationship I always wanted growing up with her.

3) **Bargaining** - Acknowledging a higher power and trying to change an outcome in exchange for something or someone as valuable to prevent or stop a loss.

Once I was finally able to distinguish between Mom as a person and Mom's deterioration, the idea of begging God to change our circumstances kept coming up in prayer and meditation time. I believe He has a plan that I am not privy to all the details, which requires quite a bit of trust to allow this journey to unfold. The twists and turns helped me grow to speak to God through the tears, asking Him to calm the rough waters. I realized I have nothing to bargain with within a moment of clarity because God does not need time, money, or empty promises. There is no spiritual ATM card to fall back on. He wants my trust and faith, which sounds simple enough but is very hard to maintain at times.

You know you are in this state of mourning when you begin to bargain with God if He will just give you the outcome you want. *"I will stop smoking, drinking, or eating less junk food if you would just..."* or *"I will go to church from now on if you will just..."* or *"I will donate to charity more or volunteer my time if you will just...."* His plans are not created with what you are willing to give up. It just does not work that way.

Taking the understanding of Mom's abnormal aging to heart made me secretly bargain with God to allow me the added time to be with her, make up for lost time, and seek out the medical attention that she deserves. I promised to let go to serve her more, but those promises were hard to keep.

My promises went against my natural abilities and limitations, which were certainly not what He wanted or planned. My bargaining became a trade-off for Mom's health in exchange for my own. Until, of course, I realized that I would not be an effective caregiver without my own strength. A parent would give anything for their child, even their sanity at times, to be the superhero that takes away the pain or gives hope.

4) **Depression -** When the loss sinks in more and the realization that bargaining for more time, health, or different outcome will not happen.

Added depression comes from stepping into a world I feel I have no business being in. During those three years, I experienced my depression from maintaining a career while still being a good wife and mother. Work-life balance was already hard enough without adding in mom's needs.

The arguments created between my sisters and me over her care made it difficult to hang on to hope for a better future relationship. Letting go of the family as I knew it added to the depression because I also began to feel abandoned even though I was the one to pull away.

Depression comes and goes when I feel defeated by the constant effort to remain positive even though I see the decline in her abilities. Each day I spend time with her, we have the same conversations repeatedly to get through daily tasks, work on daily hygiene habits, or seek fun activities to help her willingly engage more.

Every time I see another indication that the short-term memory seems shorter, I wonder how much longer until she no longer recognizes me. Each time I observe her off in an empty gaze, it worries me and makes me wonder where her mind is or what memory she might be stuck in.

5) **Acceptance -** may still be accompanied by sadness or regret, but you have more peace and less pain so you can move forward in life once again.

No matter how much I attempt to understand what she is going through, I cannot imagine the feeling of losing a sense of reality. Empathy would help me know what she needed at any given moment, but it will not stop her from actively dying. There are good days, and there are bad days. I soon appreciated the good days for what they are instead of seeing each good day as a potential turning point, opportunity for reversal, or added time altogether.

Acceptance will come when you understand that your loved

---

one passed on to another dimension but is not gone forever. Acceptance also comes when you let go of the fear of letting go. When I reflected on the years and time I wasted being angry, I realized my anger was coming from a place of fear.

Parents prepare their children to let them go someday as young adults to thrive in society. Caregivers prepare their loved ones to let them go to the other side someday until you cross over to see them again as well. It is an emotional journey.

We may go through these stages in order or out of order. The order may depend on how you process emotions and whether or not you are given the proper time to grieve at all. While my sisters seemed to be in denial and isolation, I was in a tennis match between anger and acceptance. I can only explain this as being stuck in a dream, moving forward in slow motion, or throwing limp punches that don't seem to reach your target while standing in quicksand.

Reconciling the memories of who she used to be with the misbehaved, ill-mannered child Mom was becoming left me dumbfounded on some days, angry the next, and depressed on another day. Being stuck between stages is just as normal as cycling through all of the stages in shorter periods.

I experienced true acceptance when I was finally able to forgive the past, forgive myself for choices in life when I did not know any better and wasted so much time in an angry state. When I could finally experience what letting go feels like and truly live peacefully in the present moment, I stopped regretting the past and wishing for a better future.

Now, I am not saying I stopped grieving, and life has been nothing but joy and laughter. No. I still have my moments of grieving and allow myself time to cry, if need be, or sit and reflect. I feel the emotions instead of trying to tuck them away or deny them. I wasted so much energy trying to be strong for the family by hiding my pain, which inevitably made me sick with head colds, stomach aches, and depression.

It is hard watching a parent who was once so independent become so dependent on the simplest needs. No matter how many times I reached a point of acceptance, I would eventually have another moment in denial from having a good day with her. This kind of grieving is normal and necessary, but we must also be grateful for the present.

Life is too short to live angry or depressed when God intended so much more for each of us.

Healthy ways to cope with grief include the following:

1) **Encourage laughter.** Laughing is not only a pleasant distraction; it will help release the endorphins in your body to boost your spirit and energy levels.

2) **Sleep as much as possible.** Sleeping might be difficult when life does not stop long enough for you to grieve or the demands of the family keep you on the constant go. Grieving requires energy which still burns calories for mental focus to meet your demands. You might need sleep aids from time to time but try to achieve deep restorative sleep as often as possible without the aids.

3) **Avoid junk foods.** Grieving may bring excessive cravings for comfort foods, but many of those foods will contribute to mood swings, as we covered in Chapter 14 under Foods to avoid. Grieving or not, remember - garbage in, garbage out.

4) **Get exercise.** Meditative walks would be gentle enough to burn off some anxiety, stress, or angry vibes. Similar to sleep, it will help to release endorphins to help ease any depression. Getting out of the house for a brief walk will also keep you from giving in to the urge to isolate yourself in bed beyond a healthy period, especially if you have others still dependent on your care.

5) **Call in reinforcements.** Get a babysitter, pet sitter, or house sitter to come in and help you maintain the day-to-day stuff while you slip away to attend a grief support group. Grieving alone may be necessary at first to allow the weight of life changes to reconcile in your mind. Try to give yourself a time frame alone and then venture out to connect with others grieving. You might learn something or make a new friend who helps to ease the pain.

Death Cafés

Part of my grieving before reaching acceptance came from envisioning how Mom would die. After attending so many doctor visits to maintain her defibrillator and heart health, I couldn't help but wonder what her death would be like. Then as I broke down the stages of

Dementia to determine what stage Mom was in, the concern of pneumonia or choking started to worry me more.

As much as I wanted to have more conversations with Mom beyond the daily weather or bickering about daily needs, I could not bring myself to share these thoughts with her. I tried to share these concerns with the family, but they did not understand my concerns since they were not around Mom as much or attentive to her needs. They also had a superstitious fear that talking about her death would somehow bring it about sooner. I was curious.

Finding a different type of support group will help you rather than grieve during this caregiving journey alone. If you are mourning the loss of your loved one more, even though they are still living, then you are most likely thinking about death and dying more often like me. If you are curious and comfortable enough to talk to the doctors about it, then great. If you are too afraid to talk about death and dying with your loved one, finding a death café may help you.

I remember trying to have a conversation with Mom about her wishes afterlife, but instead of understanding my need to know, she responded defensively. Mom acted as if my initiation of funeral talk, last wishes, or anything remotely sounding close to riding off into the sunset was because I wanted to rush her end of life along faster.

"Why, are you trying to put me in the ground sooner than later?" My first response was usually an eye roll. Then later, as I understood the stages of Dementia more clearly, I knew this conversation with her would be difficult no matter how I approached it without her ability to reason, form a plan, or comprehend the details.

She could not strong-arm her way through or deflect with sarcastic humor for this kind of chat. Dad used to joke by saying, *"Just bury me in a pine box."* Mom said, *"Put me in a red dress and play Louisiana-style music to celebrate my life."* That was it. There was no mention of where they wanted to be buried, what kind of ceremony, or how to pay for any of it.

Thankfully, I am not alone in wanting to have these kinds of conversations. In 2010, Jon Underwood decided to develop a series of projects about death, focusing on talking about death. The first cafe was in his house in the UK facilitated by his mother, psychotherapist Sue Barsky Reid.

After that, they continued to meet up in funky cafes, people's houses, cemeteries, a yurt, and the Royal Festival Hall. The Death Cafes caught on, so Jon and Sue created a guideline for others to create more worldwide. Death Cafes breathe life into conversations about dying for those who are not afraid to speak about the unknown.

Death cafes are also available for those who prefer to talk about the death and dying of their loved ones in a learning yet judgment-free zone. These cafes have spread quickly across Europe, North America, and Australasia. There have been 12,684 death cafes in 78 countries since 2011.

Google 'death café' in your area to see if there is one near you in person or online. They are all created on a volunteer basis. If one is not in your area, you may be interested in creating one or joining one online elsewhere.

Keep in mind this type of support group is not a grief support group for those that have lost a loved one. It is more for those curious or concerned about their loved ones who are actively dying and want to go in-depth about death.

End of Life Doula

You might have heard about birthing coaches and birth doulas, so it only makes sense when you think about the cycle of life to have an end-of-life doula as well. Joining a death cafe may be helpful to speak with others who are experiencing similar situations. Still, a doula will work with you more individually or with your family to help all involved understand what to expect during the end of life.

Though Hospice and an End of Life Doula offer similar services centered around the transition from life to death, the doula can spend significantly more time with you and your family in various ways. Hospice care is a type of healthcare for patients to receive medical assistance wherever they call home to tend to their pain and symptoms.

Through the End of Life Doula Association, members are taught a foundation for a doula to approach their clients. These members are taught deep active listening techniques, common issues with facing death, meaning and legacy work, vigil planning, guided imagery, signs & symptoms in the dying process, reprocessing the dying experience, early grief work, and even their self-care.

After this training, a doula can assist in facilitating conversation with the family as a competent third party to guide your family in making informed decisions. They also provide emotional support and companionship to give you an emotional pause and spiritual support for your loved one. An End of Life Doula is trained to provide support while prioritizing comfort and quality of the patient's life without medical assistance.

When our loved ones are nearing the end of life, the need for

---

different knowledge about their physical and mental state arises. Understanding what your loved one's wishes in their final moments will be, as we discussed during Chapter 16 under Caregiver Compliance.

Even though you may know of their final wishes, the physical expectations of comfort care must be addressed to avoid as much emotional distress as possible. Your doula will be able to explain what the body does as it begins to shut down and be able to speak on your behalf if the moment becomes too overwhelming.

It can be difficult for your loved one to advocate on their own and similarly difficult for you to answer medical questions in those remaining moments as your loved one releases their hold on life.

During these final yet precious moments with your loved one, it is extremely helpful to have a competent third party with an objective to provide you with clarity continually. You may also experience the added benefit of understanding or receiving assistance managing medical and personal affairs so you can be with your loved one or have support yourself if you have no one else.

From the beginning of a diagnosis and through to the end, a doula acting as your patient advocate can help set up doctor visits and other medical appointments. They can also help patients get the financial, legal, and social support related to and needed for the end of life. Many advocates have resources for attorneys, CPAs, and other providers who can assist the patient or MPOA & POAs during this time.

Many doulas already have a background in the healthcare industry to assist you in navigating discussions and decisions around making the call for Hospice. They must understand your loved one's wishes, conditions, and needs to help craft a plan around their remaining time left.

We may be mourning our loved ones before their last breath but keep in mind that our loved ones, especially those who have not lost most of their mental capacity, are also mourning their life as well.

Whether they understand what is happening to them or not, a doula may also be able to provide massage therapy to ease their aches and pains. I am not suggesting a full body massage or deep tissue because that may be unwanted or too painful to bear. A gentle touch to stroke their arm or foot with essential oils can benefit their psychological and physiological state of mind and relieve pain.

The caregiver's journey may be stressful right up to the very end. It does take a village to raise a child just as much as it does to help our loved ones experience the quality of life through to their last breath.

You are not alone and do not have to be because others worldwide want to connect through death cafes and others trained to help as an end-of-life doula. No matter the illness your loved one is actively dying from, sometimes there are twists and turns along the way when we do not have any answers. An End of Life Doula can shine some light onto your dimming light.

I believe in life after death and that God has a plan for each of us. I also now understand how a caregiver's journey brings us together in ways we naturally try to avoid. There is a reason individuals are called to this kind of profession as a doula.

Death does give life more meaning.

Chapter 23
Living in the Present Moment

Job 21:23-25 (NIV)
One person dies in full vigor, completely secure and at ease, well-nourished in body, bones rich with marrow. Another dies in bitterness of soul, never having enjoyed anything good.

It is easy to allow life to run away with our dreams when we get stuck in a reactive state within our mundane routines. Working to pay bills, striving to raise kids, and spending more time daydreaming of a life I wish I were living made me seek out all sorts of research as I adapted to my caregiving journey with Mom.

The research kept me hopeful about my future health, but life with Mom also pulled me back to the past when we could have changed our approach to living a healthy lifestyle. Regret is not a healthy mindset and can keep you from going forward in a positive direction.

What made me feel more positive was doing the opposite of what Mom had learned as a young adult through food and exercise. I was hopeful about maintaining a healthy heart, but I also worried Mom's way of living with mixed Dementia would eventually become my life in years to come in terms of my brain. I did not want to buy into the genetics approach when our environment is even more powerful.

I came across a world-renowned neurologist, Dr. Dale Bredesen. His clinical trials focus on new therapeutics based on his understanding of an imbalance in nerve cell signaling. Once the nerve cell is suppressed, it causes shifts in memory, making connections to memory break, which results in memory loss. Hopes for discovering what can be done to stop the connections from breaking are still high.

Then in a more hopeful discovery, I came across a headline that reads "New Alzheimer's Treatment Fully Restores Memory Function." Australian researchers successfully regained memory function in 75% of mice that received the treatment. Yes, mice, but the possibility for humans is not far behind since this treatment focused on using therapeutic ultrasound or non-invasive sound waves instead of drug therapeutics.

What we have learned to this point is that pharmaceuticals are not only extremely expensive for those who have Dementia; they only treat symptoms but do not actively cure Dementia. We know that many kinds of Dementia are incurable, yet science wants to provide more drugs. Aside from the therapeutic drugs to maintain behavioral symptoms, we should not depend on more drugs.

As of June 8, 2021, The New York Times published an article explaining the Food and Drug Administration approved a new Alzheimer's drug from Biogen called Aducanumab. This drug will be marketed as Aduhelm, with a monthly intravenous infusion that Biogen has currently priced at $56K per year.

Most people living with Dementia barely receive $35K in social security or do not have any other means to afford this type of drug in addition to specialized costs of living. There has been no word on whether or not Medicare or Medicaid will cover any costs at all.

Only two days later, on June 10, 2021, The New York Times published a follow-up article explaining that due to the rush to approve this drug, three scientists resigned from the independent committee that advised the agency on the treatment. *"This might be the worst approval decision that the F.D.A. has made that I can remember,"* said Dr. Aaron Kesselheim as reported by Scott Eisen from the Associated Press.

Dr. Kesselheim is a professor of medicine at Harvard Medical School and Brigham and Women's Hospital, who submitted his resignation after six years on the committee. Kesselheim claimed the approval was wrong *"because of so many different factors, starting from the fact that there's no good evidence that the drug works."* So even though they had clinical trial data supportive of the ineffectiveness of the drug, the F.D.A. rushed to approve it with 9 out of 11 committee members opposed to the drug.

There were many reasons previous studies failed and were abandoned before Biogen's attempt. As infuriating as this news sounded, it proves society has lost connection with the present moment. We can connect on a higher level, stress-free, which simply requires us to sharpen our senses without more pharmaceuticals.

Before we can become hopeful about the future and what science will honestly be able to provide to fight Dementia, we must not lose sight of our human capabilities now. We must sharpen our senses to begin preparing, starting with two of the five senses through sound and smell.

One of the capabilities I applied to my caregiving journey was received as an intuitive mind of an accountant. This perspective helped me come full circle because I connected the basic Accounting equation of Assets = Liabilities + Equity with Dementia. It sounds bizarre until you realize Dementia is a process of accountability that holds an equation of our Personal Assets = Experiences + Thoughts. Our thoughts dictate our feelings. Our feelings dictate our actions, which become our experiences. Our experiences become our assets.

My thoughts behind those experiences are to share these feelings to collectively connect on a higher level and reduce our stress as caregivers.

Back to Basics - Sharpen Your Five Senses

SOUND - Healing Tones

According to *Music as Medicine: The Impact of healing harmonies* from The New Research Building Harvard Medical School, *"In ancient*

Greece, music was used to ease stress, promote sleep, and soothe pain."

Healing Frequencies – Meditative Binaural Music:

I understand hearing impairments for some may create a challenge, but if your hearing is not an obstacle, you can purchase a good pair of earbuds or turtle shell-style headphones to start. Go online to Youtube.com, for example, and search for Binaural Meditation music.

For starters, search for Angelic Tones or Angelic Meditation Music in 417 Hz, 432 Hz, 528 Hz, and 639 Hz. These meditative sets may be as short as 15 minutes or as long as 8-10 hours. They can work as sleep music, study music, work music, meditation music, or plain relaxing music at the end of a challenging day.

Why these frequencies?

417 Hz – Known to wipe out all the negativity inside us by bringing change so powerful it can reverse and undo negative happenings.

432 Hz – Known to give clarity to feel calmer, happier, and more relaxed; also known as the frequency of the universe, to have cosmic healing powers.

528 Hz – Known to be the musical mathematical matrix of creation. The Love frequency resonates at the heart of everything, making it known as the DNA Repair frequency.

639 Hz – Known as the frequency filled with love, radiance, and positive energy for balancing and healing the heart chakra.

During my Caregiver journey, my lower back, lumbar L4-5, ruptured, and the vertebrae just below it, known as the L5-S1 or Sacral 1, was bone on bone. I could no longer walk, drive, or relieve my body of waste without severe pain. After my surgery, I was prescribed a belt for 30 minutes a day that administered ultrasonic sound waves to my spine to stimulate bone growth.

Using sound as a healing mechanism is not new technology. During the 1920s - 1930s, American Scientist Royal Raymond Rife invented the Rife Machine. This machine produces energy similar to radio waves. According to Healthline, Christina Chun, MPH, who medically reviewed the machine in Jaquelyn Cafasso's article on June 25, 2018, explaining Rife's machine was inspired by Dr. Albert Abrams.

Cafasso shares that Abrams believed every disease has an electromagnetic frequency. He suggested doctors could kill diseased or cancerous cells by sending an electrical impulse identical to the cell's unique electromagnetic frequency, a theory also known as radionics. This sound technology was believed to work on viruses, bacteria, and cancer cells effectively.

At the time, few people believed his claims. And limited studies were able to prove his findings. However, in the 1980s, author Barry Lynes reignited interest in Rife machines. Lynes claimed the American Medical Association (AMA) and government agencies covered up evidence about Rife machines. However, researchers did not have solid proof that the Rife machines were successful. They continued to work on the theories from the 1980s to the 1990s. Now researchers are experimenting with radiofrequency EMFs to treat cancer.

How Brain Frequencies Work:

The human brain is more than just an organ; it's more like our supercomputer recording, storing, and retrieving data through electrical impulses. All areas of the brain communicate through neurons, which are like small electrical stations. Our brain functions in one of four different brainwave frequencies during the day, depending on the activity in which we engage.

Delta Waves – The deepest psychophysical relaxation. We typically reach this brain wave frequency via the unconscious mind during sleep, dreams, and total deprivation. The deepest level of relaxation is also known as the self-healing restorative sleep phase. We need at least 7 hours a night of this Delta Wave frequency.

Theta Waves – Are Unexpected, unpredictable, dreamlike, but very vivid images can be seen. This wave is also known as hypnagogic images, which are typically reached just before Delta Waves. This frequency is what we relate to calm drowsiness. These images are often surprisingly real because they contain intense memories.

Alpha Waves – Associated with a state of a vigilant but relaxed mind. This wave can be experienced during meditation or light introspective moments of yoga or tai chi. In this state of mind, we are more likely to be calm and relaxed enough to solve external problems if needed. This relaxed state is the desired mindset, but not always possible based on daily caregiving demands. By increasing alpha waves, we can reduce anxiety and depression.

Beta Waves – This is our normal state of mind throughout the day with normal awareness. These waves are the fundamental activities of survival related to recording, storing, and retrieving data throughout our day.

In a state of fight or flight, we experience a release of the hormone cortisol throughout our body while the brain uses Beta Waves to keep most situations under control. Otherwise, we would freak out and lose focus.

We may not be able to control our brainwave frequency since it occurs naturally, but we can select activities to stimulate our brain to help trigger brainwave frequencies. Listening to the meditative binaural frequencies will help induce a state of calm, relaxation, and detachment from daily stressors. Our temples (bodies) are designed for many different tasks. Each of us is gifted with a talent or more that requires us to raise our vibrations, remove vibration blockages, and find the present moment of joy. It truly is by divine design.

The Discovery of balancing my frequencies made living in the present moment less of a challenge for me. This type of music did not only relax me; it allowed my blocked energy to flow more freely. Starting the day with a silent meditation routine and finishing it with meditative music to fall asleep helped me keep a routine with positive energy flowing into the next day.

SMELL - Essential Oils

As we know it today, aromatherapy is the practice of using natural oils extracted from flowers, bark, stems, leaves, roots, or other parts of a plant or tree to enhance psychological and physical well-being. Our sense of smell is a powerful motivator. Think of how often you walked through a festival or indoor mall past booths or stores with fresh baked goods or sweets. They make your mouth water or even allow a childhood memory to surface because of a familiar scent. Realtors know this all too well when they stage open houses with inviting scents such as baked cookies, fresh pine, lemon, vanilla, or lavender to create a pleasant experience.

Essential oils are not to be taken lightly and require understanding for best results and avoiding harm. For centuries, they have been used by Chinese, Indians, Egyptians, Greeks, and Romans for cosmetics, perfumes, drugs, and even as currency.

Although essential oils have been around for so long, they were not

---

called Aromatherapy until the 1920s. The first book to mention Aromatherapy did not come to be until 1937 by René-Maurice Gattefossé, a French chemist. His book was later revised in English in 1993, becoming the first modern work on this subject. The editor of the 1993-second edition titled "Gattefossé Aromatherapy," Robert Tisserand, is often referred to as the father of modern Aromatherapy since he was the one to bring this practice into popularity.

How Aromatherapy works:

Studies done on both mice and humans have proven essential oils can enter the bloodstream by being inhaled. The delicate membranes in our nose provide a direct pharmacological effect via the blood supply to the brain—and an indirect effect via the olfactory nerve pathways to the brain, touch receptors affected by massage. The powerful placebo effect, according to Martin Watt, as published in Aromatic Thymes 2006.

Aromatherapy has many uses. The form I am referring to is intended to be inhaled or topical application. The Molecules in oils enter the nose, mouth, and skin then pass to the lungs and bloodstream, which take it to other parts of our body.

According to *21 Drops Essential Oil Therapy* the science behind essential oils is related to the oils containing volatile aromatic molecules. Volatile, meaning the oils dissipate quickly once applied or inhaled. *"When essential oils are inhaled through the nose, aromatic molecules are carried through the lining of the nasal cavity via tiny olfactory nerves, located in the roof of the inner nose, to the part of the brain called the limbic system. The limbic system, in turn, influences the endocrine system and the autonomic nervous system."*

Top Essential Oils to Consider:

- **Lavender** – Versatile oil gives off a light aroma to uplift spirits while transitioning moods to a state of calmness by reducing stress, emotional pain, and anxiety.

- **Tea Tree** – Clove spice infused with pine aroma is a powerful antiseptic for healing wounds, prevents future infection, and naturally disinfects the air while creating a refreshing at-home scent.

- **Eucalyptus** – Gives off a mixed aroma of sweet mint and spicy pine. Most are familiar with the cough drops made in this flavor because it is a natural anti-inflammatory, which remedies any skin irritation while naturally hydrating damaged tissue. It is also well known for improving respiratory issues.

- **Orange (Citrus)** – A sweet aroma with d-limonene aids in maintaining normal cellular regeneration while it gives off a natural calming effect. This aroma promotes positive attitudes and induces relaxation for a calm spirit.

- **Lemongrass** – Has a fresh light lemony aroma with earthy undertones. This oil helps relieve muscle pain and aches with many great vitamins for the skin externally and kills harmful bacteria. When inhaled, this oil helps to relieve aches and boost energy.

- **Peppermint** – Gives off a minty and refreshing aroma. We are also familiar with it for soothing colds and coughs or sprucing up a mocha, but it is great for many health restorative properties. It is used as a medicinal and calming aroma to treat gastrointestinal issues, reduce muscle pain, and relieve anxiety. When inhaled, this oil will liven up the mind, body, and soul.

- **Cinnamon** – Known in the winter holiday months as a warm and comforting aroma to spice up beverages and pies. Cinnamon is now being used worldwide to treat health problems, including respiratory problems, skin infections, blood impurities, menstrual problems, and various heart disorders. This spice is rich in minerals such as manganese, iron, and calcium while having a high fiber content. It also helps to remove nervous tension. The list goes on.

- **Rosemary** – Stimulates hair growth, boosts mental activity, relieves respiratory problems, and reduces pain. This oil is very popular in Mediterranean regions as a culinary herb. This oil comes from a part of the mint family, including basil, lavender, myrtle, and sage.

- **Frankincense** – Is extracted from the gum or resin of olibanum trees called Boswellia Carteri. Found in ancient Egyptian and Anglo-Saxon civilizations. Mostly associated with Christian traditions, this aroma can boost the immune system with antiseptic and disinfectant qualities even when inhaled.

  Topically, it can improve oral health, hair roots, tones, and lift skin, aids intestinal tract and blood vessels, and protect from premature loss of teeth and hair. Other perks include reducing scars, promoting digestion, stimulating urination, reducing respiratory issues, and relieving stress.

Some of these oils were used as remedies centuries ago as perfumes to reduce the unpleasant body orders from lack of bathing. These same perfume oils were helping to prevent sickness by harnessing natural antibacterial properties.

It did not take long for essential oils to be viewed negatively and seen as witchcraft, causing herbalists to be burned or persecuted. Thankfully, in modern-day, the use of oils is trusted and used by those who understand their powers for the greater good to heal the mind and body in hospitals by Naturopathic Therapists.

Combining sound through soft earbuds with a soothing smell at bedtime in a diffuser proved to be even more relaxing and stress relieving. The thoughts of the day lingering seemed to melt away at the end of every day with a binaural meditation and scents to fill our room at bedtime to induce a peaceful state of mind.

I was waking up the next day energized and still feeling at peace. I was going through seasons without head colds or annoying allergies. The oils were creating cleaner air to breathe and helping to boost my immunities. I could even see a difference in my complexion when I combined a couple of different oils such as Citrus, Peppermint, Lavender, and Eucalyptus.

Pure form is a bit trickier to handle because it varies from person to person with different tolerance levels or reactions. You must be careful and read up as much as possible before using any oil in pure form. Some may have skin reactions such as Dermatitis, which appears in rashes, burns, and itchy scaly skin if the pure oil is not diluted. Others may have no problem at all.

Carrier oils in most lotions and soaps cannot penetrate further than the epidermis's top 2-3 cellular layers. When essential oils are applied directly to the skin, the oil can be absorbed into the bloodstream because these types of oils have a much smaller molecular weight. For this reason, they are far more effective in massage therapy as well.

TOUCH - **Massage therapy to relieve pain and blocked energy**

When we give care consistently without a break, our stress can break down our immune system, as discussed during chapter 6, Domino Effects under Heal the Heart to Heal the Mind. You might agree if you find yourself with a burning tension in your neck and shoulders or an ache in your lower back and glutes from sitting with your loved one for long periods. The lack of exercise and excess cortisol in your muscles will make your body ache in ways you might dismiss to aging.

Massage therapy might be considered a luxury to some, but caregivers now need to relieve stress, decrease anxiety, and reduce irritability. If you are suffering from situational depression, a massage may also provide supportive treatment for relief and regain a sense of empowerment through a mind-body connection.

For those having problems sleeping, combining massage with essential oils could drastically improve your ability to achieve restorative sleep. Caregivers suffering from insomnia, migraines, or severe pain can find relief from receiving regular massages weekly or bi-weekly. Your loved one experiencing a chronic illness or disease may also be experiencing higher levels of stress. They may not be cured of their chronic illness or disease, but they will most likely experience a better quality of life.

In a study on the effects of trigger point therapy by the American Massage Therapy Association, they witnessed a significant decrease in heart rate with systolic and diastolic blood pressure. Measures of oxygen consumption and cortisol levels were lower after 15 minutes of a chair massage. Massage is also beneficial to relieve headaches, shoulder tension, fatigue, muscle, and joint pain. If not for massage therapy, my lower back pain before surgery would have surpassed the typical pain scale on a 1-10 to be a 12 regularly.

By becoming too sedentary as we sit with our loved ones or work long hours away from them, we allow emotional energy to become blocked in our bodies. The more you pay attention to your body and understand the aches and pains, you can appreciate a massage to improve your mental health. The sense of touch will help with pain management, and it helps to keep our mind and body connected overall.

Aside from massage, giving and receiving hugs throughout the day is extremely beneficial. When you can hug your loved one, you reduce cortisol levels which boosts heart health and reduces stress by showing support. Hugs help us to reduce fear and pain too. When words are too hard to express, a hug can communicate to others through a silent embrace.

TASTE - Bad Dental hygiene and blood

When the caregiving days feel like they are becoming longer and all you want to do is sleep, you might be tempted to skimp on dental hygiene. If you think you are saving time by not putting in the effort or doing better next time, you are only creating more problems and stress later down the road, especially when poor dental hygiene has been linked to Dementia.

Our mouth can carry about 700 species of bacteria, including periodontal gum disease, which has been linked to vascular dementia and Alzheimer's. Gum disease results from infection of the oral tissues holding teeth in place. Bacteria and infections in the mouth can get into the bloodstream and travel to the brain.

The National Center for Health Statistics conducted a study with 26 years of follow-up compared to the antibodies present in the diagnosis of Alzheimer's. The results of a more recent study suggested that plaques of beta-amyloid protein may be produced as a result of periodontal disease.

Bad taste, also known as dysgeusia, is a common symptom of gastrointestinal reflux disease, salivary gland infection (parotitis), sinusitis, poor dental hygiene, and can even result from taking certain medicines. Not flossing and brushing twice a day can cause gingivitis, which can cause a bad taste in your mouth. Dental problems, such as infections, abscesses, and even wisdom teeth coming in, can also cause a bad taste.

Of course, the occasional indulgence with a chocolate chip cookie became more of a nice reward than my stress-related comfort food. Having water on hand with lemon to wash the cookie down helped keep a bad taste out of my mouth, freshen my breath, and make my skin glow from staying hydrated.

Pay attention to the taste in your mouth throughout the day. You might need to drink more water, swish with mouthwash, or make an appointment with a dentist. Dental care is proactive preventative maintenance, which is why we are supposed to go twice a year when a routine physical is only once a year.

SIGHT - Nature walks, sunrises, and sunsets

Caregivers might not realize how isolated their lives have become as they care for their loved ones until they need more social interactions. Looking at someone else other than your loved one is not a bad thing to wish. By going out for a walk in nature, you are not only getting a chance to break your isolation, but you are also getting a change of scenery overall.

Walking near water or designated nature paths can also provide similar results from our sense of smell and touch. Feel a breeze on your face, breathe in the fresh air around you instead of the stagnant indoor air. We lose sight of this sense when we get what is considered tunnel vision. Your main focus becomes your loved ones and their needs, as your own needs slip away. What happened to your bike, surfboard, golf clubs, or outdoor gear? Are you lost in your tunnel vision, maybe?

I had tunnel vision that opened my eyes in a traumatic event after my lower back surgery when I experienced a pulmonary embolism one month later. The moment of having a panic attack because I was in pain and could not breathe was when I felt the universe holding me.

God is in everything, everywhere, all the time. I grew up being taught this but did not truly experience this concept until I could not catch my breath. Then in an instant, thoughts of damage to my brain or not getting to say goodbye to my loved ones overwhelmed me. I kept seeing nature scenes with lush green rolling hills with varieties of closed doors tucked away within the hills.

I survived one of the scariest moments in my life and thankfully lived to share this with you. Life without breath is like a world without God. When we lose touch with nature, we also lose touch with Him. Distractions and pains from our caregiving journey pull us into the material world when we need to stay connected to His. Taking the time to marvel at nature is transcendent healing for depression, anxiety, stress, overwhelm, and hopelessness.

When the universe exhales, we inhale. It is that simple. Healing could be as close as your backyard or apartment balcony.

So, you see, by sharpening our senses, we do not have to be dependent on pharmaceuticals. I will even suggest our senses can help us avoid major medical situations like heart attacks, degenerative joints, or diabetes by sharpening our senses. As I sharpened my senses, I became more self-aware of my environments, the people, and the elements that contributed to my mood and energy flow. I had a stronger sense of self.

I feel God attempts to do for each of us, as what we think are random events taking place in our lives to refocus us on our temples and what they were intended to be. In Hindsight, He has used my caregiving journey to teach me this and so much more.

Over the years of caring for Mom, I slowly realized today eventually became yesterday, and tomorrow has not yet come. Although I was stressing and worrying as if it had, it affected my health negatively. I had to take the time to process my past, which helped me gain a better perspective to let it go to live in the present moment peacefully.

All we should be concerned with is the present moment. It sounds so simple, but it took a few years for me to practice this and feel comfortable with focusing on only the present moment in gratitude. I challenge you to engage your senses more daily and fall in love with Yourself in the present moment.

Chapter 24
Redefining Our Expectations

Romans 12:2 (NLT)
Don't copy the behavior and customs of this world but let God transform
you into a new person by changing the way you think. Then you will
learn to know God's will for you, which is good and pleasing and perfect.

Our expectations and mindset will need to change if we truly seek change for the better while living in the present moment. Change does not mean you cannot prepare for a future event, such as tracking doctor appointments or anticipating the next grocery trip. We need to practice focusing on the moment given to share with our loved ones each day.

If I experienced a bad day with Mom, I immediately had negative expectations for our uncertain future. *Is this how it is always going to be? Or worse, as she declines?* My thoughts and feelings needed to match up to accept reality and help shape a reality not yet in existence.

The more I understood her form of Mixed Dementia as time passed, the more I felt informed and worried I would eventually be living with these illnesses. If Vascular and Frontotemporal Dementia symptoms started in her mid-40's, then it's around the corner for me. *Right?* The reality of this logic made me fearful of what my husband and family would be facing. What my next 20 to 30 years could be.

By allowing this worry to settle into my daily thoughts as I observed her movements or lack of, I invited undue stress and anxiety into my life. I was too frazzled to recognize that my stress created a cycle of fatigue that caused tiny slips of memory that had nothing to do with aging.

Thankfully, a full night of rest or even a refreshing nap was all I needed for a sharp mind again. Clarity returned, and worries subsided as if God placed his hand on the back of my head to say, *"Rest my child, I have this under my control."*

Worries subsided even more, when I realized Mom had what appeared to be the perfect storm of symptoms, which came from life or an environment that I did not have. We share genetic makeup, but it is not definitive for my health. Although I felt guilty for being concerned with my wellbeing, at this point, I desperately wanted to understand her path to early-onset Alzheimer's and FTD, outside of genetics.

As we lived through one season after the next, I meditated outside as much as possible. By observing the trees in the fall shed their leaves to budding flowers blooming in the spring, I could see that nature goes through this process of change every year, as do we all. These changes of renewal are to be expected, not feared. Even if stores put Christmas decorations out in August, it just means change is on the way. We can fight it, ignore it, or go with the flow.

These seasonal changes bring about signs of hope all around us if we look for them. If you take the time to sit near some trees, you will see how the winds push change through the branches. The push can be gentle, or it can be quite abrasive.

Either way, the tree remains strongly rooted while it flexes and bends to flow with the winds. I had to learn how to change my daily habits and expectations so I, too, would flex and bend while living as a mother, spouse, and caregiver.

Caregivers are like trees planted to care for their loved ones. Some care without a doubt with so much compassion they instinctively know how to bend and flex day by day. Others care with resistance which creates worry, stress, and reluctance to flex and bend as moments arise. Finding a balance between compassion and resistance is no easy task, so being present at the moment will provide opportunities to remain compassionate without resistance.

Resistance is not all bad when it comes to finding balance. It can be a healthy reminder to set boundaries, understand our limitations, and avoid burnout.

My friend and Caregiver, Meriam Boldewijn, understands the need for healthy resistance, which is the basis for her book *Caregiver 2.0 From Burnout to Powerhouse*. She breaks down her story with added boundaries and how burnout took her to a dark place as she cared for her husband living with diabetes and brother after having a stroke. Meriam became lost on her journey and depleted her wellspring of hope until she found a way out of the darkness.

I found myself in a similar dark place after spending a weekend building a garden for Mom with hopes of encouraging her to venture outside. When my intent to help her was met with repeated rejection as she allowed the garden to die, my thoughts of creating the garden instantly became *"this was a waste of time, and that it was all for nothing."* These looped thoughts created a deep sense of defeat and resentment. I lost sight of my purpose.

In this present moment of defeat, I created a reality of hopelessness. I opened the door for a future, which had not happened yet, making me dread spending time with Mom. My mindset invited additional negative thoughts, which led to depression. What was happening here? My thoughts and feelings were allowing me to become what I stressed about before.

This process was easier to accept and cope with when I had explanations to rely on, whether spiritual, medical, or scientific. The more knowledge I gained, the less my thoughts ran away to the dark side. I was guided to this information which shed much-needed light on positive reinforcement.

Dr. Joe Dispenza explains how our thoughts and feelings have a specific link between our emotional states and our heart rhythms.

"When we have negative emotions (such as anger and fear), our heart rhythms become erratic and disorganized. In contrast, positive

emotions (love and joy, for instance) produce highly ordered coherent patterns that HeartMath researchers refer to as heart coherence."

When I became angry with Mom for not maintaining the garden, I became consumed with fear of her falling due to muscle atrophy. When she refused to get off the couch, I became stressed, defeated, and depressed. I let the situation take over and ran with my emotions without a fight. I was tired of playing indoor board games and needed us to go outside for a few moments to refresh more often.

I wanted to apply the concepts of healing the heart to heal her mind, but she would not try to save her life or appease me. Our heart health is dependent on our commitment to make healthy choices in achieving a better understanding of our emotions. Being stuck on autopilot and expecting life to be more fruitful does not work. We have to be willing participants to engage in our journey in ways that support our loved ones yet guard our health.

As I continued to pray and meditate during these troubling times of stress and depression, I received guidance, which led me to further understanding. My spiritual guidance went beyond recognizing the behaviors or symptoms of what living with Dementia looked like and confirmed Dr. Joe Dispenza's concept of changing and creating my reality. To do so, I had to begin by changing my habits in the present moment.

"Since every potential in the universe is a wave of probability that has an electromagnetic field and is energetic in nature, it makes sense that our thoughts and feelings are no exceptions." Another reminder to stop worrying about a future I can change for myself, even if I cannot change Mom's or help her broken will to mend. We may be on similar paths now, but I am not headed in the same direction as she is in the long run. I embrace this concept now.

Thoughts are the language of the brain, and feelings are the language of the body. We need to train our thoughts (brain) and feelings (body) to be similar instead of thinking one thing yet feeling another. I cannot think I am in control of my health and feel helpless and defeated about the future of my health at the same time.

Track backward for a moment with me. In the first half of this book, we touched on initial symptoms, which eventually led to a medical diagnosis in some cases. The listed symptoms and behaviors are caused by the breakdown of an autonomic nervous system in the brain. Our cells are made up of molecules and atoms made up of subatomic particles composed of energy. Our physiological temple comprises the same stuff as the rest of the universe – subatomic particles.

I found peace in Dr. Joe Dispenza's explanation of *"this potential energy lowers itself as a frequency of wave patterns until it appears as solid."* My understanding is, individually, we are the frequency in solid form. My thoughts and feelings change my frequency, raising or lowering, but my awareness can aid in accepting the change or creating change.

When we lead a healthy lifestyle and consume value-added nutrition, we consume energy, which keeps our guts, hearts, and brains healthy. Dr. Dispenza continues to explain how this same energy is connected to intelligence, which keeps our hearts beating and our stomachs digesting food and oversees an incalculable number of chemical reactions per second that take place in every cell.

The same consciousness prompts trees to grow fruit and causes distant galaxies to form and collapse. Because it exists in all places, times and exerts its power within us and all around us, it makes change both personal and universal.

I accepted the divine timing of receiving this information as a universal nudge to change my expectations. You reading this book may be your divine timing.

From the smallest to the grandest universal level, I can now see where I fit into the larger picture. I see how this is not about me and how I am meant to be there for Mom in her greatest time of need. I can visualize the larger picture: we are all connected and only separated by our consciousness, a thought process.

Hinduism refers to this quantum field through the opening and clearing of chakras to allow the flow of our energy to connect us to the divine. As much as I tried to keep spirituality separate from science, it became impossible. Why may you ask?

Dr. Joe Dispenza helps explains this answer through universal inquiry as, *"How can consciousness that has created all of life, expends the energy and will to consistently regulate every function of our bodies to keep us alive, has expressed such a deep and abiding interest in us, be anything but pure love?"*

I could only match this answer in response to my findings, which included a biblical approach. The one pure love that comes to mind is the Holy Spirit. If you have ever been fortunate enough to experience it as I have, you would understand the frequency or vibration on a much higher level than your own.

Dr. Joe Dispenza continues, *"When we emulate the properties of this awareness, we are becoming creators. When our will matches its will, when our minds match its mind, when our love for life matches its love for life, we are enacting this universal consciousness. We become the elevated power that transcends the past, heals the present, and opens the door to the future."*

My lack of understanding of Dementia in past years as we learned about Bipolar tendencies gave way to so much resistance because it forced me to recount a painful past. To understand Mom in her state of Mixed Dementia, I had to heal in this present time, which in turn opened my eyes and opened the doors to a future I now know is guided by the Holy Spirit, the love of God.

I am the child that became the parent who is also a creation becoming a creator.

Each caregiver aids a loved one with a broken will, which is given the power to create a better quality of life until they depart from this dimension. We can create a negative environment when we do not let go of the past or avoid taking better care of ourselves. We can create a positive environment when we forgive and choose to love them through to the end with the best of our abilities.

Redefining your expectations has to start somewhere - one step at a time, by one day at a time. Learn to clear your gut of toxic inhibitors through changing lifestyle habits. Then seek therapy to heal in the present from the past to align your thoughts and feelings. Include meditative practices to connect to the universe and invite the Holy Spirit into your daily routines. Stop reacting to life and start living proactively.

When I was giving off a stench of defeat, I received more moments to react with defeat. As I consciously changed my lifestyle habits with nutrition, restorative sleep, exercise, and meditative practices, I began to return a positive signal that invited more positive moments.

Later, when Mom moved in with us, my thoughts and feelings remained more positive since I now had more control over our environment. Keeping a clean house, monitoring her television selections, and finding time to sit near my meditation tree as needed gave me more hope for our unknown future.

Maintaining balance comes from a place of hope. It is easy to be hopeful when I am well-rested, nourished, and energetic. When either of those is low, my hope tends to wane, and caring for Mom becomes a chore or more of a burden than I would like to admit. Trying to find the bright side of situations was another fun challenge to help me focus. Being able to come from a place of gratitude instead of only acceptance helped keep hope alive and allowed me to empathize with the kind of life she existed in.

Returning to the outdoors to meditate has become extremely important over these past couple of years. Spending time with the Holy Spirit in nature renewed my strength and reminded me we were not alone on this journey.

I was not meant to fear these unexpected life changes but to embrace them. *"This too shall pass"* became my second mantra to hold onto my faith strongly as the unknown rattled me along our way.

As Dr. Joe Dispenza states, *"When you change your mind, your brain changes; and when you change your brain, your mind changes."* Mom used to tell me that I could do anything I set my mind to when I was younger. I knew she was trying to encourage me to think beyond my perceived limits as a child, but her words still ring true for me today.

Caregiving made me feel limited in the beginning. Now, I am pushing my intellect as if I have no limitations at all. Dr. Joe Dispenza helped me to understand on an academic level by pointing out, *"We live by habit when we're no longer aware of what we're thinking, doing, or feeling; we become unconscious. The greatest habit we must break is the habit of being ourselves."*

I encourage you to take the time to examine your habits. Are you living the life you dreamt of, or are you habitually allowing life to pass by?

Chapter 25
Let Go, Let God

Philippians 4:6-9 (NIV)
Do not be anxious about anything, but in every situation, by prayer and petition, with thanksgiving, present your requests to God. And the peace of God, which transcends all understanding, will guard your hearts and your minds in Christ Jesus.

Finally, brothers and sisters, whatever is true, whatever is noble, whatever is right, whatever is pure, whatever is lovely, whatever is admirable – if anything is excellent or praiseworthy – think about such things. Whatever you have learned or received or heard from me, or seen in me - put it into practice. And the God of peace will be with you.

Watching how Mom and Dad coexisted around each other, absorbing their ideas of morality, was confusing from what I learned in CCD classes at Church. There certainly was a disconnect from *"due unto others as you would have done unto you."* I tried to keep the golden rule in mind when I realized I would fulfill my calling as a caregiver. Set my previous mindset and feelings of animosity aside and focus on Mom's needs regardless.

I had two parents I loved but felt caught in the middle and forced to choose one over the other for various reasons. I was able to see both sides of their stories and still could not choose who was right or wrong or if they were good or bad for the choices they made. Both were hurt by each other. Both wanted something from the other they were unwilling to give themselves.

I have learned a tremendous amount of information regarding our mind, body, and soul because I accepted fiduciary responsibility and the caregiver role. If I had to sum it up in the simplest of ideas, I would have to say Dementia is not to be taken lightly or dismissed. Next, I would remind you of the significance your God-given temple is for a greater plan. Finally, I will encourage you to open your mind and accept YOU are not alone in this universe.

When I was working in the corporate world, the interactions left me feeling empty and lost. Life with Dementia would happen in such a way to challenge me, break me, and yet still fill me up. I will never question the existence of a higher power ever again. Because I found the courage to ask why I was here and what my purpose in life was. I was given unique visions through my dreams and ultimately a moment to feel the Holy Spirit combine with my spirit.

The answer to my questions did not come quickly. Over several nights I had a dialogue while trying to find my comfort level with speaking to the Spirit. I did the only thing I knew to trust at this point - Pray. This Q&A went on like this over weeks of repetitive dreams.

Holy Spirit: "Let Go"
Me: "Of what?" (what am I holding onto so tightly)
Holy Spirit: "Let Go"
Me: "Of what, my job? Career? Money? Dreams? Life?"
Holy Spirit: "Let Go and seek a more spiritual career."
Me: "Are you kidding me? I just spent ten years getting 2 degrees and two more years for the CPA license. I cannot imagine what I would do otherwise. How will we meet our bills?"
Holy Spirit: "Let Go and seek a more spiritual career. All your material needs will be met."

Me: "Okay, but I have no idea what a spiritual career entails or how to start one."

Holy Spirit: "Let Go and seek a more spiritual career. All your material needs will be met. It will be better for you in the long run."

Me: "Okay, but I need help deciding what a spiritual career is. I love my church, but I cannot imagine working in it. I will go where you lead me."

I had several sleepless nights trying to figure this out. How could I step away from all the hard work, time, and money put into the 2 degrees and one license towards setting up an accounting career? To do what? Pray for a living. As Mom would say, I needed an attitude adjustment. Especially when telling the truth did not set me free when I was 16 as it brought about more turmoil.

Searching for the truth for Mom and I initiated a life-changing transformation that felt like a mid-life crisis but brought about a much-needed change in me. The interesting thing about God is He has all the time in the world and is patient with us. Through my eyes, with a mindset solely focused on chasing dreams of romance, career, and adventure, I completely lost sight of who truly is in control. Rather than continue to chase the ghost of my future self, I fell in love with who I am, who He intended me to be.

Stepping away from the corporate career I was building was scary, but it was the first leap of faith in trusting God. What I did for a living was not the only part of me He created in me because the life I thought I was creating was simply the training for life as a caregiver.

I was thinking about the simple side of helping to maintain her daily like meals, picking up groceries or Rx refills, and taking her to a doctor's appointment now and then. I was not thinking about the emotional impact of caring for her and what it would feel like to change my work routine and life around her needs.

Who would I be without the career I was building? What was I giving up? There was no way of knowing until I turned in my notice at work in October 2017 and took the leap.

Of course, the first few weeks were nice to sleep in and catch my breath for a change. It felt like I was just on vacation and kept waiting for a call asking me to return. Although I was asked to remain on a consulting basis, I had a strong feeling I was not supposed to entertain that idea at all. Something was shifting inside me, and I knew I would be okay once I stopped feeling like I was standing in quicksand.

Within three months of stepping away from the corporate world to care for Mom, my Big Sis called with some news. By the dismal tone of her voice, I knew it had to be related to Mom or Dad. Ironically, it was neither because it was about my aunt Martha, Dad's younger sister, who had passed away. The way life had been going for Mom, I expected the call to be about her. I was ready for the call to be about her in a strange way.

The news took us all by surprise, as the loss of a loved one often does. What was peculiar about this news was Mom's reaction. Death seemed to have plagued her life over the prior year with little to no mourning at all.

First, her eldest brother passed at the beginning of the year, in January 2016. He had similar heart issues with a defibrillator placed as well as mixed Dementia. Although he was not officially diagnosed before he died, I suspected he was living with Lewy Body Dementia from the description of his behaviors shared with me.

Next, her sister, Vilma, who was only one year older than Mom, passed away in July 2016. Only seven months later, from her brother's passing, she did not express any grief after either of her siblings passed. Her response was, "well, we all die eventually, right?"

Vilma was taking similar medications for her heart as Mom. Since Mom assumed the bad heart ran in the family, she would sigh and say, "well, she had a bad ticker like Grandpa too, so it was expected anyway." I could not tell if she was still putting up the strong survivor front or if she was incapable of crying, showing grief, or comprehending the loss.

Then her youngest brother passed only six months after Vilma in January of 2017 after finally receiving a heart transplant. This 3rd family death was only three weeks before Martha. Again, barely any sadness and no true grieving after three deaths in roughly one year.

And Yet, when Martha died, three weeks later, in February of 2017, it was not only another death; it was a loss she could have shared with Dad.

We sat in a local Tex-Mex restaurant after church one Sunday afternoon as our meals were being prepared when I tried to explain to Mom about Martha delicately. I had no way of knowing how the news would affect her, but I made an assumption based on her lack of mourning from her siblings that she would do the same with this news.

Mom believed in an old wives' tale that deaths happened in threes. I don't know where this originated from, but it's something she would say after watching the news every time they announced the death of a celebrity for whatever reason.

The look on her face after I mentioned Martha's passing was shocking. It was like I threw cold water in her face or told her one of my sisters had passed. I can only imagine she felt panic over who the other two deaths would be to follow Martha's to complete her wives' tale this time. The dilemma of wanting to reach out to Dad but not giving way to years of silence seemed to be causing some traumatic decline in her.

Something seemed to be unsettling with Martha's passing for Dad as well. He was shocked, angry, and full of guilt. He did not answer her last phone call. Martha was his second younger sibling to die before him. I believe intense grief settled into his lungs quickly in the form of pneumonia (the element of water or fluid) within a month of her passing. Only a couple of months after I had finally asked God what my purpose in life was or, more directly, "Why am I here?" Dad had begun to ask, "Why am I still here?"

He also assumed since his father had died at such a young age of 55, he would not live much longer after. Even still, he made it to his 70th birthday. He did not consider health factors and the differences in lifestyle habits. He failed to acknowledge that he was not a chain smoker as his three other siblings had been. He exercised quite often until their divorce and made an effort to try different food diets but living with Mom and her huge, sweet tooth made it hard to maintain lifestyle changes for the better.

A week later, Dad and I went to lunch after Martha's passing when he expressed guilt for missing Martha's last call but could not wrap his mind around why he was still alive while his two younger sisters passed before him. His younger brother had a heart attack the prior year at age 50, and Dad never had one.

Doctors were astonished at Dad's health status in prior years. They could not figure out how he had not had a stroke himself. He listened to whatever advice he was given for some time until he, too, felt defeated by life with Dementia. He started to say the same thing as Mom did about how we are all going to die someday, so we might as well die happy. Another excuse to overindulge with food and whatever he wanted and as much as he wanted.

When we returned from lunch, he settled into his corner on the couch under a blanket and fell asleep. Although he was exhausted from the outing and emotional turmoil, he sat and slept so peacefully. I started to think about his mortality while watching him sleep and began to feel an unsettling panic of my own because I could not imagine him past his current age. My Dad, friend, and mentor was only 70 years young to me. I was not ready to imagine life without him.

During the previous three years, I was able to reconnect with Dad in such a way we revived our father-daughter relationship as it had been so long ago before. I was Daddy's little girl again. He had the opportunity to explain to me just how proud he was of me for pushing through to achieve so many goals he never had the courage to do while creating a beautiful family. I had the opportunity to express sincere gratitude for all his sacrifices, which helped me reach my goals.

There was a mutual moment of forgiveness and acceptance. We were able to share many meals discussing the highs and lows of our lives, which gave me a better understanding of Mom's many emotional issues. My life reached a point of peace and joy, allowing me to feel whole like I had never felt before.

I started to finally understand God has a plan, even when we cannot see the plan. This understanding was a feeling deep inside that I could only describe as an intuitional connection with the Spirit. More was shifting within me, but I had no clue what to do with it all. This time I did not have to worry about maintaining a work-life balance and greatly appreciated the time I was given to allow the shifting within to begin the work I set in motion once I asked why I was here.

Then Dad's fiancé called on a Sunday afternoon on Mother's Day 2017 to inform us we needed to get to the hospital immediately. Things were not looking well at all as he was struggling to breathe even more. I sped up the highway as fast as I could from North Austin to the Temple, TX Baylor, Scott, and White hospital while attempting to calm myself by saying, "this too shall pass."

The gravity of this moment speeding against time and distance to be by his side was resting heavily on my chest. Once I arrived and walked into his room, I had to remain calm so he could see my strength instead of the fear taking over like the messenger of death itself.

He pulled my hand to kiss the back of my hand, smiled with as much strength as possible. Seeing him in the hospital bed in his pajamas with an IV in one arm and an oxygen mask on his face made my strong, burly "Tanco" father look so small and frail.

I picked up his hand to kiss the back of his hand as well and then said, "This is all temporary. It will pass soon enough." He knew it was his time because, in response, he said, "I can't believe I am going to go out like this." I had a brief moment of clarity when the image of him sleeping on the couch in his red sweater after our last lunch together flashed through my mind once again. There was a reason I could not imagine him past that moment in time.

When I said it was all temporary, I meant the doctors would do what needed to be done so he could go home again. I could feel the panic and denial creep in and take hold of me because I felt like I could not breathe as they took him away to the ICU. The concept of temporary now held a new meaning.

Dad's pneumonia was proving to be much more severe than previous times he endured it. I wanted to spend as much time as possible with him, so I willingly turned my back on Mom. I could not be in two places at once. Little Sis and I took turns checking in on her morning and night while Big Sis and I took turns sleeping at the hospital next to Dad's bedside. My husband filled in the gaps wherever he was able to give us more time.

For the next three weeks, I tried to remain hopeful and positive, but Dad's health continued to decline. I prayed more daily than I had ever prayed before, hanging on to the present moment out of fear of letting go. First, I prayed for his recovery, and then I began to accept what was happening, so I prayed for him to be at peace.

I struggled to make meaningful connections with God throughout my life, but I was now connecting with Him daily, hourly, and feeling the strength and guidance.

Dad eventually had to be intubated until a tracheotomy replaced the intubation with full life support. We were still in suspense of this temporary transition. I wanted so desperately to hear his voice again. I wanted his eyes open, at least so he could look into my eyes as I told him I loved him one more time. It had never occurred to me that telling him this would be temporary would be my last words to him, or the last moment I would see the sparkle in his eyes.

I prayed for Dad to be without pain. I prayed for Dad to be given a choice to stay and continue living his life in this new state of normal. I strangely knew I had to let go, yet I was hanging on tightly to his hand, to my memories, to hope for a better outcome.

Then I slowly accepted a little more each day and prayed for him to be painlessly set free from this world. He had been more than enough for me in this world of unfair challenges and heartbreak. All the while, I secretly worried about how I would manage caring for Dad in one city and Mom in another at the same time.

Friday of Memorial Day weekend, before God opened His arms to welcome Dad home, I sat by his hospital bedside writing this book, trying to remain calm yet distracted from the uncomfortable grief knocking on the door of my heart. As I looked up to check in on him, I caught him peacefully laying there, eyes closed with a smile on his face. I realized, at that moment, our family members, who had gone on before him, were coming to greet him. I felt it without a doubt. I could see his lips pucker as if he were greeting someone, a kiss hello.

Then in the early morning hours of Memorial Day 2017, while I was still asleep, I began to see glowing white crosses. I felt a kiss on the side of my mouth as I lay in bed—a kiss goodbye.

When I opened my eyes, laying in darkness while looking around the room from the warmth of my bed, expecting to see him. I knew the choice we had to make next, no matter how hard it was to verbalize. His spirit was not free until his physical body was allowed to let go.

Six months after leaving the corporate world to take a leap of faith, I had to let go of Dad to become Mom's full-time caregiver and guardian.

Shortly after arriving at the hospital on Memorial Day, my siblings and I decided to begin comfort care to set him free. No matter how well informed we were about what to expect, it did not seem to change the feeling of time standing still in disbelief as we watched the light flow upwards and out of his body.

My husband drove me home while I stared out of my car window, gazing at the crescent moon in a surreal state of mind, half expecting to return to the hospital the next day to find it was all a strange dream. I held my gaze on the moon while we drove home for the focal point of light. The image of Dad's spirit leaving his body made me wonder where he had gone.

Was he blending into the moonlight? I could not stop staring, searching for him even now. Normally, my mind exhaustingly analyzes every detail, possibility, alternatives of every moment like a perpetual five-year-old - why, how, where. Thankfully, this became one of the only times in my adult life when my thoughts were numb yet primal. Shower, then sleep.

The next two mornings were painful as I woke to the sunlight pouring into the room. The hole in my chest felt heavy yet hollow at the same time.

Now what? How do I go on from here? What kind of spiritual career is God guiding me towards, and how will I know it's the right one?

At this point, anything was possible, I supposed. I paid close attention at the funeral home, answering a multitude of random preference questions. For a moment, I wondered if working in a funeral home would be considered my spiritual career. My analytical mind was back in sync, which quickly came to a resounding 'NO.' We had the next day planned for the cemetery, and I quickly decided my spiritual career had to be with the land of the living to make a difference long before the end of days in this dimension.

On the third night, since Dad had passed, I crawled into bed emotionally exhausted. As I drifted from alpha to theta sleep, I could feel a presence by my bedside. Then I felt a warm tingly sensation in the shape of a hand slide straight into my chest. During the moment this tingly warmth lingered, I felt the hollow space filled with peace and warmth while the heavyweight of grief and despair dissolved. All I remembered thinking was, "Thank you, Jesus," and then I drifted away into deep delta sleep for a mindless restorative slumber.

To my surprise, as the sunlight poured into our bedroom the third morning after, I felt no pain or heavyweight of grief. Sadness, yes, but an unexpected calming acceptance. Shortly after I started preparing for the trip to handle business at the cemetery, my phone rang. On the other end, Mom is calling in an unfamiliar voice. Her voice was full of energy, with an added edge of anxiety and irritability.

She stopped calling me on the phone since she became accustomed to me checking in on her regularly. If she wanted or needed something, she simply waited until I arrived at check-in. This time I could hear the anxiety in her voice as she asked, "Hey Jess, hey, uh, um, so listen, how did things go at the funeral home? Oh wow. So, Jess, I was, uh, I wondered if I could tag along with you to the cemetery, you know, just in case there is something I could do, you know? Something I could help pay for, anything really."

The Bipolar Manic episodes had begun again. Mom transitioned from a bitter divorced woman to a grieving widow overnight. It had been 48 hours since she last slept. Mom had reached a breaking point after so much death, and now it was the loss of her lifetime love. Whether she admitted it or not, shock and regret were taking a toll on her.

Although Mom and Dad had been divorced ten years before his passing, this was not just another death she was trying to comprehend or accept. After all, they were married for 37 years and shared a significant part of life.

The week before Dad passed, we asked Mom if she wanted to see him. We worried how this would affect Mom but felt the need for her to say goodbye, even though they had not seen each other since the last time she pushed him away ten years ago.

One day her response to our inquiry about going to see him was, "I'm fine and good riddance." The next day she would ask about his status, no longer hiding the survivor facade. The third day after, she explained in a melancholy way that she did not want to go because the hospital is still a source of traumatic grieving over her father. By the fourth day, Little Sis texted me saying Mom decided she wanted to see him. She showered on her own, put on a pretty white and blue floral dress, and asked to see him.

To our surprise, she walked into his hospital room, greeted his fiancé, who graciously stepped back to give her space with Dad. Seeing her standing next to the bed, I was reminded how petite she is and how strong she can be. She held his hand and leaned in to kiss his forehead, saying, *"It's okay, Baby, I'm here now."*

For a brief moment, it was beautiful seeing her reach out to him.

That little kid in me, deep down inside, still hoped they would get back together to have the happily ever after till death do them part. Whether it was part of God's plan or not, they both were very stubborn, and hurt feelings kept them apart from each other. Life with Dementia made little sense to both of them, making everything seem like personal attacks instead of mental breakage.

By the grace of God, Dad gained another eight years to his life because my stepmother took wonderful care of him. God blessed Dad with a woman he wanted and needed. God also blessed me with a beautiful stepmom and new friend to share memories of Dad.

The brief moment was over when the nurse quickly came in to adjust his meds. Dad's blood pressure started to rise quickly the longer Mom stood next to him. We asked Mom if she was hungry or wanted to step away to the lobby to get her to step away from Dad politely. She did without a tear or shock in her eyes.

I can only assume she was still processing, in her way, all of the deaths from the prior year. She also experienced a step-down with each death, as referred to with the decline of living with Dementia. She may not have visibly expressed grief or mourning, but her body was reacting, struggling to process mentally.

Dad's death made it final. He was never coming home. Mom had kicked him out two other times before the third and final time, but Dad returned to her each time. It is what she grew up witnessing between her mother and father. Her father always returned. So, she expected Dad to always return no matter what.

The third and final time for Dad, he asked, *"Are you sure? Because I am not coming back this time."* Mom was not in her right mind back then or even a fair mind. Having a sense of logic, judgment, and reasoning had already begun to deteriorate drastically.

Mom said, *"Yes, leave."* No longer having a true concept of time, she did not realize how long it had been since they last saw each other.

The Bipolar episodes continued to flare in waves for the next six weeks, making it critical for us to take over. After trying to make sense of everything from leaving the corporate world to the timing of Dad's death and then moving Mom in with us, the idea of a spiritual career still perplexed me. My identity was still linked to the corporate world, so I struggled to know what to expect spiritually.

I am a visual learner—a researcher and notes taker. The application would come later, so for now, I was in true survival mode. I knew one thing for sure: this was all happening for a reason.

Regardless of His reasoning, the family drama between my sisters and I escalated to the worst it had ever been as the weeks passed. I lost

Dad, in a sense Mom, my baby sister theoretically, and then what felt like my freedom. Lost, confused, and beginning to regret my leap of faith because life was not making any sense to me anymore. I wanted the corporate cube again for the comfort of normalcy and isolation.

Why was this happening now? If this is what a spiritual career entailed, pain and confusion, I could only think of doubt.

How? How in the world do you make a career out of caring for loved ones or strangers to end their time on earth sooner than later? I was still thinking like an analytical accountant and could not feel my way through to the answers. I was shifting into this survivor mode when I needed to be in observer mode. I needed to find the answers now.

Living through the rest of 2017 brought challenges for the entire family, and no one was prepared. Continuing to pray and finding ways to stay grounded became a priority. All I could do was reflect and analyze the data available to me like an accountant. It was all I knew at this point. I completed God's training, yet all the skills I had at the time did not beam with light towards a potential spiritual career to me.

Pray and reflect, decipher a dream, pray, and reflect, meditate, pray, reflect, rinse, repeat. Then I remembered the dialogue with the Holy Spirit. "Let go, find a spiritual career, and all your material needs will be met." I took a leap of faith because the feeling of trust was so strong. I realized I was ready to trust Him with more than changing careers. I trust Him with my life.

In the spring of 2018, I chose to be baptized in a non-denominational church because God is not a brand. Mom told me right away this choice meant I was giving up my baptism from birth. She feared this also meant I was no longer Catholic, but I assured her that making this choice on my own reaffirmed what they did for me at birth. I was no longer a self-proclaimed or practicing Catholic anyway, but my faith was stronger now than it had ever been my entire life.

I chose God, not a religion, as an adult and trusted Him to guide my life. If I were going to figure out what my intended spiritual career would be, more importantly, my purpose in this lifetime, then I needed to live purposefully and no longer passively.

The Proactive Caregiver was born, or more importantly - I was reborn into a new life of purpose. *Proverbs 20:27 The spirit of man is the lamp of the Lord, searching all his innermost parts.*

God was pulling me out of the material world mindset and answering my questions of who I am by guiding my words written and spoken. The Spirit was now connected with my spirit, helping me to shine my light. So many times throughout my life, I searched for the light. Interestingly enough, I can now embrace the light in me, waiting to shine bright, as it is in you too, dear caregiver.

So here is one more proactive lesson learned to share.

Dad did not have any life insurance or a living will at the time of death which created an unexpected financial burden. Other than his sarcasm throughout life that he did not need much more than a pine box and a few kind words about him in the end, he did not want or plan for much else. That might have been an easy decision to make, knowing he wanted to be buried rather than cremated, but it is not that simple with funeral regulations. Even if you decide to bury your loved one on private property, you must still have a funeral director present, which is not done pro bono.

The questionnaire we were required to complete for the funeral home presented another opportunity for our family drama to intensify further. Disagreements were expected, but when it came to the cost of the funeral, suddenly, the burden of making legal decisions escalated when I felt it could not possibly continue to get worse.

Because Dad did not have a living will and was divorced, the funeral director said the decisions fell to the firstborn. In this case, Big Sis took this also to mean she was entitled to the flag placed on his casket for the Airforce military funeral honors ceremony instead of Mom or his fiance.

Big Sis also decided where his final resting place would be, as close to her as his remains could be. I was fine with that decision simply because I know Dad is with me everywhere I go in spirit. I did not need to keep tabs on his remains.

Even if Dad did not feel the need to create a living will, at the very least, he could have completed a personal preference form for the disposition of his body.

Nothing is more certain than death and taxes in this lifetime, but even in death, there is just as much red tape as is presented with filing taxes. Using sites such as Funerals.org, you can find your legal form by the state under the Funeral Consumers Alliance to predetermine who has the legal right to make decisions about your loved one's funeral. This proactive step will help any estranged families or families experiencing multiple marriages with children or stepchildren.

The next thing to do proactively is purchase funeral insurance. I know how bizarre this sounds and even annoying when considering how many different insurance types we purchase throughout our lives. Funeral insurance is like purchasing a college plan or a 529 plan for your kid only; it helps cover funeral expenses, but unfortunately, not tax-deductible.

The questionnaire we went through included details about Dad and his family history through preferences such as flowers, type of casket, transportation to the cemetery, the cost for a police escort for the funeral procession to the cemetery, and much more. This type of insurance locks in the funeral cost, which is important when you consider inflation.

If your loved one does not prefer cremation, you can expect funeral expenses to be anywhere from $3,000 to $25,000. Dad's funeral was still around $15,000 after selecting what we felt were the must-haves.

By the way, if you get tons of flowers, you also must pay for a vehicle to transport those flowers to the cemetery. If at all possible, select a family fund or request charitable contributions to be made in honor of your loved one in leu of gifting flowers.

Even though Dad had a veteran's burial benefit of $10,000, we still had to agree to split the remaining cost. Once again, this created more turmoil when we should have been able to mourn together.

I realized I needed to make an appointment to return to the funeral home after Dad's funeral. Having Mom's funeral planned out gave me the peace of mind that we would not have to endure another unplanned funeral out of pocket or fight over any more details.

With all the proactive measures in place, you create a life where you and your loved one can keep making memories while enjoying the present moment.

I know I will see Dad again eventually. I expect him to be the spirit I kiss hello to invite me home. I hope sharing my journey thus far has given you more food for thought. Until the end, I will continue to be the Proactive Caregiver.

Peace be with you, Dear caregiver.

Dad, A.K.A. "Tanco" or Tank
In Vietnam

Mom, A.K.A. "Mi Vida"
Awaiting Dad

Dad's Airforce Dress Blues photo

Dad kissing Mom
During their engagement
period. Blessed.

Mom at Little Sis' wedding

Dad in Brazil celebrating his
70th Birthday

Mom in her Eeyore pajamas while playing games on her tablet. In her element, oblivious to all around her.

Mom and I, together on Mother's Day 2017, just before Dad passed.

Content Resources

Chapter 2: What We Know About Dementia
Dementia gets its name from the Latin words – English Dictionary

What is Dementia? Subtitle - Genetics vs. Lifestyle
https://qbi.uq.edu.au/dementia/what-is-dementia

Harvard Health Publishing - Harvard Medical School Article published November 2019
Blood test may find early signs of Alzheimer's
https://www.health.harvard.edu/mind-and-mood/blood-test-may-find-early-signs-of-alzheimers#:~:text=A%20new%20study%20found%20that,before%20Alzheimer's%20disease%20symptoms%20appear

US National Library of Medicine National Institutes of Health – Article published March 2003, titled *"The Discovery of Alzheimer's disease"* Alois Alzheimer, a German psychiatrist PMCID: PMC3181715; PMID: 22034141
https://www.ncbi.nlm.nih.gov/pmc/articles/PMC3181715/

US National Library of Medicine National Institutes of Health – Article published October 24, 2008, titled *"Oskar Fischer and the study of dementia"* another German psychiatrist PMCID: PMC2668940; PMID: 18952676
https://www.ncbi.nlm.nih.gov/pmc/articles/PMC2668940/

Brain and Life.org magazine article published August/September 2019, by Gina Shaw titled *"General Anesthesia Tips for People with Neurologic Disorders"* general anesthesia may carry certain risks – postoperative hallucinations, delirium, and cognitive difficulties.
https://www.brainandlife.org/the-magazine/articles/2019/august-september-2019/general-anesthesia-may-carry-certain-risks-postoperative-hallucinations-delirium-and/

Springer Link article published February 2020 titled *"Updated nomenclature of delirium and acute encephalopathy: statement of 10 Societies"* Slooter, A.J.C., Otte, W.M., Devlin, J.W. *et al.* Updated nomenclature of delirium and acute encephalopathy: statement of ten Societies. *Intensive Care Med* **46**, 1020–1022 (2020). https://doi.org/10.1007/s00134-019-05907-4
https://link.springer.com/article/10.1007/s00134-019-05907-4

"How Not to Die," – *Discover the Foods Scientifically Proven to Prevent and Reverse Disease* by Dr. Michael Greger, published 2015 by Flatiron Books; chapter 3 How Not to Die from Brain Diseases Pages 53-61

Dr. Joy Poskozim, owner of Joyful Dental Care in Chicago

Chapter 3: How the Stages of Dementia Get Dismissed
Eli and AstraZeneca PLC study article published June 12, 2018, titled *"Update on Phase III clinical trials of lanabecestat for Alzheimer's disease"*
https://www.astrazeneca.com/media-centre/press-releases/2018/update-on-phase-iii-clinical-trials-of-lanabecestat-for-alzheimers-disease-12062018.html#

Reuters Healthcare & Pharma published January 7, 2018; article titled *"Pfizer ends research for new Alzheimer's Parkinson's drug"* https://www.reuters.com/article/us-pfizer-alzheimers/pfizer-ends-research-for-new-alzheimers-parkinsons-drugs-idUSKBN1EW0TN

Eisai Global published article October 23, 2017, titled Biogen and Eisai Expand Existing Collaboration Agreement to Develop and Commercialize Investigational Alzheimer's Disease Treatment including phase 3 Aducanumab https://www.eisai.com/news/news201760.html

Alice Park of TIME Health magazine issue fall of 2018 referencing Eisai, a Japanese company partnered with Biogen

Bloomberg article published June 7, 2021, by Lisa Du and Grace Huang titled *"Biogen's Japanese Partner Has Second Alzheimer's Drug Coming"* https://www.bloomberg.com/news/articles/2021-06-08/biogen-s-alzheimer-drug-nod-may-bode-well-for-eisai-s-efforts

"Silence is the language of God. All else is poor translation." – Rumi (Samadhi) http://www.edwardradev.com/ulterior-romanticism-thesis

Silence and Serenity published Article September 5, 2020, by Chicago Gnosis, The Gnostic Academy of Chicago https://chicagognosis.org/lectures/silence-and-serenity

Untangling Alzheimer's The Guide for Families and Professionals. A conversation in Caregiving by Tam Cummings, PhD Gerontologist. Published in the United States by The Dementia Association LLC. Stage of Dementia pages 216-258. Tool for stages of Dementia, the Dementia Behavioral Assessment Tool (DBAT)

Judy Cornish, the author of The Dementia Handbook and Dementia with Dignity, founder of the Dementia & Alzheimer's Wellbeing Network (DAWN®)

Michael Greger, M.D., FACLM, founder of nutritionfacts.org

Journal of Clinical Investigation (JCI Insight) article published on August 17, 2017, noninvasive detection of Alzheimer's Disease

Chapter 4: Creating a Cultural Shift
Figure A Image Maslow's Hierarchy of Needs – Image provided by Saul McLeod in Maslow's Hierarchy of Needs article published December 29, 2020, https://www.simplypsychology.org/maslow.html#gsc.tab=0

Figure B Image Food Pyramid provided by Free Food at KU

Figure C Image Vegetarian Food Pyramid provided by Loma Linda University

Figure D Image provided by Healthy Eating Pyramid – Food Pyramid UK 2017 https://www.nicepng.com/ourpic/u2q8i1t4q8t4u2y3_healthy-eating-pyramid-food-pyramid-uk-2017/

Free Radicals Author Dr. Edward Group DC, NP, DACBN, DCBCN, DABFM. Article "What are Free Radicals?" published February 6, 2017 https://www.globalhealingcenter.com/natural-health/what-are-free-radicals/
Lobo, V. et al.

"Free Radicals, Antioxidants and Functional Foods: Impact on Human Health."
Pharmacognosy Reviews4.8 (2010): 118–126. PMC. Web. 14 Dec. 2016.
Cadenas, E, and KJ Davies. "Mitochondrial Free Radical Generation, Oxidative
Stress, and Aging." Free Radical Biology & Medicine., vol. 29, 18 Oct. 2000, pp.
222–30. Accessed 14 Dec. 2016.

Pham-Huy, Lien Ai, Hua He, and Chuong Pham-Huy. "Free Radicals, Antioxidants
in Disease and Health." International Journal of Biomedical Science: IJBS 4.2
(2008): 89–96. Web. 14 Dec. 2016.

Rahman, Khalid. "Studies on Free Radicals, Antioxidants, and Co-Factors. "Clinical
Interventions in Aging 2.2 (2007): 219–236. Web. 14 Dec. 2016.

Free Radical Theory of Aging – Antioxidants & Redox Signaling article published
by US National Library of Medicine February 1, 2014, titled *"The Free Radical
Theory of Aging is Dead. Long Live the Damage Theory!"* PMCID: PMC 3901353;
PMID: 24159899 https://www.ncbi.nlm.nih.gov/pmc/articles/PMC3901353/

May 2020 AARP Caregiving in the U.S. Figure 1. Prevalence of Caregiving by Age
of Care Recipient, 2020 Compared to 2015 page #4 II. Executive Summary

May 2020 AARP Caregiving in the U.S. Figure 5. Percentage of Caregivers of
Adults Who Are in Each Generation, 2020 vs. 2015 page #11 III. Detailed
Findings

AARP Public Policy Institute article published May 2018: The Emerging Generation
of Family Caregivers by Brendan Flinn - Exhibit 1-Millenial Family Caregivers by
Age Group; Exhibit 2-Millenial Family Caregivers by Race/Ethnicity
https://www.aarp.org/content/dam/aarp/ppi/2018/05/millennial-family-
caregivers.pdf

May 2020 AARP Caregiving in the U.S. Figure 87. Demographic Summary of
Caregivers of Adults, 2020 and 2015 page #89 III. Detailed Findings

National Alliance for Caregiving: 2015 Report Caregiving in the U.S.; Research
Report published June 2015 conducted by AARP Public Policy Institute
https://www.aarp.org/content/dam/aarp/ppi/2015/caregiving-in-the-united-
states-2015-report-revised.pdf

Evercare Study of Caregivers in Decline "A Close-up Look at the Health Risks of
Caring for a Loved One" Report of Findings published September 2006 in
conjunction with National Alliance for Caregivers.
http://www.caregiving.org/data/Caregivers%20in%20Decline%20Study-FINAL-
lowres.pdf

Chapter 5: Protect Your Future with The Caregiver's Trinity
"The Power of Now: A Guide to Spiritual Enlightenment" by Eckart Tolle published
by Namaste Publishing in Canada and New World Library in U.S.

Pareto Principle as published online by Investopedia, Economics section
https://www.investopedia.com/terms/p/paretoprinciple.asp

Internal Revenue Service Publication 502 Medical and Dental Expenses (including
the Health Coverage Tax Credit) deduction in excess of 7.5% (rate as of 2020
thru 2025) https://www.irs.gov/pub/irs-pdf/p502.pdf

Long Term Care Insurance – When to Purchase a policy, Limitations on retirement contributions
https://www.irs.gov/retirement-plans/plan-participant-employee/retirement-topics-401k-and-profit-sharing-plan-contribution-limits

What Is the Best Age to Get Life Insurance? Published by Investopedia author Thom Tracy, reviewed by Michael J. Boyle on March 27, 2021; Life Insurance section https://www.investopedia.com/articles/investing/072816/what-best-age-get-life-insurance.asp#ixzz5E1qBXJFG

Chapter 6: The Domino Effect
Euro Stem Cell publish article *"The heart: our first organ"*
https://www.eurostemcell.org/heart-our-first-organ#:~:text=The%20heart%20is%20the%20first,needs%20directly%20from%20its%20surroundings

2021 812 Superfast Ferrari of Austin Image provided by
https://austin.ferraridealers.com/en-US/812-superfast

1972 Ford Pinto Image provided by https://www.oldcarsweekly.com/features/car-of-the-week-1972-ford-pinto

https://www.webmd.com/heart-disease/news/20130125/heart-problems-dementia

US National Library of Medicine, National Institute of Health – Dementia presenting as postpartum depression; Published May 2002 by Dell DL and Halford JJ. https://www.ncbi.nlm.nih.gov/pubmed/11975961

The American College of Obstetricians and Gynecologists published by Elsevier Inc. January 17, 2004, case report titled Dementia Presenting as postpartum depression by Diana L. Dell MD and Jonathan J. Halford MD

AgingCare.com Expert Minding our Elders article posted October 2007 titled Thirty Percent of Caregivers Die Before the People They Care for Do
https://www.agingcare.com/discussions/thirty-percent-of-caregivers-die-before-the-people-they-care-for-do-97626.htm#:~:text=Rough%20statistics%20show%20that%2030,Some%20studies%20show%20deaths%20higher.&text=Caregivers%20often%20don't%20find,to%20their%20own%20doctor%20appointments

Author Sharon Feiereisen from *"Eat This, Not That!"* published an article on 20 Foods That Put You in a Bad Mood https://www.eatthis.com/bad-mood-foods/

Enneagram www.enneagraminstitute.com/type-descriptions

Author Kim Stanley has two books to consider reading - "How to Make a Downsize Move" and "Step by Step to Right Sizing."

Chapter 7: One Hot Mess
Mayo Clinic Article covering Long Qt Syndrome: National Heart, Lung, and Blood Institute. https://www.nhlbi.nih.gov/health-topics/long-qt-syndrome. Accessed April 29, 2020, in connection with overview article
https://www.mayoclinic.org/diseases-conditions/long-qt-syndrome/symptoms-causes/syc-20352518

American Heart Association
http://www.heart.org/HEARTORG/Conditions/Arrhythmia/AboutArrhythmia/About
-Arrhythmia_UCM_002010_Article.jsp#.Ws436IjwbIU

Chapter 9: Sibling Rivalry – All is Not Well
"Anatomy of the Spirit," author Dr. Caroline Myss published by Three Rivers
Press, a division of Crown Publishers, Inc. The wounded child archetype, page
202. Woundology page 209; page 69 Figure 3: Seven Power Centers or Chakras
of The Kundalini System.

Lord of the Flies novel by British author William Golding published 1954 and
republicized December 16, 2003, by E.L. Epstein as order collapses without adult
supervision.

Chapter 10: When We Know Better, We Do Better
Nicole M. Gage, Bernard K. Baars in Fundamentals of Cognitive Neuroscience
(Second Edition) 2018 https://www.sciencedirect.com/topics/medicine-and-
dentistry/frontal-lobe 5.1 The Fragile Frontal Lobes

Vascular Dementia https://www.mayoclinic.org/diseases-conditions/vascular-
dementia/symptoms-causes/syc-20378793

Brain Cross-Sections Image:
https://www.brightfocus.org/sites/default/files/styles/full_width/public/Brain_Cro
ss-Sections.jpg?itok=Ib0yHbOp

Pet Scan Brain Normal versus Alzheimer's Disease Images:
https://www.mayoclinic.org/tests-procedures/pet-scan/details/why-its-done/icc-
20319683#! – Mayo Foundation for Medical Education and Research

The Association for Frontotemporal Degeneration ttps://www.theaftd.org/what-is-
ftd/disease-overview/ Disease Overview

Lewy Body Dementia Association (LBDA) https://www.lbda.org/go/what-lbd-0

Key differences between FTD and Alzheimer's https://www.alz.org/alzheimers-
dementia/what-is-dementia/types-of-dementia/frontotemporal-dementia

"Teaching medical students about dementia: a brief review" Dementia &
Neuropsychological published Web 2015 Apr-Jun; 9(2): 93-95 PMCID:
PMC5619346 PMID: 29213949
https://www.ncbi.nlm.nih.gov/pmc/articles/PMC5619346/

Health Central Image: http://turnkey-publishingtool.s3-website-us-east-
1.amazonaws.com/stories/7b7047ca-b63c-48be-b32a-
b3c55f295fdf/photo/AlzheimersFacebook.jpg

Jacinto AF, Brucki SMD, Porto CS, Arruda MA, Nitrini R. Detection of cognitive
impairment in the elderly by general internists in Brazil. Clinics. 2011; 66:1379–
1384.

Keller I, Makipaa A, Kalenscher T, Kalache A. Global Survey on Geriatrics in the
Medical Curriculum. Geneva: World Health Organization; 2002. Available from:
http://www.who.int/ageing/projects/en/alc_global_survey_tegeme.pdf.

Tsolaki M, Papliagkas V, Anogianakis G, et al. European Alzheimer Disease Consortium: Consensus statement on dementia education and training in Europe. J Nutr Health Ageing. 2010; 14:131–135.

Chapter 11: Medical Referees
Anosognosia Dementia Daily Caring Article titled "6 Ways to Help Someone Who Doesn't Know They're Ill: Anosognosia in Dementia" https://dailycaring.com/6-ways-to-help-someone-who-doesnt-know-theyre-ill-anosognosia-in-dementia/

Forensic psychiatrist as published by NHS https://www.healthcareers.nhs.uk/explore-roles/doctors/roles-doctors/psychiatry/forensic-psychiatry

Early-Onset (Young-onset) Alzheimer's https://www.mayoclinic.org/diseases-conditions/alzheimers-disease/in-depth/alzheimers/art-20048356

Chapter 12: Proactive Measures
Rosanna Lee, RD, MS, MHSC, PHEC, practicing registered dietitian with the College of Dietitians of Ontario in the greater Toronto area, specializing in senior nutrition. Article published by Costco Connection titled "Listening to Your Gut" https://www.costcoconnection.com/connection/202101/MobilePagedArticle.action?articleId=1649893#articleId1649893

Mayo Clinic and Alzheimer's Association – Articled published May 20, 2021, titled *"Diabetes and Alzheimer's linked."* https://www.mayoclinic.org/diseases-conditions/alzheimers-disease/in-depth/diabetes-and-alzheimers/art-20046987

Make Your Body Work article titled *"Eating vs. Exercise: Why Your Food Changes Always Win"* published by Dave Smith http://makeyourbodywork.com/eating-vs-exercise/

Precision Nutrition article titled *"The Paleo Problem: Examining the pros and cons of the Paleo Diet"* by Brian St. Peirre, MS, RD https://www.precisionnutrition.com/paleo-diet

https://livinghistoryfarm.org/farminginthe40s/life_24.html
Written by Claudia Reinhardt and Bill Ganzel, the Ganzel Group.

"Let Food Be Your Medicine" Author Dr. Don Colbert 2016 published by Worthy Books, a division of Worthy Media, Inc.

http://main.poliquingroup.com/ArticlesMultimedia/Articles/Article/1474/Pros_Cons_of_A_Ketogenic_DietMany_Benefits_Includi.aspx

"How Not to Die" Discover the Foods Scientifically Proven to Prevent and Reverse Disease, co-author Michael Greger, M.D., FACLM founder of Nutritionfacts.org with Gene Stone
Grant WB. Trends in diet and Alzheimer's disease during the nutrition transition in Japan and developing countries. J Alzheimers Dis. 2014; 38 (3); 611-20.

Chan KY, Wang W, Wu JJ, et al. Epidemiology of Alzheimer's disease and other forms of dementia in China, 1990-2010: A systematic Review and analysis. Lancet. 2013; 381 (9882): 2016-23.

Grant WB. Trends in diet and Alzheimer's disease during the nutrition transition in Japan and developing countries. J Alzheimer's Dis. 2014; 38 (3); 611-20.

Roses AD, Saunders AM. APOE is a major susceptibility gene for Alzheimer's' disease. Curr Opin Bitechno. 1994;5 (6):663-7.

Okereke OI, Rosner BA, Kim DH, et al. Dietary fat types and 4-year cognitive change in community-dwelling older women. Ann Neurol. 2012; 72(1):124-34.

Shukitt-Hale B. Blueberries and neuronal aging. Gerontology. 2012;58(6):518-23. Cherniack EP. A berry thought-provoking idea: the potential role of plant polyphenols in the treatment of age-related cognitive disorders. Br J Nutr. 2012;108(5):794-800.

Johnson EJ. A possible role for lutein and zeaxanthin in cognitive function in the elderly. Am K Ckin Nutr. 2012; 96(5):1161S-5S.
http://www.eatthis.com/bad-mood-foods/ Sharon Feiereisen from "Eat This, Not That!" published article May 5, 2020, titled *"20 Foods That Put You in a Bad Mood"*

Chapter 13: Brain & Gut Food for Thought

Fiber –Harvard Health Publishing article titled *"Making one change – getting more fiber- can help with weight loss"* published February 2015 by Nancy Ferrari, Managing Director and Executive Editor
https://www.health.harvard.edu/blog/making-one-change-getting-fiber-can-help-weight-loss-201502177721 -

Water – Medical News Today article titled *"What are the health benefits of cucumber water?"* published November 15, 2018, by Kat Gál and medically reviewed by Katherine Marengo, LDN, R.D.
https://www.medicalnewstoday.com/articles/323694

Hot water and Lemon – Flushing Hospital Medical Center article titled *"The Surprising Benefits of Hot Water and Lemon"* published April 16, 2015, by Sage Robinson https://www.flushinghospital.org/newsletter/the-surprising-benefits-of-hot-water-and-lemon/

"Urinary Tract Infections and Dementia" article published by Alzheimer's Society https://www.alzheimers.org.uk/get-support/daily-living/urinary-tract-infections-utis-dementia

Fiber – Kathleen M. Zelman, MPH, RD, LD - Article in Nourish by WebMD titled Fiber: How Much Do You Need? Closing the Gap. Published from WebMD Archives.
https://www.webmd.com/diet/guide/fiber-how-much-do-you-need#1

Fiber – *"Closing America's Intake Fiber Gap"* published by American Journal of Lifestyle Medicine on July 7, 2016, online PMCID: PMC6124841; PMID: 30202317
https://www.ncbi.nlm.nih.gov/pmc/articles/PMC6124841/

Fiber – Article titled Increasing Fiber Intake published by University of California San Francisco
https://www.ucsfhealth.org/education/increasing-fiber-intake#:~:text=The%20American%20Heart%20Association%20Eating,about%20half%20the%20recommended%20amount.

Garlic – Healthline article titled "11 Proven Health Benefits of Garlic" published June 28, 2018, by Joe Leech, MS https://www.healthline.com/nutrition/11-proven-health-benefits-of-garlic

Chapter 14: Superfoods, Protein, & Vitamins

Mushrooms – Healthline article titled *"Are Mushrooms Good for You?"* published October 12, 2017, by Rena Goldman and medically reviewed by Natalie Butler, R.D., L.D. https://www.healthline.com/health/food-nutrition/are-mushrooms-good-for-you

Mushrooms - WebMD article titled *"Health Benefits of Mushrooms"* https://www.webmd.com/diet/health-benefits-mushrooms#1

Coconut – Healthline article titled "5 Impressive Benefits of Coconut" published July 23, 2019, by Anne Danahy, MS, RDN https://www.healthline.com/nutrition/coconut-nutrition

Coconut – Everyday Health article titled *"What is Coconut? How to Enjoy the Fruit-Nut Seed and What It Offers Your Health"* https://www.everydayhealth.com/diet-nutrition/diet/coconut-nutrition-facts-health-benefits-beauty-benefits-recipes/

Avocado – Healthline article titled *"12 Proven Health Benefits of Avocado"* published June 29, 2018, by Kris Gunnars, BSc https://www.healthline.com/nutrition/12-proven-benefits-of-avocado#TOC_TITLE_HDR_2

Pomegranate – WebMD article titled *"Pomegranate Power"* by Elaine Magee, MPH, RD https://www.webmd.com/food-recipes/features/pomegranate-power

Pomegranate – Healthline article titled "12 Health Benefits of Pomegranate" published August 15, 2018, by Joe Leech, MS https://www.healthline.com/nutrition/12-proven-benefits-of-pomegranate#TOC_TITLE_HDR_12

Vitamin C - https://www.mayoclinic.org/drugs-supplements-vitamin-c/art-20363932

Vitamin D - https://www.mayoclinic.org/drugs-supplements-vitamin-d/art-20363792

Vitamin K - https://www.webmd.com/vitamins-and-supplements/supplement-guide-vitamin-k

Vitamin A - https://www.mayoclinic.org/drugs-supplements-vitamin-a/art-20365945

Vitamin E - https://www.mayoclinic.org/drugs-supplements-vitamin-e/art-20364144

Vitamin B12 - https://www.mayoclinic.org/drugs-supplements-vitamin-b12/art-20363663

Folate or Vitamin B9 - https://www.mayoclinic.org/drugs-supplements-folate/art-20364625

Choline – Article *"Choline Deficiency is a thing. Here's why you need it"* written by Dave Asprey, published online by Bullet proof https://www.bulletproof.com/supplements/dietary-supplements/choline-supplement-benefits/?gclid=EAIaIQobChMI98Wru8ft8wIVS2pvBB0QWgfpEAAYAyAAEgKdoPD_BwE

Omega 3 - https://www.mayoclinic.org/diseases-conditions/heart-disease/in-depth/omega-3/art-20045614

Red Wine – Prevention article titled *"8 Reasons to Love Red Wine"* published October 1, 2012, by Stephanie Castillo https://www.prevention.com/health/healthy-living/health-benefits-of-red-wine/slide/9

Raspberry – Berry Health Benefits Network article titled *"Red Raspberries"* published by Oregon Raspberry & Blackberry commission http://berryhealth.fst.oregonstate.edu/health_healing/fact_sheets/red_raspberry_facts.htm

Cucumber – Web MD article titled *"Cucumber"* published September 3, 2020, by Mary Jo DiLonardo https://www.webmd.com/food-recipes/cucumber-health-benefits

Pumpkin Seeds – Healthline article titled *"Top 11 Science-Based Health Benefits of Pumpkin Seeds"* published September 24, 2018, by Mary Jane Brown, PHD, RD (UK) https://www.healthline.com/nutrition/11-benefits-of-pumpkin-seeds#section1

Sunflower Seeds – Web MD article titled "Health Benefits of Sunflower Seeds" under Diet & Weight Management https://www.webmd.com/diet/health-benefits-sunflower-seeds#1

Saffron – Healthline Article titled *"11 Impressive Health Benefits of Saffron"* published January 7, 2019, by Ryan Raman, MS, RD https://www.healthline.com/nutrition/saffron

Moringa – Medical News Today article titled *"What makes moringa good for you?"* published January 2, 2020 by Bethany Cadman and medically reviewed by Debra Rose Wilson, Ph.D., MSN, R.N., IBCLC, AHN-BC, CHT https://www.medicalnewstoday.com/articles/319916#what-is-in-moringa

Sage – Healthline article titled *"12 Health Benefits and uses of Sage"* published December 14, 2018, by Ryan Raman, MS, RD https://www.healthline.com/nutrition/sage

Rosemary –Web MD published article titled *"Health Benefits of Rosemary"* https://www.webmd.com/diet/health-benefits-rosemary#1

Olive Oil – Healthline article titled *"Why Extra Virgin Olive Oil is the Healthiest Fat on Earth"* published on December 20, 2019, by Kris Gunnars, BSc https://www.healthline.com/nutrition/extra-virgin-olive-oil

---

Avocado Oil – Healthline article titled *"8 Evidence-Based Health Benefits of Avocado Oil"* published on July 26, 2021, by Hrefna Palsdottir, MS and medically reviewed by Katherine Marengo LDN, R.D. https://www.healthline.com/nutrition/9-avocado-oil-benefits

Spirulina – Healthline article titled *"10 Health Benefits of Spirulina"* published October 5, 2018, by Joe Leech https://www.healthline.com/nutrition/10-proven-benefits-of-spirulina

Chia Seeds – Healthline article titled *"11 Proven Health Benefits of Chia Seeds"* published August 8, 2018, by Kris Gunnars, BSc https://www.healthline.com/nutrition/11-proven-health-benefits-of-chia-seeds#TOC_TITLE_HDR_6

Quinoa - Healthline article titled *"11 Proven Health Benefits of Quinoa"* published June 28, 2018, by Kris Gunnars, BSc https://www.healthline.com/nutrition/11-proven-benefits-of-quinoa#TOC_TITLE_HDR_2

Turmeric – Healthline article titled *"10 Proven Health Benefits of Turmeric and Curcumin"* published May 10, 2021, by Kris Gunnars, BSc and medically reviewed by Kathy W. Warwick, R. D., CDE, Nutrition https://www.healthline.com/nutrition/top-10-evidence-based-health-benefits-of-turmeric

Dark Chocolate – Healthline article titled *"7 Proven Health Benefits of Dark Chocolate"* published July 27, 2021, by Kris Gunnars, BSc and medically reviewed by Kim Rose RDN, CDCES, CNSC, LD, Nutrition https://www.healthline.com/nutrition/7-health-benefits-dark-chocolate#TOC_TITLE_HDR_3

Green Tea – Medical News Today article titled *"What are the health benefits of green tea?"* published May 18, 2021, by Megan Ware, RDN, L.D. and medically reviewed by Kathy W. Warwick, R.D. CDE https://www.medicalnewstoday.com/articles/269538#_noHeaderPrefixedContent

Chai Tea - Healthline article titled *"How Chai Tea Can Improve Your Health"* published July 20, 2017, by Alina Petre, MS RD (NL) https://www.healthline.com/nutrition/chai-tea#TOC_TITLE_HDR_4

Peppermint Tea – Healthline article titled *"12 Science-Backed Benefits of Peppermint Tea and Extracts"* published on October 12, 2018, by Melissa Groves https://www.healthline.com/nutrition/peppermint-tea#TOC_TITLE_HDR_8
"Wheat Belly: Lose the Wheat, Lose the Weight, and Find Your Path Back to Health" written by Dr. William Davis published Trade paperback June 2014 by Rodale, Inc

Web MD article titled *"Wheat Belly Diet Review: What to Expect"* published by Lisa Schweitzer   https://www.webmd.com/diet/a-z/wheat-belly-diet-review

Whole Grains - https://www.mayoclinic.org/healthy-lifestyle/nutrition-and-healthy-eating/in-depth/whole-grains/art-20047826

Natural News article titled *"Non-GMO corn offers far more nutrition without poison, study shows"* published April 28, 2015, by Ethan A. Huff https://www.naturalnews.com/049515_GMO_corn_nutrient_content_glyphosate.html

Natural News article titled *"GMO corn is failing; pesticides only exacerbate the problem, scientists say"* published May 5, 2016, by Ethan A. Huff https://www.naturalnews.com/053898_GMO_corn_insecticide_resistance_pesticides.html

Web MD article titled "Leaky Gut Syndrome: What is it?" published August 14, 2013, by Matt McMillen https://www.webmd.com/digestive-disorders/features/leaky-gut-syndrome

Chapter 15: How to Effectively Switch Roles
Amazon description: SVINZ Newest 5 Alarms Dementia Clock, Day Clock w/ Snooze Button, 2 Auto-Dim Options, Large 8" Display Wall Digital Calendar Alarm Clock for Vision Impaired, Elderly, Memory Loss, Black, SDC008

Psalm 23 - https://www.bible.com/bible/111/PSA.23.niv

Chapter 16: Caregiver Compliance: Legal Documents, Trusts, Probate, & Estates
Statutory Durable Power of Attorney (DPOA) – Texas State Law Library article titled *"Durable Powers of Attorney"* https://guides.sll.texas.gov/powers-of-attorney/durable-powers-of-attorney

Declaration of Guardian – Rania Coms Law PLLC article titled *"Can I Appoint My Own Guardian in Case I Become Incapacitated?"* published April 17, 2019, by Rania Combs https://texaswillsandtrustslaw.com/resources/can-i-appoint-my-own-guardian-in-case-i-become-incapacitated

HIPAA Authorization – HIPAA Journal article titled *"What is HIPAA Authorization?"* published February 9, 2021, https://www.hipaajournal.com/what-is-hipaa-authorization/

HIPPA Security – HHS.gov article titled "Summary of the HIPAA Security Rule" https://www.hhs.gov/hipaa/for-professionals/security/laws-regulations/index.html

Advance Directive to Physicians – U.S. Department of Health & Human Services article titled *"Advance Care Planning: Health Care Directives"* published by National Institute on Aging https://www.nia.nih.gov/health/advance-care-planning-health-care-directives
Medical Power of Attorney (MPOA) – Texas Law Help.org article titled *"Medical Power of Attorney: Information and Answers to Common Questions"* published on October 13, 2021, by Legal Hotline for Texans (TLSC) https://texaslawhelp.org/article/medical-power-of-attorney-information-and-answers-to-common-questions

Revocable & Irrevocable Trust – Investopedia article titled *"Irrevocable Trust"* published April 28, 2021, by Julia Kagan and reviewed by Ebony Howard https://www.investopedia.com/terms/i/irrevocabletrust.asp

Probate – Nolo.com article titled "How the Probate Process Works: Information for Executors" subtitle "Learn the steps needed to complete the probate process" by Mary Randolph, J.D. https://www.nolo.com/legal-encyclopedia/how-probate-process-works-information-32438.html

Chapter 18: In Hindsight
WebMD Article titled *"What are Chakras?"* published by on June 28, 2021, and medically reviewed by Dan Brennan, MD https://www.webmd.com/balance/what-are-chakras

"Anatomy of the Spirit," author Dr. Caroline Myss published by Three Rivers Press, a division of Crown Publishers, Inc. Part II: The Seven Sacred Truths, page 93; page 73 Figure 4: The Ten Sefirot: The Tree of Life; page 79 Figure 5: The Divine Power Within Our Biological Design

Chapter 19: Spousal Distress
AARP article titled *"When Caregivers Fall Out of Love"* published on July 31, 2017, by Barry J. Jacobs https://www.aarp.org/caregiving/life-balance/info-2017/spousal-caregiving-divorce-fd.html

Chapter 20: Finding the New Home
Genworth article titled "Cost of Care Survey" published National averages 2020 https://www.genworth.com/aging-and-you/finances/cost-of-care.html

Assisted Living – A Senior Living Resource article titled "Learn About Assisted Living" published August 11, 2021, by https://www.whereyoulivematters.org/assisted-living-defined/

Memory Care – Assistedliving.org article titled *"What is Memory Care and How Much Should It Cost?"* updated 2021 https://www.assistedliving.org/memory-care/

Nursing Homes – Seniorliving.org article titled "What is a Nursing Home?" published on July 13, 2021, by Scott Witt Elder, Home Care Expert and Jeff Hoyt, Editor in Chief https://www.seniorliving.org/nursing-homes/

Hospice Care Services – Hospice Foundation of America article titled *"What is Hospice?"* https://hospicefoundation.org/Hospice-Care/Hospice-Services

Chapter 21: Surviving the Holidays
Elderly Plane Travel – Arizona Center on Aging article titled "Fit to Fly? Older Adults and Air Travel" published April 2018 by Christian E. Gausvik, MD and Jeffery D. Schlaudecker, MD https://www.uofazcenteronaging.com/care-sheet/providers/fit-fly-older-adults-and-air-travel

Chapter 22: Mourning the Living
Elisabeth Kübler-Ross & David Kessler – On Grief and Grieving: Finding the Meaning of Grief Through the Five Stages of Loss published through Scribner 2014 after 2005 Elisabeth Kübler-Ross Family Limited Partnership and David Kessler Inc.

Sue Barsky Reid – Founder of Death Cafés - https://deathcafe.com/what/

End of Life Doula Association - https://www.nedalliance.org/scope-of-practice.html

Chapter 23: Live in the Present Moment
The New York Times article published June 8, 2021, and updated June 10, 2021, by Pam Belluck and Rebecca Robbins titled *"Three F.D.A. Advisers Resign Over Agency's Approval of Alzheimer's Drug"* https://www.nytimes.com/2021/06/10/health/aduhelm-fda-resign-alzheimers.html

American Academy of Neurology resource AAN Publications article titled "How to Talk to Your Patients About Aducanumab (Aduhelm) https://www.aan.com/tools-and-resources/practicing-neurologists-administrators/aducanumab-resources/how-to-talk-to-your-patients-about-aducanumab-aduhelm/

Taste – National Institute on Aging featured research article titled *"Large study links gum disease with dementia"* Published July 9, 2020, on; Reference: Beydoun M, et al. JOURNAL OF ALZHEIMER'S DISEASE. 2020;75(1):157-172. doi: 10.3233/JAD-200064.

Music as Medicine: The impact of healing harmonies published April 14, 2015, by The Joseph B. Martin Conference Center. The New Research Building Harvard Medical School.

Sound – Healthline article titled *"Do Rife Machines Cure Cancer?"* published on June 25, 2018, by Jacquelyn Cafasso and medically reviewed by Christina Chun, MPH https://www.healthline.com/health/rife-machine-cancer

American Scientist Royal Raymond Rife – *"Sound Therapy"* article for integrative medicine, anti-aging, and cancer clinic https://www.bionuu.com/rife/
"The Cancer Cure that Worked! Fifty Years of Suppression" by Barry Lynes published January 1, 1997, by Marcus

Delta Waves – Very Well Mind article titled *"Deep Sleep and the Impact of Delta Waves"* published on October 6, 2021, by Kendra Cherry and medically reviewed by Daniel B. Block, MD https://www.verywellmind.com/what-are-delta-waves-2795104

Theta Waves – Healthline article titled *"What is the Purpose of Theta Brain Waves?"* published on July 1, 2020, by Jennifer Larson and medically reviewed by Alana Biggers, M.D., MPH https://www.healthline.com/health/theta-waves
Alpha Waves – Very Well Mind article titled *"What are Alpha Brain Waves?"* published on April 1, 2021, by Kendra Cherry and medically reviewed by Huma Sheikh, MD https://www.verywellmind.com/what-are-alpha-brain-waves-5113721

Beta Waves – Science Direct article titled *"Beta Wave"* published 2007 from Clinical Neurology for Psychiatrists (Sixth Edition), Abstract by Juri D. Kropotov 2016 https://www.sciencedirect.com/topics/medicine-and-dentistry/beta-wave

U.S. National Library of Medicine article titled *"Reversal of Cognitive Decline: A novel therapeutic program"* published on September 27, 2014, in connection to renowned neurologist Dr. Dale Bredesen PMCID: PMC4221920; PMID: 25324467 https://www.ncbi.nlm.nih.gov/pmc/articles/PMC4221920/

Frequency Meditation Music - https://www.learning-mind.com/brainwave-frequencies/

Frequency Meditation Music - Science Translational Medicine Article published 11 Mar 2015: Vol. 7, Issue 278, pp. 278ra33; DOI: 10.1126/scitranslmed.aaa2512

Smell - Aromatherapy: Rene-Maurice Gattefosse and Robert Tisserand, second edition of book title Gattefosse's Aromatherapy. Published by C.W. Daniel, 1993 ISBN 0852072368, 9780852072363 https://books.google.com/books?id=cdZ5Wj3fRpIC&q=inauthor:%22Ren%C3%A9-Maurice+Gattefoss%C3%A9%22&dq=inauthor:%22Ren%C3%A9-Maurice+Gattefoss%C3%A9%22&hl=en&sa=X&ved=0ahUKEwiUp5O2hIvcAhUMWq0KHS8bCIkQ6AEIJzAA

Aromatherapy application and blood stream from Lorraine Dallmeier: http://www.herbhedgerow.co.uk/can-essential-oils-get-into-your-bloodstream/

Aromatherapy Skin absorption: Article *"Essential Oils – Their Lack of Skin Absorption, but Effectiveness via Inhalation"* by Martin Watt. Original version published in Aromatic Thymes. 1995. Vol. 3 No.2 11-13. Original copyright 1995 Martin Watt. Revised 2006.

"Medical Aromatherapy: Healing with Essential Oils" by Kurt Schnaubelt, published by Frog Books 1999
"Natural Toxins in Traditional Medicines some Myths removed" by Matt Watt first published by Aromatic Thymes Vol 3 No.4 1995 revised 2006

Article *"How Aromatherapy Works"* https://www.21drops.com/pages/about-aromatherapy John Hopkins Medicine article titled *"Aromatherapy: Do Essential Oils Really Work?"* https://www.hopkinsmedicine.org/health/wellness-and-prevention/aromatherapy-do-essential-oils-really-work

Lavender Essential Oil – Very Well Mind article titled *"The Health Benefits of Lavender Essential Oil"* published on December 9, 2020, by Cathy Wong and medically reviewed by Caitilin Kelly, MD https://www.verywellmind.com/lavender-for-less-anxiety-3571767

Tea Tree Essential Oil - Very Well Mind article titled *"The Health Benefits of Tea Tree Oil"* published on June 28, 2020, by Cathy Wong and medically reviewed by Emily Dashiell, ND
Eucalyptus Essential Oil - Very Well Mind article titled *"Essential Oils That Ease Bronchitis Symptoms and How to Use Them"* published on June 25, 2021, by Michelle Pugle and medically reviewed by Arno Kroner, DAOM, LAc https://www.verywellhealth.com/essential-oils-for-bronchitis-5179761

Orange (Citrus) Essential Oil – Healthline article titled *"The Benefits of Orange Essential Oil and How to Use"* published on October 3, 2019, by Jill Seladi-Schulman, PH. D and medically reviewed by Cynthia Cobb, DNP, APRN, WHNP-BC, FAANP https://www.healthline.com/health/orange-essential-oil-uses

Lemongrass Essential Oil - Very Well Mind article titled *"The Health Benefits of Lemongrass"* published on October 11, 2021, by Malia Frey and medically reviewed by Melissa Rifkin, MS, RD, CDN https://www.verywellfit.com/lemongrass-benefits-side-effects-and-preparations-4178847

Peppermint Essential Oil - Healthline article titled *"About Peppermint Oil Uses and Benefits"* published on April 25, 2019, by Jill Seladi-Schulman, Ph.D. and medically reviewed by Debra Rose Wilson, PH. D, MSN, R.N. IBCLC, AHN-BC, CHT
https://www.healthline.com/health/benefits-of-peppermint-oil#pain

Cinnamon Essential Oil - Very Well Mind article titled *"Health Benefits of Cinnamon"* published on February 26, 2020, by Cathy Wong and medically reviewed by Barbie Cervoni MS, RD, CDCES, CDN
https://www.verywellfit.com/cinnamon-for-health-89013

Rosemary Essential Oil - Very Well Mind article titled *"Essential Oils That Ease Bronchitis Symptoms and How to Use Them"* published on June 25, 2021, by Michelle Pugle and medically reviewed by Arno Kroner, DAOM, LAc
https://www.verywellhealth.com/essential-oils-for-bronchitis-5179761

Frankincense Essential Oil - Very Well Mind article titled *"Essential Oils That Ease Bronchitis Symptoms and How to Use Them"* published on June 25, 2021, by Michelle Pugle and medically reviewed by Arno Kroner, DAOM, LAc
https://www.verywellhealth.com/essential-oils-for-bronchitis-5179761

Touch - American Massage Therapy Association – AMTA article titled *"Massage and Trigger Points"* published on March 2, 2015, by Christian Bond
https://www.amtamassage.org/publications/massage-therapy-journal/massage-and-trigger-points/

Taste - The National Center for Health Statistics – U.S. Department of Health & Human Services featured research article titled *"Large study links gum disease with dementia"* published on July 9, 2020, by National Institute on Aging

Chapter 24: Redefining Our Expectations
Author Dr. Joe Dispenza *"Breaking the Habit of Being Yourself - How to Lose Your Mind and Create a New One"* published 2012 by Hay House, Inc.

Chapter 25: Let Go, Let God
Funeral Consumers Alliance found at Funerals.org article titled *"Your Funeral Rights"* under Legal/Your Rights
https://funerals.org/?consumers=your-funeral-rights
Find a Local Funeral Consumer Alliance by state https://funerals.org/local-fca/

Jessica Lizel Cannon

To learn more about Jessica and her caregiver's journey, visit **https://www.jessicalizelcannon.com**.

The Proactive Caregiver Podcast

with Jessica Lizel Cannon
www.jessicalizelcannon.com

New Episodes weekly!
Subscribe on your favorite podcasting app or listen in at:
www.jessicalizelcannon.com

Other titles by Jessica Lizel Cannon:

Becoming Proactive

Subscribe to the website at **www.jessicalizelcannon**.com to get your
copy of this e-book for free or purchase at
www.jessicalizelcannon.com/books.

The Proactive Journey

Volume 1

by Jessica Lizel Canon

www.cannonlightmedia.com

The Proactive Caregiver
Stop Reacting to Life, Start Living Proactively

www.ingramcontent.com/pod-product-compliance
Lightning Source LLC
Chambersburg PA
CBHW060857120626
46553CB00001B/111